ABOUT THE AUTHOR . . .

MARCUS L. LOANE, M.A., D.D., is bishop coadjutor in the Sydney Diocese of the Anglican Church in Australia. He has had extensive ministries in Africa, Asia and Latin America speaking to missionaries and local pastors. He served for 23 years as vice principal and principal of Moore College before taking up his present duties in 1958. He has written six books, including *Oxford and the Evangelical Succession* and *Makers of Religious Freedom*.

LIFE THROUGH THE CROSS

LIFE
THROUGH
THE CROSS

by

Marcus L. Loane

ZONDERVAN PUBLISHING HOUSE

Grand Rapids, Michigan

To

Dorothy Abbott

A faithful secretary
and generous friend

Foreword

The first half of this book follows the course of events from our Lord's anguish in Gethsemane to His condemnation by the Sanhedrin. It moves toward the great drama of His death on the cross. Such a drama had elements of tragedy, of emotion, and of human appeal which are just as vivid now as they have always been for thoughtful readers. But that is by no means all. If His death were only a heroic example of devotion and sacrifice, it would have no comfort for a troubled sinner. If it did no more than illustrate the character of divine love or of human sin, it could not lift mankind beyond guilt and despair. The bare fact of His death could be of no value for the needs of the mid-twentieth century unless it were clear that it was "a full, perfect, and sufficient sacrifice, oblation, and satisfaction, for the sins of the whole world." He died the death that we deserved to die; it was just as though we ourselves were put to death. The Son of God loved us and gave Himself for us.

But His Death and Passion were not isolated, nor can they be rightly interpreted apart from His Resurrection. The second half of this book is concerned with the events from morning till evening on that third day when He rose from the dead. A contrast between the restoration of Lazarus and the Resurrection of the Lord Jesus helps to make the latter stand out in its unique preeminence. Lazarus came forth, bound hand and foot with the graveclothes; Jesus left the shroud and napkin in the tomb. Lazarus was subject once more to infirmity and mortality; Jesus "dieth no more." Lazarus had to pass a second time through the gates of death and he is still waiting for the better resurrection; Jesus rose again after the power of an endless life. Jesus is He that liveth and was dead; and now He is alive for evermore: He is the Prince of Life who is able to save all who will come to God by Him.

"Worthy is the Lamb that was slain to receive. . . . honour, and glory, and blessing" (Revelation 5:12); for He that was slain now "liveth for ever and ever" (Revelation 5:14).

INTRODUCTION

When Henry Drummond, author of the little classic called *The Greatest Thing in the World,* lay dying, it came over him that in his years of Christian witness he had not made as much of the cross as he should have done. The cross had been in the background of his faith and thinking, but it was not the "chief word of his ministry." In his dying hour, his physical pain intense and unremitting, a friend played softly some of Drummond's favorite hymns. At last came the simple verse, sung to the old Scots melody of Martyrdom:

> *I'm not ashamed to own my Lord,*
> *Or to defend His cause,*
> *Maintain the glory of His cross,*
> *And honour all His laws.*

His dying spirit was inspired. Tapping time with his hands, he joined softly in the words. When the song was finished, he said, "There is nothing to beat that!"

No one who works his way through the pages of this book will be left wondering whether his Grace, the Archbishop of Sydney, makes the cross the "chief word of his ministry."

Those of us who have known Marcus Loane, who have felt the fiber of his mind, the heartbeat of his preaching, the "magnificent obession" of his life, know full well that he has brought to the writing of this volume the ripened fruits of years of preparation. The "shadow" of the cross has been his "abiding place."

In such of his works as *Cambridge and the Evangelical Succession,* and the biography of Archbishop Howard Mowll he has exhibited unusual talent as a biographer. But the field in which he writes of the Passion of our Lord is the one that obviously evokes the full range of his gifts and the full measure of his devotion. The mood of his writing is generally calm, seldom tempestuous; but it is a calmness that gathers force from its clarity. His style is always chaste, rarely abrupt, and at times rises to artistry by reason of the rhetorical balance that is achieved. An example will be found on page 21: "On the surface crest of human feeling He could not help but wish for some relief; in the ocean depth of sacred longing there was nothing which He would so gladly do as to submit to God."

It is, however, the *content* of these chapters by which they will at last be judged. On that ground alone they deserved to be heard. They are ribbed with Scripture, the relevant passages being carefully selected and illuminatingly handled. They are alive with the "mind of Christ" — that "mind" of the self-emptying Servant, of whom St. Paul tells us that He "became obedient unto death, even the death of the cross," and for this reason He has been "highly exalted" and given a name that is above every name."

To say more is needless. The publishers will have done themselves a high honor and their readers a signal service if many thousands of them make *Life Through the Cross* their literary pilgrimage from the first chapter to the last.

PAUL S. REES

Minneapolis, Minnesota

CONTENTS

Part One

The Man of Sorrows

Part Two

The Crown of Thorns

PART ONE

THE MAN
OF
SORROWS

Chapter 1

THE OLIVE GROVE

Then cometh Jesus with them unto a place called Gethsemane, and saith unto the disciples, Sit ye here, while I go and pray yonder. And he took with him Peter and the two sons of Zebedee, and began to be sorrowful and very heavy. Then saith he unto them, My soul is exceeding sorrowful, even unto death: tarry ye here, and watch with me. — MATTHEW 26:36-38 (see MARK 14:32-34; LUKE 22:39, 40; JOHN 18:1, 2).

WE ARE never on more holy ground than when we linger in the olive groves of Gethsemane, for it is a thing most sacred to pause awhile near this scene of unexampled sorrow. Gethsemane was a garden which lay on the lower levels of the western slopes of the Mount of Olives, and it was a favorite rendezvous for the Man of Sorrows and His inner circle of friends. It took its name from an oil press where the olives used to be crushed for oil — fitting emblem for the lifeblood so soon to be wrung drop by drop from the Saviour while He was held in the vicelike grip of terrible agony!

It was nearly midnight when the band of twelve came by moonlight to the outskirts of the Garden: "Then cometh Jesus with them unto a place called Gethsemane, and saith unto the disciples, Sit ye here, while I go and pray yonder." Thus eight of the disciples were left near the gate while He passed on with Peter and the sons of Zebedee, three who had been His chosen and honored companions in the home of Jairus and on the Mount of Transfiguration. Now once again they were to see Him change in mien, and hear Him speak in prayer; but the aspect which His face now assumed and the accent which His voice now betrayed were as far as could be from the light and splendor

13

which had been their hallmarks before. The Son of Man was weighed down by a grief and gloom so dark, so unrelieved, that the disciples were lost in a maze of awe and wonder.

His face was enough to tell the story of His Sorrow of Soul; His was mental anguish. "And he began to be sorrowful, and very heavy." But the English words fail to bring out the full force and emphasis of the original, for the anguish of soul which they reflect went far beyond all that He had yet encountered. He had no doubt suffered many a pang ere this, for He was the Man of Sorrows, and He knew the meaning of grief. But His sorrows *began* in a new sense amid the shadows of Gethsemane, for His death and passion were now at hand. He who was so calm and full of controlled reserve *began to be* in such distress of soul that He could not hide it from the eyes of others. All that had gone before was now to be intensified; His whole experience of pain was to be raised to the superlative degree. The sphere of His vision as to sin had never been so vast and terrible as it was now to become, and the corresponding sphere of thought and feeling would be stirred and agitated with a violence unknown to His emotions before. It was as though some vast wave of sorrow, sudden in its rush, tidal in its force, began to break over His soul; it swept aside all His human reserves, and left in its wake a sense of bewilderment and of consternation.

The two gospel accounts of this scene are identical in this verse except for one word. He "began to be sorrowful" (Matthew 26:37); He "began to be sore amazed" (Mark 14:33). The calm and serene light which had shone from His eyes in the Upper Room had gone. The sweet and tranquil tone which had breathed through His voice by the Kidron's stream had gone. The whole cast of His soul was so overshadowed that it betrayed itself in His features, and the inner conflict found a vent for itself in His visible appearance. The vivid word picture drawn with a single stroke in Mark's account tells us that He was "sore amazed"; He was staggered, so one might say, in the sacred region of His human feelings. He was like the Hebrew Patriarch, on whom the horror of that strange darkness once fell (Genesis 15:12); He was like the pilgrim Christian, on whom the pressure of that great burden once lay (*Pilgrim's Progress*, page 1). The root idea of this word is that He was stunned; He was both shocked and stunned at the prospect of all that

was now to transpire.[1] He felt the first blast of that dread storm
which was soon to burst over His head, and it shocked Him out
of His calm, and stunned Him with this grief.

But how shall we reflect on the insight which this affords into
His very soul? "And He . . . began to be sorrowful and very
heavy." The last phrase is rendered in the Revised Version as
sore troubled, and it occurs in the text with the stress and force
of a climax. It was one thing to be *sorrowful*; it was worse still to
be *astonied*; it was even more grievous to be *sore troubled.* So
this word adds another element to His sorrow, and brings it to
a new point of intensity. It is of uncertain origin, and it only
occurs in one other New Testament passage; Epaphroditus, at
death's door in a strange city, longing for the well-known face
of a friend, was said to be "full of heaviness," or "sore troubled"
(Philippians 2:26, A.V. and R.V.). Bultmann argued, and many
have agreed, that the root idea is "to be away from home," far
from one's own people; and that adds a graphic touch of color
to the meaning in each case where the word occurs.[2]

The Lord Jesus must have felt a sense of oppressive loneliness
in the Garden that night; it was with Him in the shades of
Gethsemane as it was with Epaphroditus when in Rome he hun-
gered for the comfort of friends. He felt like one who was away
from home; He was homesick for His Father's presence. He was
alone when He came to tread the wine press of the weary, and
there was none with Him in the final ordeal (Isaiah 63:3).

His voice was enough to tell the story of His sorrow to Death;
His was mortal anguish. "Then saith he unto them, My soul is
exceeding sorrowful, even unto death." It is almost a rule in the
gospel memoirs to find that a veil has been drawn over His inner
life. What may have passed within has been curtained off from
the scrutiny of eyes too curious. It was seldom indeed that He
ever opened His lips to speak of His deeper feelings, and most
rarely did He ever lift the veil to disclose the secrets which belonged to that internal world of emotion. Once, when He stood
by the grave of Lazarus, He groaned in the spirit and was
troubled; and His pent-up feelings found a partial escape in
tears: "Jesus wept" (John 11:35). Once, when He marked out
the road to Calvary, He spoke of the grain of wheat which must

---

[1]James Morison, *St. Mark* (1887), p. 399.
[2]James Morison, *St. Matthew* (1885), p. 542.

die; and His inmost feelings found a human outlet in words: "Now is my soul troubled" (John 12:27). But the secret of the agitation which had broken up His emotional calm in Gethsemane was to wring from Him a cry of pathos which we can but haltingly apprehend. There is a dark abyss of woe into which it dimly lets us look with awe and trembling; but there are depths in that chasm which must ever remain unsearchable.

No mild explanation of these words can convey a clear idea of their sense of terror.[3] Then saith he unto them, "My soul is exceeding sorrowful, even unto death." "My soul," He said; and it was a phrase which He had only once used before, and that once when He was troubled (John 12:27). He was speaking of the spiritual center of His human nature, for His body was as yet in no wise concerned other than as it might share His distress of mind. It is never so clear that His anguish was pain of mind and not of limb, for the hour had yet to come when He would actually drink the cup of sorrow.

But the horror of soul in the Garden was due to His foresight of the burden of sin on the gallows, and the darkness in Gethsemane was no more than a faint shadow of a greater darkness in separation from God. It was the clear prospect of this which now made Him "exceeding sorrowful," and in Greek a single word is enough to express this feeling. It means to be beset with sorrow all around, and the idea is well expressed in the Psalter: "The sorrows of death compassed me, and the pains of hell gat hold upon me" (Psalms 116:3; cf. 18:5). His soul was hemmed in on all sides with grief; sorrow soaked in through all its pores. He was in a state of siege, and there was no escape from its subtle infiltration. It was like a moonless midnight in the interior region of His human spirit; not one solitary gleam of light could break through at a single point in all its circumference.

That clear foresight could not conceal from Him how things were to end on the cross. "Then saith he unto them, My soul is exceeding sorrowful, even unto death." This last phrase is the more suggestive in view of its brevity; it tells a fact, but adds no more. The weight of woe that had fallen upon Him seemed enough to crush out life itself, and He felt His body sink beneath the burden. If joy flows on the stream of life, sorrow runs on the line of death; and if its pain to be too intense, it may run

---

[3]H. B. Swete, *The Gospel According to St. Mark* (1913), p. 342.

right into the fact of death itself. It would seem that the Lord Jesus felt like one who stood at the last limit of his power to endure. He was hard by the gates of death, and He had as it were "grazed the edge" of the world to come.[4] His whole human nature was so distraught that it seemed not far off from the point of dissolution.

But why? What was the cause of such sorrow? A question not lightly to be put, and but partly to be met. The load of sin was now about to be laid on Him with its sense of shame and sore sorrow, and He began to feel as though He could hear the footfall of death as sin's just due. Was it not this very sorrow which did at length lead to His death from a broken heart hours before the time in which the cross itself would have slain Him?

Thus the sorrow of His human spirit found a vent for itself even in the look on His face; and that face was not yet so marred more than the sons of men. Or it found an outlet through a tone in His voice such as they had not heard before; and that voice had yet to utter its worst and most dreadful cry of desolation. The fact which stands out is that this sorrow could not contain itself; it did seek an outlet, even if in looks and words of distress. Sir John Cheke gives us a version of His lament which is as true as it is free: "I am even like to die for sorrow!"[5]

The Man of Sorrows, like all other men, found relief in the telling of it to others, and He went on to add something further with an eye on His friends: "Tarry ye here, and watch with me." His grief was so overwhelming that He would get away to a distance; yet His heart clung to them even when He most felt that He must go aside. Thus out of the darkness He reached a hand, feeling for the grasp of a friend; He would have them near Him, even though He were a little removed.[6] How exquisitely human! Does not such a High Priest become us, who was like us in all things save sin alone?

---

[4]Alexander MacLaren, *The Gospel of St. Matthew* (Bible Class Expositions, 1905), vol. ii, p. 182.

[5]James Morison, *St. Matthew* (1885), p. 543.

[6]Alexander MacLaren, *The Gospel of St. Matthew* (Bible Class Expositions, 1905), vol. ii, p. 182.

Chapter 2

THE BROKEN CRY

And he went a little farther, and fell on his face, and prayed, saying, O my Father, if it be possible, let this cup pass from me; nevertheless not as I will, but as thou wilt. — MATTHEW 26:39 (see MARK 14:35, 36; LUKE 22:41, 42).

IT WAS step by step that the Lord Jesus withdrew from the warmth of human companionship that He might keep the most lonely vigil ever known in human experience on the eve of the cross. He had led the eleven disciples out of the Upper Room, away from the crowded city; then eight of these were left beside the gate of the Garden while He passed on with three. There was nothing novel in this desire to be alone; He had often retired for the sake of solitude in His hours of communion with God. But not even the three could share the more private side of His need in that supreme hour of sorrow, and He went on alone.

"And he was withdrawn from them about a stone's cast, and kneeled down, and prayed" (Luke 22:41). He moved into the thick shadows of those gnarled trees to be quite alone with God, though His face and figure were still dimly within view of the three whom He had left behind. His was now the sorest sorrow ever to wring human heart or nature, and it was as though He would not even let the moonbeams play too freely on a grief so sacred. He had to go where no other can go in pain or in sorrow of soul, and a comparison of the gospel records helps us to trace His grief in detail. Matthew begins with the remark that "He went a little farther" (Matthew 26:39), and Luke's account goes on to say that He "kneeled down" (Luke 22:41); Mark says that He was bowed down "to the ground" (Mark 14:35), and the final detail is supplied by Matthew who says that He "fell on His face" (Matthew 26:39). He knelt in that shaded retreat till His

18

feelings forced Him down on His face; and then, prostrate on the bare earth, He breathed the most poignant prayer ever heard.

The first half of this prayer was in words of most touching entreaty: "O my Father, if it be possible, let this cup pass from me." We pause instinctively, and ask if this could be the voice of one whose faith had failed? And the answer is No! He groaned in the spirit, but it was the spirit of one who knew himself to be the Son. His strong sense of filial devotion was never perhaps more active than in that dread hour of crisis. Matthew's record has it, "O my Father" — an appeal so wistful! And Mark's account is still nearer to the original, "Abba, Father" — an address so tender! Abba is one of the few words in His native patois which has come down to us just as it was spoken, and it was no doubt a word of intimate endearment in the home life of His childhood. "Abba, Father" was a bilingual form of address current in some home circles, and His spontaneous combination of the Greek and Aramaic would reach out to Jew and Gentile alike (cf. Romans 8:15; Galatians 4:6). "O my Father!" It was a cry soaked in agony, fraught with entreaty, hard to resist, harder still to deny. John had once leant on the breast of the Lord Jesus; but there was no breast now save one on which the Lord Jesus could lean.

This most wistful form of address led up to His cry of yearning desire: "O my Father, if it be possible, let this cup pass from me!" There is a sense in which it must have been possible; "all things are possible unto thee" (Mark 14:36). This was just the echo of His teaching in bygone days, and it simply applied to His own need the gist of what He had said to others (Mark 10:27). It shows how much He longed to be spared from the hour at hand, and there were more than twelve legions of the angel host which could have hastened to His rescue.

Was it not weakness on the part of the Son of Man that He should speak as if it were desirable at all? It was weakness, perhaps, in the same sense as when we read that "He was crucified through weakness" (II Corinthians 13:4). But it was not moral weakness; for of moral weakness there was neither trace nor hint in the whole of His being. There was no last-minute wish to default in that cry of anguish, nor was it as though He would shut God up to one line of action. The *if* was an unfaltering limitation to His request; the one condition which His own words imposed was *if* it were possible. He would not press the suit, even with His Father's consent, unless it were possible; and that word meant unless it were "within reason" in view of His mission on earth for us men and for our salvation.

Yet He was in the throes of an awful conflict as His cry came to its climax: "O my Father, if it be possible, let this cup pass from me." The Old Testament metaphor of the cup is confined in the gospel memoirs to the idea of pain; so it was then in the case of "this cup," with its contents of trembling and sorrow, the cup of wrath and death. There was more than one dark potion in that bitter chalice of grief and pain, and we can still discern some trace of the mixture from which He was to drink. At the very bottom of the cup there was death, and that worse by far than death by hemlock; it was death as sin's due, death in all its blackest features. It was death in its most awful reality, stark and naked as the final act of judgment which sin deserves. But close to the surface there were many other bitter acids which would float in that cup: the traitor kiss, the pagan scourge, the crown of thorns, the cross of shame.[1] That cup was filled to its brim with the wrath of God against the sin of man. Must He drink it, dregs and all? Could it not pass from His lips?

The next half of this prayer was in words of most perfect surrender: "Nevertheless not as I will, but as thou wilt." It was as though He had almost begun to taste the cup, even as He asked if it might be removed. His cry had gone to the utmost limit to which the soul of man can go, and yet not go beyond the will of God. There was no sin in His intense desire to be spared from that cup of anguish; it was in fact the mark of one who wore the robe of a nature that was identical with ours. How could we say that the mantle of our manhood was His, or yet that the pattern of His sorrow was ours, if His heart and flesh had not shrunk from the ordeal which that cup and its dark contents entailed? His cry was the recoil of a truly human instinct from the dregs of the cup; His woe was the revolt of a truly mortal nature from the pains of the cross. But those dregs had to be consumed and those pains had to be endured, if He were to atone for sin. That is why there was a *nevertheless*; His prayer had to be conditional on the will of God.

He knew that the cup would not be placed in His hands at

[1]James Morison, *St. Matthew* (1885), p. 545.

all if it were not at the wish of a most gracious Father: "Nevertheless not as I will, but as thou wilt." The two wills which meet us in these words throw light on the whole drama, for it was His human will which is in contrast, not in conflict, with that of His Father. We catch a glimpse of His will as the Son of Man distinct from His will as the Son of God, and we see it in the act of reverent submission to the will of God His Father. "Not as I will," He said, and that refers to the will that forms a wish rather than to that which makes a choice. We may wish, yet not choose, for a wish is not so rigid as a resolution. It was His wish that if it were within the range of what was possible that cup might be removed; but He never faltered in His own will His strong resolve, to die for the world and its sin. His wish was that He might be spared from that cup as far as might be within reason; but His will was to bow to the will of our God, and to drink and drain that cup if need must be.

Thus underneath His agony, there lay this one supreme desire: "Nevertheless not as I will, but as thou wilt." There was a sense in which we might say that He both desired and yet did not desire that cup to pass, for by far the strongest desire of His inmost heart was that God's will should be done. On the surface crest of human feeling He could not help but wish for some relief; in the ocean depth of sacred longing there was nothing which He would so gladly do as submit to God. Thus the surrender of His will to the will of God set new harmonies at play, and the disorder of that grief was to melt into the calm of glad and free submission to Him. That cup was not to pass away until the last drop had been quaffed, and He now saw that it was for Him to accept that cup as His portion with all that it contained. Thus He resolved to take the cup which the Father had willed that He should drink; He would grasp it firmly in His hands, hold it calmly to His lips, and drain it, dregs and all.

How long the Lord Jesus remained prostrate in the Garden, absorbed in that anguish of soul, we do not know, but the gospel memoirs make use of a tense which implies that He had just begun to pray when these words were uttered. This is a hint which may account for the minor variations in their report of what He said, for it may be no more than a fragment which has come down to us. We may quote that prayer once more in the form which it takes in Luke's gospel: "Father, if thou be willing, remove this cup from me: nevertheless not my will, but thine, be done" (22:42). Was there ever a cry from earth which could be more certain to reach the ear of God than this? Who would be heard, and whom would the Father shield from evil, if not His own dear Son?

Yet the echoes of that cry still linger in the ears of mankind, for the tremendous elements of mystery and suffering meet and mingle in its words and motives. It could only be the shadow of the cross which had made Gethsemane so dark; that is the one explanation we can offer for these words of ineffable sorrow. The guilt of the world was upon His heart; the shame of the cross was before His eyes. For the cup which He had to drink was that which would atone for the sins of the world. What that cup held was not mere death, but Death as sin's last due; and it might not pass from Him that it may pass from us for ever. The wrath of God was in that cup; the pains of Hell were in that cup. But He would drain the last chill drop from the sinner's cup of guilt that we may drink forever from the Father's cup which is full of grace and has neither brim nor bottom.

Chapter 3

THE FATHER'S WILL

He went away again the second time, and prayed, saying, O my Father, if this cup may not pass away from me, except I drink it, thy will be done. — MATTHEW 26:42 (see MARK 14:39).

And there appeared an angel unto him from heaven, strengthening him. — LUKE 22:43.

PERHAPS an hour would slip slowly away while the Lord lay prostrate on the bare ground, wrestling in prayer just as Jacob had once wrestled till break of day. An hour at least seems to have been implied in His word of rebuke to the three whom He found asleep: "What, could ye not watch with me one hour? Watch and pray, that ye enter not into temptation" (Matthew 26:40, 41). He had prayed His way through that first distress to a calm mind, ever the true companion of full surrender. Then He had risen to His feet, retraced His steps, found His three friends asleep, and stirred them from slumber. How did He look on His return from the scene of sorrows so sore? Had the cloud of trouble spread its wings and fled from His face?

It seems clear that the hour of prayer had brought Him a sense of profound relief; the conflict and turmoil had died away in the growing reality of the Father's design. The swift current of His inner feelings had changed, so that no more than a shadow of that anguish of soul would now remain.[1] But He had not yet come to the end of that night of sore distress, for this relief was no more than momentary. It was just a brief lull in the storm of sorrows which had begun to burst, and a fresh cloud, dark with trouble, was soon swept up over His head. He left them once more to renew the old conflict alone: "And again, he went

---

[1]William Hanna, *Our Lord's Life on Earth* (1882), p. 449.

23

away, and prayed, and spake the same words" (Mark 14:39).
Matthew alone records the words which broke from His lips as
He knelt in prayer, and Luke alone refers to the help which God
sent Him by the hand of an angel.

We catch a glimpse of the struggle, and see how it welled
up and overflowed in prayer: "O my Father, if this cup may
not pass away from me except I drink it, thy will be done."
There is, just as before, that clear sense of the Saviour's need,
joined with that strong grasp of the Father's hand. "O my
Father"; wistful words of appeal, full of tenderness and devotion,
rich in entreaty and submission. If Mark's version of His mode
of address in the first prayer be still fresh in our minds, it will
enhance our sense of the solemnity in that hour of crisis. "Abba,
Father." It may faintly remind us of the cry which had once been
addressed both to Elijah and to Elisha: "O my father, my father,
the chariot of Israel and the horsemen thereof!" (II Kings 2:12;
13:14). Trembling hands had been reached out to lay hold
on each of the prophets in turn, for it was felt that the hope of
Israel was bound up with their lives. And this was now as
though the Lord Jesus would lay hold on God with both hands,
like one whose faith would grip reality with all its power. A yet
darker hour was to come when the double form of address would
make itself heard in even more urgent tones, for then the dear
name of Father would fail or be suppressed in the wider terms
of appeal to God. "Eli, Eli, lama sabachthani," He would then
cry in His Aramaic patois; "My God, my God, why hast thou
forsaken me?" (Matthew 27:46).

The one reason for this further appeal was that the old dread
had returned: "O my Father, if this cup may not pass away
from me except I drink it, thy will be done." The strong secret
shrinking of His human instinct had been subdued, though not
erased, and this second prayer was yet more deeply rooted in
a yielded spirit than the former. It was not as though He had
lost the ground which had been won in that other conflict; it
was rather that He had to fight to retain it, and fighting meant
this renewed travail of soul. But He could build on that other
supplication, and He could take His stand on a higher level.[2]

His words were now framed in a way which shows how He

---

[2]Alexander MacLaren, *The Gospel of St. Matthew* (Bible Class Expositions,
1905), vol. ii, p. 185.

had come to see that He could not avoid the cup. This is clear from the text in the English Version: "If this cup *may* not pass away." But the original is not so mild, for it runs in stronger channels: "If this cup *can* not pass away." There was of course to the very last a sense in which that cup could have passed away, just as there was a sense in which He could have come down from the cross (Matthew 27:42). But He had come to see that there was a higher sense in which the cup could not be removed at all if He were to atone for the sins of the world; for in that sense the cup which could not pass undrunk would pass away from Him at last in the very act of drinking.

But His sense of Sonship was in the ascendant as this second prayer rose to its climax: "O my Father, if this cup may not pass away from me, except I drink it, thy will be done." This was no mere passive resignation of His will to the will of His Father, as if there were no help for it. We dare not treat His cry as though it were uttered only in the spirit of one who saw that he could not escape his fate. He had Himself once taught His friends how to approach the same Father as His children, and the last clause of this prayer in Gethsemane was a direct verbal echo of the words he had used in that pattern of prayer: "Our Father which art in heaven . . . *thy will be done* in earth, as it is in heaven" (Matthew 6:9, 10).

Jesus was Himself the one who had ever felt the strongest desire to do God's will on earth: "Then said I, Lo, I come (in the volume of the book it is written of me,) to do thy will, O God" (Hebrews 10:7; Psalm 40:7, 8). We do not share at all in the mind of Christ as He breathed this prayer in the Garden if we dare to limit His words to mere resignation to a lot that was inevitable. It was by far the most intense desire, the most active thought in His whole being, that the will of God should be done; and since it was God's will that the cup should not pass undrunk, He chose God's will, and took that cup, and willed to drink it all.

We catch a glimpse of the angel, and see how he drew near and fortified the Lord: "And there appeared an angel unto him from heaven, strengthening him." God did hear that cry of anguish, even though the cup might not pass away; and though He would not grant it as to its letter, He was more than ready to meet Him as to its spirit. The deep shadows in the Garden were thus lit up by the visible appearance of an angel, for the words "from heaven" would not have been added if it were in fact no more than some strange subjective impression.[3] He who was Lord of the angel hosts in glory had been made a little lower than the angels on earth. Yet He came not into the world without this voice: "Let all the angels of God worship him" (Hebrews 1:6).

There is most remarkable economy in the gospel memoirs with regard to angels in the life of the Lord Jesus; there are in fact only four points in His earthly story at which we read of such angelic ministries. He who came as the Son of God was to receive a full measure of worship from the angels: thus there was the angel choir to hail His incarnation at Bethlehem, and there was the angel host to mark His exaltation on the Mount of Olives. He who came as the Son of Man would also need comfort quite as much as worship: thus there was the angelic ministry in the desert after His temptation, and there was the angelic strengthening in the Garden during His agony.

But it was in answer to the stricken cry of a soul in need that this angel was sent: "And there appeared an angel unto him from heaven, strengthening him." The most suggestive parallel to this experience was the incident at the outset of His ministry which is described in the temptation narrative. He had spurned the prince of darkness, but His toil in spirit had left Him faint and spent in His strength of body; and it was then that the angels of God came and ministered unto him (Matthew 4:11). He had now been engaged in an even darker conflict with the unseen powers of evil, and once more an angel from God came to strengthen Him that He might stand and withstand.

We are not told how the angel was to impart to Him this strength divine, or what manner of strength it was, whether for soul or for body. But the word *to strengthen* is rare enough, and is only used of bodily strengthening in the New Testament (cf. Acts 9:19). Was it that the angel would look with a sort of wonder on this Mysterious Man who had thus entered into single combat with the hosts of darkness and had foiled their prince and captain twice with the will of God? Was it perhaps the awe and the worship of that angel which now strengthened him in body and soul? It would at least help Him to descry the joy

[3]Alfred Plummer, St. *Luke* (1922), pp. 509-10.

that was set before Him so that He might endure the cross and despise the shame.

Thus God heard that cry and came to His help by means of this angelic ministry: "And there appeared an angel unto him from heaven, strengthening him." There is at least one who knew in himself something of this conflict and this succor, for Paul was driven to like extremities of need and pain by the thorn in his flesh. The real nature of that thorn in the flesh cannot be known, but it made him feel like one who had to suffer the agonies of impalement. It was something sharp and painful, something which he knew would never leave him; it was so dark and so malign that he dared to change the image, and to speak as if it were an agent of hell. It was like an angel from the pit of darkness, for it was just as if Satan himself stood and smote him with clenched fist in the face. He could see no purpose of love or grace behind it all; he was conscious only that it left him in pain of soul as well as of body. It was almost unbearable, and he felt at last that he could go no further unless he were set free. It brought on a crisis in mind and soul; it drove him to his knees in anguish and despair.

We are not told the words in which his prayer was framed, but it matters little; not once, nor twice, but three separate times, being in an agony, his cry went up. God did not grant him the letter of his desire, but He more than granted it in spirit: "And he said unto me, My grace is sufficient for thee, for my strength is made perfect in weakness" (II Corinthians 12:7-9). Nor did He grant the Lord Jesus His prayer on its own terms, but He sent an angel to strengthen Him.

A stone's cast was all that separated Him from the three in the Garden; but who can mark out the distance that lies between Him as the Man of Grief and the rest of our race? These words remind us that there is no one who can wholly follow Him in Gethsemane; He far outstrips all men in the degree of His sorrows in the Garden. Yet though He went so far beyond us all, we may at least hear His call to follow, and there is a sense in which we are called to share in the fellowship of His sufferings. "Are ye able," He asked the sons of Zebedee, "to drink of the cup that I shall drink of?" And they answered, hardly knowing what it would mean: "We are able" (Matthew 20:22). Shall we not then accept the cup which the Father wills to place in our hands? Shall we not take it and hold it, drink it and drain it, for Jesus' sake? And if angels came to strengthen Him who is our Elder Brother, are they not all ministering spirits sent forth to help those who are the heirs of glory? But if we are to know the comfort or succor of this angelic ministry, we must learn from our hearts to pray as He would have us pray, "Thy will be done."

Chapter 4

THE DARKEST HOUR

And he left them, and went away again, and prayed the third time, saying the same words. — MATTHEW 26:44.

And being in an agony he prayed more earnestly: and his sweat was as it were great drops of blood falling down to the ground. — LUKE 22:44.

IT IS SAFE to believe that the second season of prayer in the shades of Gethsemane had come to an end with a new sense of peace and self-possession. He had returned to the three, only to find them asleep as they had been before. He tried in vain to stir them up, and then a fresh wave of sorrow rolled in upon His soul. "And he left them, and went away again, and prayed the third time, saying the same words." There was not the least hint of sin in this struggle for peace, nor would such prayer be wrong in the heart of the least of His brethren. Neither Mark nor Matthew gives us any details of this last and greatest crisis, but Luke's account has drawn the whole picture in a single verse which we can never forget. Once more His soul was crushed with pain, and He was bowed with grief upon the ground; and He was seized with an anguish so sore that the beads of sweat broke out on His brow like drops of blood.

It is remarkable that this terrible prostration of strength followed on the angelic ministry which had strengthened Him as if for fiercer combat. It is not less remarkable that the only author to give us these details was that "beloved physician" whose mind was trained in a school of exact observation and who wrote with technical interest in terms which are never found in any other part of the New Testament. We can only look from afar and read with eyes of awe this quiet medical narrative, knowing that its spirit is as reverent as the language on the whole was reticent.

The first words confront us with a problem as to the real nature of His anguish: "And being in an agony he prayed more earnestly." The word *agony* was used by Luke alone in the New Testament, but it was a common term in medical documents in the Classics. Its root idea was that of fear, and it was an agony of fear that we are here meant to understand. The Lord Jesus had been in an acute state of distress before; His soul had been in the grip of mortal sorrow. Twice He had recoiled from that cup as if by instinct; twice He had returned with that cup as if in accord. But now the old conflict broke out again with a tenfold degree of pain and fear; it was the same mental anguish, but in intensified power and severity. The long struggle, the twice-fought fight, had now come to its last crisis, and this final round must have been the one supreme contest with the powers of darkness. It was like the last scene in the temptation narrative, when the Evil One stood fully unmasked; the Lord Jesus spoke the peremptory word of command that drove him from the field (Matthew 4:10). So now it was not just that His human nature shrank back; it was rather the fact that He had now been caught in the death throes of His fight with the prince of the powers of darkness.

But the sorer conflict drove Him on to pray with desperate vehemence: "And being in an agony he prayed more earnestly." The word *earnestly* had its basis in a physical conception, and is used in the Acts, as in this verse, to set out the spirit in which prayer was being offered. It is a stock adverb, derived from the verb "to stretch out," and the meaning is made clear in the words of the gospel healing: "Then saith he to the man, *Stretch forth* thine hand. And he *stretched it forth*; and it was restored whole, like as the other" (Matthew 12:13). Thus a literal translation of the adverb would be "more extendedly," and an easy passage of thought from this would be to treat it as "more persistently."[1] So when Simon Peter lay in prison with the threat of execution at the hands of Herod, "prayer was made *earnestly* of the church unto God for him" (Acts 12:5, R.V.).

The Church was at full stretch in the spirit of prayer; those who prayed were keyed up to the highest tension. But the same word is raised to the comparative degree for the Lord of the Church; He prayed *more earnestly, more strenuously.* Jacob's

---

[1]Alfred Plummer, *St. Luke* (1922), p. 510.

prayer at the Brook Jabbok was intense and earnest as he wrestled with the unknown angel; but when Jesus strove and wrestled in this agony, it was the prayer of a Suppliant whose pains know no equal. Just how strenuous was that prayer in agony may be seen from another reference to the Son of Man "Who in the days of his flesh . . . offered up prayers and supplications *with strong crying and tears*" (Hebrews 5:7).

But why did He feel so crushed by sorrow in the gloom of Gethsemane? Was it nothing greater than the common load which falls on all men's shoulders? There are many others who have braved both death and torture with a heroic fortitude that would not let them shrink; how then can we think that this agony was no more than dread for what lay between Him and the grave? Clear and perfect vision of all that He must needs endure would not conceal the gloom or terror of the cross; yet that vision had been before His eyes, and the shadow of death upon His path, ever since He had been about His Father's business. This agony, this sense of fear, would not have been worthy of Him if that were all; but what if it were part of His pain and passion for the sins of the world? What if it were not the fear of death and dying, but the sense of God's wrath and judgment? The sorrows of Gethsemane were not merely a pale copy of the darker woes of the cross; the fact is that we find ourselves shut up to the belief that this agony was part of the Atonement. It may be true that in some sense He bore our sins in His body from the cradle to the gallows; but the cup of trembling and the pain of passion were in effect condensed and shared between Gethsemane and His death on the cross.

The next words confront us with a problem as to the real nature of His Passion; "And his sweat was as it were great drops of blood falling down to the ground." The word *sweat* was used by Luke alone in the New Testament, but it was a common term in medical documents in the Classics. The nature and degree of perspiration were closely observed by the ancients in cases of illness, so that it was perfectly natural for Luke to take both into account. Aristotle and Theophrastus both refer to sweat as the result of keen mental anguish, so that it is by no means out of place in this sacred record. But the feature which so impressed Luke was the fact that this sweat was like great drops of blood, and it is clear that this was no idle figure of speech, no mere flight of fancy, as when we speak of "tears of blood." How could he mean that those beads of sweat were somehow like clots of blood if all the time they were only simple sweat-drops? And why should he refer to blood at all if there were no blood in those great beads of perspiration?

There are historic examples which prove that a physical disorder of this kind may result from a violent disturbance in the nervous system; the stream of blood may be forced out of its proper channels so that it will at length ooze out through the cutaneous excretories. Thus it would seem that His was so sore a conflict between opposite emotions that in the end the blood was forced out of its own normal system so as to break through the pores on the surface of that sacred body.[2]

This must have meant that His human power to endure was strained to the utmost limit: "And his sweat was as it were great drops of blood falling down to the ground." The word for *falling down* was in common use for medical description, and was applied to the descent of the humors of the body. Thus Luke says that His sweat was literally mingled with blood, colored by blood, in His anguish beneath those trees; more still, he says that it was so profuse that it fell in great drops from His face to the ground. The whole picture grows with each point in a way that makes us feel how His power to bear was put to its supreme ordeal, for it meant that His whole humanity was tried and taxed to a degree which we can scarce conceive. We might have thought that a common sweat while He was out of doors in the cold night air, prostrate on the ground and hidden in the shadows, would have been a striking phenomenon; for the night was so cold that those who were in the courtyard of the high priest's palace stood in need of a fire to warm themselves. But what are we to think of such anguish as this, and of the strain which it must have imposed, when it made beads of sweat stand out like drops of blood upon His brow, rolling down with a splash like that of rain upon the ground?

Do we ask in awe and wonder what it was that shone both wet and red, like some strange dew, at the feet of that kneeling Figure? Would those sweat-drops, tinged with blood, be visible to the disciples at a little distance in the pale light of the Paschal

---

[2]C. J. Ellicott, *Historical Lectures* (1876), p. 330, footnote 1. Compare William Stroud, *Treatise on the Physical Cause of the Death of Christ* (1871), pp. 115, 380.

moon as it straggled through the trees? That strange phenomenon must have been due to some abnormal commotion in
His nervous system; and what that was we can only understand
when we dimly consider that He was to pay our debt with
His blood. In the absence of all outward trouble, in the quietness
of that shaded garden, the pain of His Passion so took hold
of His soul that He was bowed with strong crying and tears.
Before ever a thorn had touched His brow, or scourge His back,
or nails His hands and feet, the truth of His travail so swept
in on His soul that He broke out in sweat like drops of blood.
This was an integral part of His suffering; it was a manifest
side of the Atonement. The cup which He prepared Himself
to drink in the Garden, like the pain which He had yet to endure
on the cross, was primarily spiritual, both in essence and in
reality. It was something inward, something unique; mysterious
to ponder, impossible to fathom. But it proves the truth of the
old saying that the sufferings of His soul were the soul of His
sufferings.[3]

Not one of the gospel memoirs has left us a record of the
words which were used in that final crisis of prayer. Matthew
only says that He prayed in *"the same words"* while the other
two are silent altogether. We are not to suppose that He merely
voiced a single phrase again and again; it means rather that
the burden of His prayer was the same as it had been before.
But there is a faint hint as to the form of that prayer in the
words that were spoken when He was placed under arrest: "The
cup which my Father hath given me, shall I not drink it?"
(John 18:11). Prostrate on the bare ground, with strong crying
and tears, all His raiment moist with sweat, stained with blood,
in words brief and broken, wrung from a heart torn with sorrow,
He wrestled in agony, and wrestled alone.

Thus did He lift up His heart and all its desires, until at all
points those desires had melted into the master desire to do
God's will. It was in the Garden through the Eternal Spirit
that He offered Himself to God; and that offering, that self-
surrender, was not without pain and tears, blood and sweat.
Shall we not, like vassals of old, kneel at His feet and place
our hands within His hands as the sign that we yield ourselves
up forever?

---

[3] William Hanna, *Our Lord's Life on Earth* (1882), p. 453.

Chapter 5

THE HEEDLESS THREE

> Then cometh he to his disciples, and saith unto them, Sleep on now, and take your rest: behold, the hour is at hand, and the Son of man is betrayed into the hands of sinners. Rise, let us be going: behold, he is at hand that doth betray me. — MATTHEW 26:45, 46 (see MARK 14:41, 42; LUKE 22:45, 46).

THE HOUR of agony was by now accomplished, and the Lord turned away for the last time from that scene of solitary intercession. The strong crying and tears with which He had laid hold on Him that was able to save Him from death had not been in vain, for He "was heard in that He feared" (Hebrews 5:7). He was to be saved, not from death, but out of death, for the answer to that prayer seems to have been the pledge of Resurrection. This was the Joy which buoyed Him up and bore Him on, for His Resurrection from the dead would be far better than His preservation from death itself.[1]

But what was He to say to the three whom He found asleep at the post of vigil? He had assigned eight of the disciples to the task of picket duty near the gate of Gethsemane; then He had left the three within eyesight, if not within earshot, as watchmen and sentries. They were to guard His hours of prayer against surprise by the sudden approach of foes; they were to watch and pray for their own sakes lest they too should succumb to temptation.[2] Perhaps we are the less surprised that He should have found them asleep after His first lonely vigil in prayer; they were worn out with the emotions and the excitements of that long and troubled evening. It was indeed singularly like their conduct on the Mount of Transfiguration when

---

[1]Hugh Martin, *The Shadow of Calvary* (n.d.), p. 317.
[2]William Hanna, *Our Lord's Life on Earth* (1882), p. 454.

"they . . . were heavy with sleep" (Luke 9:32). That was a scene which would present the very antithesis of this experience in Gethsemane; it was as full of glory as this was steeped in sorrow. But that these three, of all others, should sink into sleep so drugged, so overwhelming, not once, nor twice, but each time He withdrew, is a phenomenon we cannot now fully resolve.

The first words of the Lord Jesus seem to have been spoken in a mood of pensive reflection: "Sleep on now, and take your rest: behold, the hour is at hand, and the Son of man is betrayed into the hands of sinners." Luke alone offers us a reason which helps us to look more kindly on this drowsy slumber, for his comment is just that of one who would spare the three: "When he rose up from prayer, and was come to his disciples, he found them *sleeping for sorrow*" (Luke 22:45). This was in harmony with the words of the Lord Jesus when He first discovered them all asleep: "The spirit indeed is willing, but the flesh is weak" (Matthew 26:41).

It is remarkable how often the medical diarists do link *sorrow* with care and loss of sleep, and the events of that night were enough to tell us why it was that "their eyes were heavy" (Matthew 26:43). Their minds had been keyed up with strong feeling, and there had been prolonged tension and deep anxiety. It was now past midnight, and they were worn out with want of sleep and sorrow. Great strain and great grief had weakened their power to keep vigil, and their minds grew more or less numb with the drugs of nervous fatigue.[3] But while sorrow made their eyelids heavy, love ought to have kept them alert. They were far from thoughts of selfish ease or heartless indifference; and yet how sad it was that He should find them a second and a third time — asleep!

Thus He stood and mused a moment or two when He returned for the last time: "Sleep on now, and take your rest." The Lord Jesus had been absorbed in a conflict with the dark and unseen hosts of Satan, and there was no human friend who could stand by His side; yet He had wished to have them near, to feel that He was still within reach of loving hands and voices. He had thought that they might look on at a little distance, and so watch with Him in spirit, for such reverent sympathy as they could give would have been His strength and solace.

---

[3]William Hobart, *The Medical Language of St. Luke* (1882), p. 84.

Perhaps He would not have stood in such need of that angelic ministry had they strengthened His hands in love and prayer; but their failure had shown once for all how inadequate was all hope of human strength and support. Thus there was a note of something like sorrowful irony and gentle reproach in His final remark on their conduct: they could sleep on now that the time to watch and pray had gone beyond recovery! All the pain of disappointed trust and contradicted love made itself vocal in that pensive complaint. He had begun to taste the gall of which David had long before spoken: "I looked for some to take pity, but there was none; and for comforters, but I found none" (Psalm 69:20).

Slumber might no longer do harm; nor could vigil do good. "Behold, the hour is at hand, and the Son of man is betrayed into the hands of sinners." That hour, so long foreseen, had come at last, and come while those who loved Him most lay like lifeless logs on the ground! It was grievous enough that they should have fallen asleep at all, but their double relapse into that dull, drowsy slumber was worse by far. It had compelled Him to face the approach of that dark hour alone, for sleep that is broken and then resumed is more torpid than if never disturbed at all.[4] He had watched the slow onward march of that hour from afar, and had never let Himself be misled (see John 2:4; 7:30; 8:20); then He had seen it draw nearer, and His language had borne a more urgent appeal (see John 12:23; 13:1; 16:32; 17:1). But now that dark hour of crisis which had for so long been in view had come; it was the hour when the sorrows of His Passion were to begin. The few moments which had still to elapse before He was betrayed at the hands of Judas were as nothing as things now stood; it was so imminent that the present tense could be used with an air of vivid simplicity. It was indeed only a matter of minutes before He would aver in the presence of His captors: "This is your hour, and the power of darkness." (Luke 22:53.)

The next words of the Lord Jesus seem to have been spoken in a mood of rapid decision: "Rise, let us be going: behold, he is at hand that doth betray me." Perhaps there was a pause in the silence of that Garden, a brief respite for the Lord and

---

[4]Alexander MacLaren, *The Gospel of St. Matthew* (Bible Class Expositions, 1905), vol. ii, p. 188.

His three disciples. Then that mood of calm reverie gave way in one vital moment to a mood of great urgency. The change is marked by His sudden alteration of speech and tone: He passed from quiet meditative soliloquy to a style that was sharp, clipped, and broken. The three might sleep no more! He would have them up on their feet at once! They were bluntly aroused by His enigmatic command, and they would then rejoin the eight who still lingered near the entrance to the Garden. The stage had changed for a new and swiftly moving scene of action, and the shaded quiet of Gethsemane was soon to be shattered with more strident sounds than the voice of prayer.

It is clear that the Lord Jesus had caught a glimpse of the flash of torches and the gleam of lanterns not far away in the Valley of Kidron; it could only mean that the band led by Judas was on its way to seize and bind the Son of Man. Therefore He had aroused the three and had returned to the others, not for flight, not for fight, but to prepare for the traitor and his party.

So then He stood and spoke as He addressed Himself to the crisis at hand: "Rise, let us be going." The five words in English are but two in Greek, and it is the same phrase as that which had brought the discourse in the Upper Room to an end (John 14:31). We could almost think that the need for some kind of action had brought a new sense of peace to His heart; it brought relief after the long strain and suspense in the Garden. He knew how thick and fast His trials and blows were now to fall, but He had spent that hour or more in watch and prayer lest He should find Himself unarmed. He had wrestled with God until faith had prevailed, and He was as serene as the moonbeams when He went forth with that cup in His hand.

Judas would find that He who had risen from the bended knees of His soul could meet arrest at the hands of wicked men with dignified composure. There was not a trace of all that recent anguish in face, or form, or gait, or mien; His eye spoke the language of a firm and conscious authority as He bade them rise and go forth to meet that band. Who can mistake the air of that unshaken constancy to which His whole demeanor now bears witness?

But it was one thing for the Lord Jesus, and quite another for the disciples: "Behold, he is at hand that doth betray me." He had tried to warn them of the storm which was bound to burst, and which would in measure engulf them all. At the table in the Upper Room they had been startled to hear Him say: "Verily I say unto you, that one of you shall betray me" (Matthew 26:21). On the way to Gethsemane He had further warned them that the force and fierceness of that storm would drive them far from His side: "All ye shall be offended because of me *this night*: for it is written, I will smite the shepherd, and the sheep of the flock shall be scattered abroad" (Matthew 26:31). Among the trees of the Garden He had warned three of them once more that the furies of hell would be loosed in that storm: "Watch and pray, that ye enter not into temptation" (Matthew 26:41). He knew that His Passion would mean trial and trouble for them no less than for Himself, for how could they escape from the shame and reproach that would adhere to Him? It would test their fidelity in a way that they could scarcely conceive, and they would need more strength than was theirs by nature if they were to survive. But their failure to watch and pray meant that they had lost their one chance to arm themselves, and that in turn left them prone to become guilty of greater sin, and laden with deeper sorrow.

Simon Peter and the sons of Zebedee were the strongest of the twelve, the flower and glory of that little company. They had been more often with Him than the others; they had been admitted when friends were excluded. Would they not take His words to heart, and do as He desired? Would they not keep vigil with Him, and watch and pray against the hour of trial? His words would hint at the slightness of their task in comparison with His; they had but to watch while He would wrestle, and wrestle in agony. If then their sleep in such circumstances was not heartless, yet was it not faithless? It was a breach of His direct command, and it ignored His plain words of warning. It did disgrace to the trust which He had freely reposed in them; it did despite to the grief which He had frankly endured before their eyes. To sleep while He suffered was to deny Him the only comfort for which He asked, and it was to cost them dear when they had to face the storm without that time of watch and prayer. Their weakness and vacillation in that dark hour was in tragic contrast with the calm and unfaltering courage of their Master; but they had slept while He kept tryst with God in prayer.[5]

---

[5]Hugh Martin, *The Shadow of Calvary* (n.d.), pp. 76-102.

Chapter 6

THE STRICKEN BAND

Judas then, having received a band of men and officers from the chief priests and Pharisees, cometh thither with lanterns and torches and weapons. Jesus therefore, knowing all things that should come upon him, went forth, and said unto them, Whom seek ye? They answered him, Jesus of Nazareth. Jesus saith unto them, I am he. And Judas also, which betrayed him, stood with them. As soon then as he had said unto them, I am he, they went backward, and fell to the ground. Then asked he them again, Whom seek ye? And they said, Jesus of Nazareth. Jesus answered, I have told you that I am he: if therefore ye seek me, let these go their way: that the saying might be fulfilled, which he spake, Of them which thou gavest me have I lost none. — JOHN 18:3-9 (see MATTHEW 26:47; MARK 14:43).

IT WAS "the night in which he was betrayed" (I Corinthians 11:23) — that long, sleepless, checkered, troubled night; the only night in which we can trace His movements step by step and follow His fate from hour to hour.[1] We can still see the rich flood of silver moonbeams and hear the soft splash of the brook Kidron; and soon after midnight in that quiet vale, amid the gnarled old trees, we see Jesus face to face with His foes. The grim struggle on His knees was over; the broken cries and bloody sweat were past. He had roused the slumbering disciples for the third time, and there He stood, calm and alert. Had He heard the sound of muffled footsteps? Had He caught a glimpse of slinking shadows? He would at least have seen the lights of the torches as they moved down the long steep hill from the city or as they danced in and out of the trees near the Garden. But He had planned to stand His ground in that place which Judas would know so well as if to smooth the

[1]William Hanna, *Our Lord's Life on Earth* (1882), p. 458.

task for His would-be captors. Thus He stood as Judas drew near with the captain of the Temple police and a band of soldiers.

"Judas then, having received a band of men and officers from the chief priests and Pharisees, cometh thither with lanterns and torches and weapons." Matthew and Mark refer to this body of men as "a great multitude," sent out by the chief priests, scribes, and elders, and armed with swords and staves; but they add no further details. It is John who takes up the story at this point to place on record the first dramatic encounter with its enthralling interest.

The first point of interest was the sudden panic which seized the motley crowd. "Jesus therefore, knowing all things that should come upon him, went forth, and said unto them, Whom seek ye?" It was as though divine necessity ruled His action, for He knew what was in progress; *therefore* He would forestall their plans, and would confront them near the gate of the Garden. They had come with torch and lantern, in case He should try to hide and they should need to search or pursue; they had come too with sword and stave, in case they should need to hunt and He should try to fight or resist. But weapons and lanterns were thrust aside by His course of action, for He *went forth* of His own accord to meet them; He stepped out from the trees and the shadows, out from the gate and the Garden, to face them in the clear moonlit valley. Once His hearers would have taken Him by force, and would have made Him their King; but He withdrew and hid Himself (John 6:15; cf. 8:59; 12:36). Now they came to take Him by force, that they might nail Him to the cross; yet He advanced and gave Himself away. They had come to find and accost Him, yet it was He who met them with words of challenge and authority: "Jesus . . . said unto them, Whom seek ye?" This was not the way in which a guilty man would hail a patrol sent out for his arrest! But it was meant to do much more than bear witness to His integrity; it was meant to fix their thoughts on Himself so as to throw a shield round His bewildered disciples.

Judas had come so as to make Him known by the sign of a kiss, but he was now forestalled: "They answered him, Jesus of Nazareth. Jesus saith unto them, I am he. And Judas also, which betrayed him, stood with them." There were some in that band, soldiers, strangers, who might not know Jesus by sight, and they met His challenge with a reply which was not without a shade of contempt: "Jesus, the Nazarene" (cf. John 19:19, Matthew 26:71). They could never believe that so bold a challenge would spring from the lips of Him whom they sought.

But were there not others in that party, Judas aside, who would know Him by sight? A sense of awe must have begun to steal across their minds; it so mastered their thoughts that not one of them had courage enough to speak out in reply: "*Thou art the man! We are in search of thee!*" As for Judas, he stood in their midst like one who had been struck dumb, unable to say what he had come to say: "This is he!" He was made to feel that the Lord whom he thought to betray was more than a match for them all, and he could not so much as find his voice before Jesus Himself told them all that they wished to know: "*I am he.*" Judas could not fail to recall how these two words in Greek had served for the revelation of His Person in days gone by, though the others would see no more in them than an indication that He was the one whom they sought (cf. John 4:26; 6:20; 8:58; 13:19).[2] Yet how absurd Judas would look and the others would feel as they stood with weapons in hand, and heard those quiet words in the cold moonlight in the Vale of Kidron!

But had some strange sight met their eyes? Or did some stark fear grip their hearts? "As soon then as he had said unto them, I am he, they went backward, and fell to the ground." They had come on a mean and treacherous errand, with a traitor for their guide. They had thought to catch Him asleep or by surprise, to take Him by stealth or in silence.[3] But He had come forth and declared Himself in the majesty of His innocence, and they recoiled in the flash of an eye, just as if they had been disarmed and stripped of all their strength. No force was put forth save the force of awe and fear, but that was quite enough; they reeled back and fell like slaked lime on the ground. There lay the armed guard, as though pinned by some unseen power to the earth; there stood the Lord Christ, calmly waiting till the prostrate soldiers should rise. He had put forth His power in a miracle which would leave His enemies without excuse; it was a

---

[2]B. F. Westcott, *The Gospel According to St. John* (18th impr., 1937), p. 253.

[3]James Stalker, *The Trial and Death of Jesus Christ* (1894), p. 7.

sign which would demonstrate for the disciples as no other sign could how free and how voluntary was His approach to all that lay in store. He could so easily have passed through the midst of that band as He had passed through the midst of the crowd, and gone His way as at Nazareth or Jerusalem (Luke 4:30; John 10:39); but He would not, for He would give Himself up of His own free will to be bound and then slain for sin.

The next point of interest was the self-surrender which ruled the kingly Christ: "Then asked he them again, Whom seek ye? And they said, Jesus of Nazareth." The air was so still in that calm moonlight that one might have heard the fall of a leaf. There lay those men, just as did the keepers of the grave who trembled and fell down like the dead whom they had been supposed to guard (Matthew 28:4). How long they lay prostrate we are not told, but a distinct pause is indicated. Then that strange spell of awe and fear which had struck them like a stroke of lightning passed clean away. They stood on their own feet once more, but they seem to have hung back from further action.

Westcott points out the force of the order in which the words occur in Greek: "Again therefore he asked them, whom seek ye?" It was left for Him to provoke them to action in words like those with which He was yet to address Judas: "*Is it this* for which thou art come?" (Matthew 26:50)[4] But it would seem that they were too shaken to do other than to reply in the old terms, "Jesus of Nazareth." He had asked them as though He would compel them to admit that they had no power of their own to make Him their captive. He had told them already that He was the Nazarene, but they had only fallen to the ground; they would in fact never take Him unless He were willing to yield Himself into their hands. But were those words also one last latent appeal to the conscience of those who had come out to take Him by force and so give Him up to death?

There was a commanding tone as well as a dignified calm in His reply: "Jesus answered, I have told you that I am he: if therefore ye seek me, let these go their way." He knew what odds there were against Him as one lone solitary figure; yet He

---

[4]B. F. Westcott, *The Gospel According to St. John* (18th impr., 1937), p. 253.

was unafraid. He knew that His hour had now come, and his mind was steeled for the cross. He would not put forth His power to send them reeling back a second time in that awed dismay; He would rather let them take Him that His wondering disciples might go free and unharmed. The spell cast by that sense of awe had made them feel that they were in His power, and they were quite ready to do just what He said. His words indeed were in effect: "Take me, but let these go their way." It was fitting that He should stand alone when He came to suffer and die; it would set His Passion in a clearer light if they were set free. He chose to yield Himself to bonds and death that they might go their way, for that voluntary self-surrender was an essential element in His death and dying as our Substitute-Sin-bearer.

Very wonderful was that spontaneous delivery of Himself into their hands: "That the saying might be fulfilled, which he spake, Of them which thou gavest me have I lost none." Those were the words which He had used that night in His great prayer on the way to Gethsemane (John 17:12), and their application by John to this scene is a hint as to the dangers which may lie in wait for the soul and lurk behind trials in the flesh. It had been no part of the plan laid by Judas and the priestly party to let some go their way; that was made clear when a little later they seized the young man who tried to follow behind (Mark 14:51, 52). It was only with great difficulty that he escaped out of their hands when he fled naked; but it was as though a mantle of love was thrown round the disciples so that not one of them was touched in spite of their helplessness. He who had loved His own which were in the world loved them to the end, and His last thought before His own arrest was to provide for their safety. He knew that some of them would one day die for Him, but that they were not fit to face so great a trial as yet. Thus He secured their freedom by His bonds, and that was in accord with His vow that He would suffer none of them to be lost.

The disclosure of majesty in the Garden at the very time when He faced arrest was all the more eloquent as a miracle because it took place in the hour of His self-humiliation. "What shall He do when He comes to judge, Who did this when about to be judged?" so once asked Augustine; "what shall be His might when He comes to reign, Who had this might when He was at the point to die?"[5] No one who was an eye-witness of that scene would ever have it to say that He was placed under arrest because there was no help for it. They could never pretend that He was put to death because that death was not avoidable. It was fresh proof that He took the path to the cross as a candidate and a volunteer for death; and the motive in His mind is pictured in the invitation: "Take me, but let these go their way." It was the true David, that great Shepherd of the sheep, who now said: "Let thine hand, I pray thee, O Lord my God, be on me; but as for these sheep, what have they done?" (I Chronicles 21:17.) He would be bound, that they might go free; He would be slain, that they might live for ever. His was a Love as strong as death, and we may trust that Love even unto the end.

---

[5]John Charles Ryle, *Expository Thoughts on St. John's Gospel* (1897), vol. iii, p. 245.

Chapter 7

THE TRAITOR KISS

Now he that betrayed him gave them a sign, saying, Whomsoever I shall kiss, that same is he: hold him fast. And forthwith he came to Jesus, and said, Hail, master; and kissed him. And Jesus said unto him, Friend, wherefore art thou come? — MATTHEW 26:48-50 (see MARK 14:44, 45).

And while he yet spake, behold a multitude, and he that was called Judas, one of the twelve, went before them, and drew near unto Jesus to kiss him. But Jesus said unto him, Judas, betrayest thou the Son of man with a kiss? — LUKE 22:47, 48.

IT IS still a dark and dreadful fact that Judas was guide to them that took Jesus. Indeed, the man and his motives form one of the darkest problems in the long and tangled story of all human affairs. The Lord Jesus had known long in advance that He was to suffer at the hands of Judas: "Have not I chosen you twelve," He had said, "and one of you is a devil?" (John 6:70.) But it would seem that it was not until the last week that Judas reached the crisis (John 12:1-8), and not until the last night of all that he made his pact with the ruling party (John 13:18-30). Then he led the Temple guard straight to the Garden where he knew that Jesus was wont to go. That in itself was a ruthless mark of contempt for the hallowed sanctuary where He had so often sought quiet and prayer. "Judas . . . knew the place" (John 18:2), and he knew well enough why it was that Jesus went there. But more ruthless still was his plan to make Him known by the sign of a kiss; that is beyond all else the sin which has made his name so dark in the eyes of all humanity.

A kiss was the token of friendship and goodwill, a sign of love and true discipleship. That was why its neglect on the part of His host had once been an item for blame: "Thou gavest me no kiss" (Luke 7:45). It may have been common as the form of

45

greeting between the Master and the twelve, but we never read of human lips that touched Him save twice in the gospel memoirs. Once it was the lips of the penitent woman who rained her kisses in love and worship upon His feet; here it was the lips of the treacherous Judas who stamped his kisses in scorn and disdain upon His cheek.

The emphasis in the first phase of this drama falls on the conduct of Judas: "Now he that betrayed him gave them a sign, saying, Whomsoever I shall kiss, that same is he: hold him fast." Perhaps the worst form that hypocrisy can take is to render a man insensible to his own deep ingratitude, and he must have been far gone in that dark form of moral oblivion when he either arranged or else agreed to such a sign. But the whole plan had gone astray when the Lord stepped out to meet them in the moonlight.

Judas, no less than the others, had been surprised by His challenge: "Whom seek ye?" He was like a man who had lost the powers of speech; he could find no words to say the thing he had come to say. He had stumbled back and fallen down in terror, and when at length he got to his feet, he had lost his poise. He heard the Lord Jesus invite them to take Him, but there was a momentary pause as if they were all afraid. Who would care to be the first to lift a finger against the one who could command powers so mysterious? Then his courage returned and he resolved to act; he stood forth to betray the Son of Man with the sign of a kiss.

There was no real need now to point Him out, but he went through with the whole plan: "And forthwith he came to Jesus, and said, Hail, master; and kissed him." Perhaps the spell of that strange awe which had felled them to the ground was still in the air and strong enough to hold them back. Therefore Judas would go on with his part as if to show them how safe it was to draw near. Perhaps it was something like a mechanical impulse which drove him on; he had fixed on the thing that he was to do, and had braced his mind to get it done. Thus, when the time arrived for him to act, he would not stop to think, he would simply let the momentum of a decision made in advance carry him through. He would step out in front of the enemy band as though he were still on terms of intimate trust; then he would hail Him with the dear name of Master, and kiss

Him with the kiss that damns. But the verb which describes that kiss is a compound form of the verb which had been used only a verse before, and it strengthens the whole force and idea behind that act. Judas sealed his greeting with the fervent kiss of a friend (cf. Luke 7:38, 15:20; Acts 20:37); it was needlessly emphatic, and that made it cruel as well as heartless.

That kiss was the final climax in a long and painful drama of sin which had long been nursed in secret. He had reached the ultimate in treachery and turpitude; there was no new depth to which he could stoop or sink. His own moral worth had been sapped by the hidden growth of greed for money, but the sale of the Lord Jesus for the sake of thirty silver coins was nothing compared with that dark kiss of shame. All that is loyal and true in our human nature loathes the thought which that word *traitor* conceals; but the one thing for which the world will not forgive Judas was the way in which that fell deed was done.

There might have been pity for the traitor, there might even have been mercy for the treason, if the crime had not been cloaked with a sign which is sacred to all mankind. But as long as love can find a home in this world of ours, his name will stand for an outrage against all the sanctities of true affection. It was a sin against the heart with all its rich capacities for tenderness and charity, and it was an act which must be abhorred by all who have ever received a kiss as the token of love. It was one of the sorest blows ever dealt by man to man, not to say by man to God.

The emphasis in the next phase of this drama falls on the conduct of Jesus: "And Jesus said unto him, Friend, wherefore art thou come?" If we may read between the lines, and if we would relate Matthew's gospel to Luke's, we may conclude that the Master spoke twice, so that Judas heard His voice in rebuke both before and after that kiss. Thus it was when Judas drew near to hail Him as Master that the saying preserved by Matthew escaped His lips: "Friend, wherefore art thou come?" It was as though He would make one final attempt to stay his hand, to make him pause, to get him to think of the thing he was about to do. The Lord Jesus knew well all that Judas had planned to do; He had known when He gave Judas the sop at the table. And Judas knew that Jesus knew; he had known it when he went out into the night. But the Master spoke in pity rather than in anger, and His words were meant to ride on the wings of love; they were in fact softened by a note of wistfulness, or of forbearance, which could only be true of the love that hath no equal. It was the last touching protest of wounded love, the last moving appeal to dastard shame; thought of, cared for, warned so often — had he really come to betray?[1]

The Lord Jesus did not refuse that kiss, though He knew what was in his heart: "But Jesus said unto him, Judas, betrayest thou the Son of man with a kiss?" There is in Luke's saying a stern, sharp note which is wholly absent in Matthew's record; it seems to mark a change of thought and front on the part of the Lord Jesus that one event alone serves to explain. Judas would not heed the words of appeal, but stamped that kiss upon His cheek as he had planned.

When Jesus felt the touch of those lips in that act of shameful hypocrisy He felt that it was more than He could bear. He could not hold back the strong rush of pain which seemed to pour in like a flood, and He spoke out once more. But He spoke now, not in tones of tender warning, but in terms of seering rebuke. "Friend," He could call him no more, not even by the widest stretch of the laws that rule human kindness. "Judas," He would call him, as if the sound of his own name ought to shock him with a sense of remorse. That name was meant to tear aside the mask of mean deceit with which he had disguised his vile intent; and the words that followed went on to mark his guilt in terms so plain that he could not escape. The majesty and sacredness of the Person who had thus been betrayed was flashed upon the mind of the traitor in words which were meant to stir and startle: "Betrayest thou the Son of man with a kiss?" The order of those words in the Greek text shows that the ultimate emphasis falls on the kiss. Was a kiss the only sign he could choose? Was there nothing else which might have served his purpose? *A kiss!*

That kiss still leaves a strange haunting sting of shame in our minds; yet no one can ever feel this today in the way that it must have been felt by the Lord Jesus. "For it was not an enemy that reproached me; then I could have borne it . . . But it was thou, a man mine equal, my guide, and mine acquaintance" (Psalm 55:12, 13). It meant that all His love for one err-

---

ing soul had now been trampled into the dust; it meant that the light which He had come to kindle in one needy mind had now been quenched in darkness. That night, and the next day, His own face was to be marred and shamed in a score of ways. It had now been furrowed by the beads of sweat that rolled like drops of blood from His brow; it would yet be bruised and beaten by the buffets of base underlings, soiled and sodden with the spittle of vile satellites. But the kiss of Judas was the wound which would leave far the deepest of all these scars. It would pierce more deeply than the thorns on His brow or the spear in His side, for it was the kind of wound that makes the soul burn and bleed.[2]

There is one faint illustration of this traitor kiss in the Old Testament. Joab had slain Absalom in spite of David's command, and had been replaced by Amasa as chief captain of Israel. But his hot spirit caught fire with anger, and he conspired against the life of this rival. He hid a sword beneath his cloak, and drew near with fair words: "Art thou in health, my brother?" (II Samuel 20:9). Then he made as if to kiss him, and plunged the sword into his heart. It was a deed that grieved David, just as he had been grieved for the death of Abner; but no heart was ever half so tender to all the wrongs of wounded love as the heart of Jesus, and the kiss of Judas in the Garden was far worse in degree than the kiss of Joab in the days of David. Yet He never lost His calm and patient dignity or His kind and gentle compassion; He strove to the last to rouse that conscience, and to save that soul from ruin.

It is the same even today when Jesus confronts the spirit of Judas in our hearts and motives; He sees all our sinful treason, and meets it still with words of most patient warning. He would fain make us see how black it is, and so wean us away before it is too late. God still commends His love toward us in that while we were yet in our sins Christ died for us; it is for us to kiss the Son now in this day of grace while He comes as our Friend, lest we should all perish when His wrath as our Judge has been kindled but a little!

---

[2]James Stalker, *The Trial and Death of Jesus Christ* (1894), p. 4.

Chapter 8

THE NAKED SWORD

Then came they, and laid hands on Jesus, and took him. And, behold, one of them which were with Jesus stretched out his hand, and drew his sword, and struck a servant of the high priest's, and smote off his ear. Then said Jesus unto him, Put up again thy sword into his place: for all they that take the sword shall perish with the sword. Thinkest thou that I cannot now pray to my Father, and he shall presently give me more than twelve legions of angels? But how then shall the scriptures be fulfilled, that thus it must be? — MATTHEW 26:50-54 (see MARK 14:46, 47; LUKE 22:49-51; JOHN 18:10, 11).

THE DRAMA in Gethsemane was now quickly moving to its predestined conclusion, for the traitor kiss had removed the last trace of lingering compunction on the part of His foes. They had recovered from the shock of that first encounter with the Nazarene, and their momentary hesitation had no sooner vanished than they bestirred themselves. The hour had come for His arrest, and they were now ready to take action. "Then came they, and laid hands on Jesus, and took him." They moved in and seized Him just as if He were a vulgar villain on the common highway, and He made no attempt either to resist or escape.[1] He whose very presence had been enough to drive back His foes in fear and alarm would not now so much as lift a finger to prevent His arrest. But the calm and serene strength of mind and purpose which He displayed shone in striking contrast with the confusion of His disciples. They had failed to spend time in watch and prayer, and this arrest now came upon them with blinding, bewildering surprise. They saw rough hands laid on Him, and their hearts were in their mouths: "When they which were about him saw what would follow, they

[1]William Hanna, *Our Lord's Life on Earth* (1882), p. 465.

50

said unto him, Lord, shall we smite with the sword?" (Luke 22:49). But then, without waiting for an answer, one of the twelve drew his sword and lashed out. All the evangelists describe this rash assault, but it is from John alone that we glean the names of Peter and of Malchus. There was just a moment of wild suspense, fraught with danger; then Jesus interposed.

The brief record preserved by Luke was mainly on account of what Christ did. "And one of them smote the servant of the high priest, and cut off his right ear." Peter's action was true to his nature as we know it — earnest, reckless, hasty. He could not bear to see rude hands laid on Christ, and he sprang to His defense. Perhaps he was spurred on by some impetuous recollection of that vow to stand by Him at all costs, even to die for Him should need arise (Luke 22:33). Perhaps he had in mind that strange conversation about the two swords which were in their hands, and the remark that these two were enough (Luke 22:38). One of those swords was his, and he promptly drew it; others might ask should they smite with the sword, but he would act. He flashed it in the air and lunged against Malchus, who must have made himself conspicuous in that moonlight arrest. Peter meant to split his skull, to kill him where he stood; but he missed the crown of his head, and did no more than slice off his right ear.

It was impulsive; it was mistaken; for what could one man do against the whole armed band? Yet we may give him the credit for a certain bravery and a ready devotion; there was an element of rightness and nobility in his action. He was prepared in the impulse of that moment to act in the spirit of his own boast, and to risk both imprisonment and death for his Master. But the impulse did not endure, and this was a gesture at the wrong time and in the wrong method.

It was untimely as an act of friendship; it was out of harmony with the purpose of His self-surrender. "And Jesus answered and said, Suffer ye thus far." There can be no reasonable doubt that Peter's blow was meant to kill that servant from the high priest's palace; it was aimed at his head. That would be one major reason for his anxiety to pass without recognition when he ventured later on inside that palace; recognition might have provoked revenge!

But what would have happened in the Garden had that blow

proved fatal we can easily imagine. One drawn sword would quickly provoke twenty others from their scabbards, and there might have been a sudden, unpremeditated attack upon the twelve. That one rash blow might have been paid for at too dear a price, had not the Lord Jesus intervened. "Suffer ye thus far," He said with perfect presence of mind, restraining the soldiers, subduing the disciples. "Thus far." As far as His own seizure and arrest, His bonds, His trial, and His execution! History knows of no example of wrong or violence which was more criminal in origin and objective than this; and if this were meekly suffered, where are we to fix the limit of passive endurance?

Luke alone refers to what He did; it was the last act of healing which He ever performed. "And he touched his ear, and healed him." Peter's action had served to place Him in the wrong; it seemed even to justify His enemies. It would make Him out to be the leader of a band of men who were a menace both to law and order.[2] Besides, this was the first time in His life that a mortal brother had been forced to suffer on His account, and this was out of line with the whole course of His earthly career. So, to undo the harm, He would repair the wrong; He stretched out His hand as if it were that of a surgeon to touch the ear and make it whole. We are not told that the ear had been shorn right off, and this seems to be a hint that it had been left to hang by a tissue of skin; for Luke was careful to say that He touched the ear, not just the place where the ear had been. At all events, this was the last act of healing ever wrought by the Lord Jesus, and it is the only case on record of the healing of a fresh wound caused by physical violence. It was a miracle wrought for an enemy, an act of true mercy, unasked, unexpected, without faith, without thanks. It was one more proof of His power and love; to the very end, He would do good to those who chose to hate Him without a cause.[3]

The more ample record in Matthew was penned mainly on account of what Christ said. "Then said Jesus unto him, Put up again thy sword into his place: for all they that take the sword shall perish with the sword." These were words of plain and downright rebuke, though the tone may have been kind and

---

[2]Alfred Plummer, *St. Luke* (1922), p. 513.
[3]John Charles Ryle, *Expository Thoughts on St. Luke's Gospel* (1896), vol. ii, p. 434.

gentle. Let him sheathe that sword once again in its scabbard, and let it be put out of sight! The Lord Jesus would meet violence with submission, would match injury with fortitude; and He would not suffer Peter's sword to provoke sudden death for the twelve! Then He lifted up His eyes to look far away from the immediate present so as to scan all the contingencies that might ever arise in time, and He went on to lay down one clear rule to guide the Church in all future circumstances. Thus He affirmed that all who take and wield the sword will be slain by its might. It was a plain warning that if men should try to promote His cause on earth by force, they would perish by the very means which they have resolved to use and trust. Those words have been verified by the facts of history time and again; the age of the Crusades in Europe and the wars of religion in Germany are a standing witness to this prophetic principle. Seldom has an appeal to the sword in Christ's Name been justified; often, if not always, it has recoiled on the head of the saints in disaster.

The next words seem to have been meant to turn Peter's mind to yet another view of the case. "Thinkest thou that I cannot now pray to my Father, and he shall presently give me more than twelve legions of angels?" Peter's rashness was in utter contrast to the unused might which was all the time at His disposal, for the disclosure of His majesty and the act of healing had been enough to show what vast powers were lodged in His hand. Had He stood in need of defense He could have asked of His Father, who would have placed angel legions at His command against His foes. The word rendered *give* (A.V.) or *send* (R.V.) means literally *to place beside*. The idea is magnificent. The Lord pictures Himself as one ensconced in the shadow of his surrounding battalions, and those battalions would be composed of angelic legionaires![4] What would become of that miscellaneous guard which must have numbered less than a tenth of a Roman legion if they were faced with the angel hosts of glory? He had no need for that puny sword when He could command the armed might of heaven; yet He would not avail Himself of it, for in that case how was He to fulfill His task on earth?

If He should be rescued from His foes by angel legions, how would He be able to go on to the cross? "But how then shall

---

[4]James Morison, St. *Matthew* (1885), p. 555.

the scriptures be fulfilled, that thus it must be?" Both the argument and the incident were brought to a close with this reference to the long file of prophecies from Genesis to Malachi which had all with one voice foretold how He must needs suffer and die if He were to conquer and reign. He would allow nothing to halt the march of events which led to the cross; neither Peter's sword, nor yet angel hosts; for He was ready to die as Scripture decreed. But all that He had done, and all that He had said, would stand as proof that His arrest and death were the result of His free and voluntary choice and consent. Even in that hour when He was betrayed, not once, but twice, He had put forth His power in a miracle; He had struck the hostile band to the ground, and had healed the severed ear with a touch. There would be no further display of the miraculous until the three hours of darkness while He hung on the cross, even although He could have called the massed armies of God to His rescue. Miracles were not enough to change men's hearts, and His enemies paid them no heed at all. But that double display of power before He let Himself be seized and bound was a final and a unique testimony to the free and voluntary nature of His arrest.

John's gospel records one more matchless saying in close connection with this incident: "Then said Jesus unto Peter, Put up thy sword into the sheath: the cup which my Father hath given me, shall I not drink it?" These words must always be read in relation to His other sayings about the cup in the Garden. It is impossible not to feel that they still preserve a hint as to the words which had trembled on His lips in His last lonely vigil. He had come to see that the cup was not to be removed; it was being *given* into His hands by the Father whose will He longed to do. Therefore now that He stood face to face with bonds and with death, He grasped that cup with a spirit almost akin to joy. He could speak in echo of that prayer of anguish, and could frame the words in perfect serenity: Simon, Son of Jonas, dost thou not know that it it *My Father* Who has put this cup in My hands? Wilt thou have Me refuse that cup? Shall I not lay down My life for sinners?[5] This was His last

[5]John Charles Ryle, *Expository Thoughts on St. John's Gospel* (1897), vol. iii, p. 250.

word to Simon Peter until after His death and the Day of Resurrection; but it was a saying of such ineffable grace that it would linger in mind and heart all through the long troubled hours that ensued. But it was more than he could grasp in that first dark hour of crisis; it would perhaps require the look that broke his heart to bring those words to life in his experience. For the moment, the twelve were all nonplussed; Peter's sword was useless, and their courage had failed. The sad record runs on without a pause: "And they all forsook Him, and fled" (Mark 14:50). But this was in the cup which His Father had given Him; would He not drink it all?

Chapter 9

THE WANTON BLOW

Then the band and the captain and officers of the Jews took Jesus, and bound him, and led him away to Annas first; for he was father in law to Caiaphas, which was the high priest that same year. . . . The high priest then asked Jesus of his disciples, and of his doctrine. Jesus answered him, I spake openly to the world; I ever taught in the synagogue, and in the temple, whither the Jews always resort; and in secret have I said nothing. Why askest thou me? ask them which heard me, what I have said unto them: behold, they know what I said. And when he had thus spoken, one of the officers which stood by struck Jesus with the palm of his hand, saying, Answerest thou the high priest so? Jesus answered him, If I have spoken evil, bear witness of the evil: but if well, why smitest thou me? Now Annas had sent him bound unto Caiaphas the high priest. — JOHN 18:12, 13, 19-24.

SEIZED and bound by the armed guard near the clear moonlit garden, Jesus was led across the brook Kidron, up the long steep ascent, through city gates and silent streets, to the hall of Annas. This old man of three-score years and ten had been high priest of Israel from A.D. 7 to A.D. 14, and was still head of the most prominent and powerful house in Jewry. He ought to have retained his high office for life, but he had been replaced by his son-in-law Caiaphas. This was due to the fact that he had defied the limits of jurisdiction allowed by the imperial authorities, and the office which he inherited by the Law of Moses had been taken from him at the word of Gratus. But he was still virtual head of the church, though his son-in-law Caiaphas was the nominal high priest. Thus we read in Luke's gospel of "Annas and Caiaphas being the high priests" (Luke 3:2), and in the Acts we are told of "Annas the high priest and Caiaphas" (Acts 4:6). He came from a long and able line of forebears, wealthy and ambitious aristocrats; he stood for the ruling caste in Israel, worldly and arrogant Sadducees. He was far too wary not to have heard of the warning words about "the leaven of the Sadducees" (Matthew 16:6), and he knew well enough that there would be no room for him or his household in that Kingdom which He proclaimed. He stood to lose all he had in this world if the Gospel were true, and he had no faith in a world to come.[1] Thus he took a leading part in the bargain with Judas and in the capture of Jesus; Judas indeed drops out of the story just at this point as though it were when the Lord came before Annas that he was paid his price. This would explain John's words: "And (they) led him away to Annas first." Annas then seized the chance to put the Lord Jesus through a preliminary interrogation which was as informal as it was illegal.

The first half of John 18:19-24 records His brief interview with Annas: "The high priest then asked Jesus of his disciples, and of his doctrine." The Lord Jesus was to stand His trial at the bar of the Supreme Council, where at least a show of law and justice would be observed. Annas could not initiate the trial apart from his colleagues, and some time would elapse before so much as a quorum of the full court could be convened. The law was most precise that there could be no trial at all until at least two joined voice in common witness against a man; it was then the task of the scribes to draw up a charge in line with these facts so that the trial could be set in motion. There was no case before the court until this had been done, and the man was neither accused nor open to question up to this point.[2] Thus, when Annas tried to prepare the way for the full court by an informal inquiry, what he did was strictly against the law. Yet he did not scruple to sound Christ out, in the hope that he would catch Him in some unguarded utterance. He asked questions about His disciples and His doctrine which seemed harmless enough, but which were meant to give a lead to the formal prosecution. The two points which he raised were a clue to the line which the Jews meant to take; they would try to embroil Him with the State as a rebel and a menace to the rule of Caesar. What was the real object of that band of twelve? What was the true import of all His teaching? Was He not the head of

---

[1]F. J. Powell, *The Trial of Jesus Christ* (1949), p. 57.

[2]F. J. Powell, *The Trial of Jesus Christ* (1949), p. 47.

a revolutionary faction? Did He not have in view a revolutionary kingdom?

But the Lord saw through this design just as clearly as He felt the breach of justice. "Jesus answered him, I spake openly to the world; I ever taught in the synagogue, and in the temple, whither the Jews always resort; and in secret have I said nothing." Hebrew law, like English law, was designed to act upon a presumption of innocence, and the onus of proof to the contrary rested on those who brought in the accusation. Annas had no legal right to question Him in private, and no moral right to try to make Him incriminate Himself. The Lord Jesus knew how easily Jewish prejudice might be roused on the score of blasphemy, and how easily Roman jealousies might be stirred on the point of sedition. But His reply was a calm and prudent statement, made with lofty self-consciousness, very unlike the tone of severe reserve which He kept for Caiaphas and the Sanhedrin. He spoke freely and boldly in the hall of Annas, for He spoke as Man to man; and His words give us a vivid picture of the whole course of His general ministry. There had been nothing clandestine or underhand, nothing that would not bear the closest scrutiny; He had spoken before the world, and there were no reserves in His public message. He had nothing new to add to all that He had taught in full view of the public, and in secret He had published nothing.

Then in words of noble and transparent ease He went on to remonstrate with Annas: "Why askest thou me? ask them which heard me, what I have said unto them: behold, they know what I said." He still felt the indignity of an arrest under the cloak of night as if He were likely to flee, and by a force so large as to suggest that He was a dangerous character. Thus He flashed His reply back in a way that told the high priest how bare and naked his own heart was: "*Why* askest thou me?" Why dost thou, the judge, ask of Me, the Man in bonds, about My disciples and My doctrine? It was in thought and in accent the voice of pure Hebrew justice, founded on the broad lines of true judicial procedure; and it was a summons to the conscience of the high priest, pointing out to an unjust judge the first duty of his great office.[3] Was it not a mean advantage that he was now trying to steal with the art of a hypocrite? Why had they planned for His

---

[3] A. Taylor Innes, *The Trial of Jesus Christ* (1899), p. 26.

arrest if they had yet to learn what He had said or done? Was he really so much in the dark? One whose spies had tracked Him for three long years! Did he really wish to know the truth? Let him ask those who had heard Him gladly! His own servants who had once been sent to arrest Him knew what He had said. Annas could ask them, and they would give their verdict: "Never man spake like this man" (John 7:46).

The next half of the paragraph describes His rough dismissal by Annas: "And when he had thus spoken, one of the officers which stood by struck Jesus with the palm of his hand, saying, Answerest thou the high priest so?" He had used a freedom which He would have spared if Annas had been on the Seat of Judgment, and His scathing rebuke had laid bare the sinister intention of the crafty old priest. It was enough to shield Him from repetition of such nuisance questions; Annas was shamed into silence, even though that reply must have galled him in the extreme. But one of the jailers who stood at hand could not restrain himself with the same practiced ease; he raised his hand and struck Him across the face: "Answerest thou the high priest so?" That was the angry, scornful pretext for the blow.

But what are we to think of an exhibition like this, when an untried captive could be struck at random? There was yet no accusation against the Lord Jesus, no case before a judge, and no court in session, and He had but recalled Annas to the Law of Israel. But this was just the first of those acts of violence which were now to intersperse the whole course of the trial. Better had it been for that man if his hand had withered and dropped ere it had struck that blow!

Out of the depths of a perfect patience which nothing could disturb, His answer came: "Jesus answered him, If I have spoken evil, bear witness of the evil: but if well, why smitest thou me?" They would swarm all round Him later on to mock and smite Him, and He would have nothing to say; but now He met challenge with counter-challenge, and His words in reply were a calm and noble protest. He took His stand on the platform of the lawful rights of every Hebrew and He asked for freedom of speech and an open accusation.[4] It was a blunt demand to be confronted with the witnesses, for there could be no case at all

---

[4]A. Taylor Innes, *The Trial of Jesus Christ* (1899), p. 27.

until their voice was heard. If He had spoken evil, let them bear witness against Him as became a court of law; and if, on the contrary, He had spoken the truth, what could excuse that wanton blow? It was almost the same as the trial that was to befall Paul before the same body of men: "The high priest Ananias commanded them that stood by him to smite him on the mouth" (Acts 23:2). But Paul could not repress a fierce retort of mingled contempt and indignation, "God shall smite thee, thou whited wall: for sittest thou to judge me after the law, and commandest me to be smitten contrary to the law?" (Acts 23:3). But the Lord was betrayed into no such loss of temper, no such heat of reply. How hard was it, even for a Paul, to imitate the gentle answer and gracious spirit of our Redeemer!

The interview with Annas was over; the first phase in His trial had failed. "Annas therefore sent him bound unto Caiaphas the high priest" (R.V.). The verb in the Revised Version has been taken in its simple aoristic meaning, so that this verse marks the end of the trial before Annas. There is serious objection to the pluperfect translation *had sent* (A.V.) on the ground of grammar alone, for the verb was one which had a regular pluperfect in use and so had no need to fall back on the aorist for that purpose. This verse simply means that Annas had failed to lure the Lord Jesus into any statement that could form the basis for an accusation, and the next stage in the prosecution could be handled best by Caiaphas and the Sanhedrin. No doubt by this time the leading members of that body had been convened, and they would have to find other ways to secure a verdict of guilty. It was as yet but two or three o'clock in the morning, and the city as a whole was still fast asleep. There might have been drastic uproar if the Galilean peasants had known of the arrest of the Prophet from Nazareth, but not a hint of what was on foot had reached the crowd of pilgrims within the city walls. The Jews dared not run the risk of action by day for that very reason; the plot must not miscarry before the Lord Jesus had been placed in Roman custody! Therefore Annas saw that He was bound once more with those thongs, and then sent Him off to that part of the palace where Caiaphas was.

There was no bitterness in the long-suffering heart of Jesus for the high priest or his servants; crafty word and wanton blow had only provoked a claim for the fairest justice. But it had been the part of truth to show Annas that He saw through his wiles, and it had been an act of grace when He stooped to reason with that callous jailer. His words could not fail to recall the grave charge in His own sermon: "I say unto you, That ye resist not evil: but whosoever shall smite thee on thy right cheek, turn to him the other also" (Matthew 5:39). The best comment on this precept was His reply to that jailer; it is a maxim that needs some reserve in its application. There are times when honor or truth compels us boldly to protest rather than tamely to submit. The Lord did not present the other cheek to that insult, because justice was still at stake; He did turn the other cheek without a word later on when all justice had been outraged. Sometimes it is right for us to turn the other cheek, to bear to the utmost, without retaliation; at other times it is right for us to take the firmest stand, to strive to the utmost, without recrimination. And if the Lord Jesus could so search and reveal man's soul in that hour of travail, what will He do when He comes as Judge with eyes like flames of fire?

Chapter 10

THE FALSE WITNESS

And they that had laid hold on Jesus led him away to Caiaphas the high priest, where the scribes and the elders were assembled. . . . Now the chief priests, and elders, and all the council, sought false witness against Jesus, to put him to death; But found none: yea, though many false witnesses came, yet found they none. At the last came two false witnesses, and said, This fellow said, I am able to destroy the temple of God, and to build it in three days. And the high priest arose, and said unto him, Answerest thou nothing? what is it, which these witness against thee? But Jesus held his peace. — MATTHEW 26:57, 59-63 (see MARK 14:53, 55-61).

PERHAPS the Lord Jesus had been screened in private before Annas partly to give the Jews time to convene a full court for His trial, and the servants of the high priest would scour the streets of the city in spite of the midnight hour to call the Sanhedrin together. No one could tell what would happen if the pilgrim crowds woke to find Him in their hands, and the only safe course which they could see was to get Him tried and lodged with the imperial authorities before daybreak. This would mark the second stage in His trial at the hands of the Jews, and it was to take place in a formal court of justice under the direction of Caiaphas. Judge and scribes would all be men trained in the Law of Moses and the Mishna, and they would know the strength of its mighty sanctions as well as the nature of its endless scruples. They were not the men to dispense with the form or process of law, even though the soul of justice might be flung to the winds as in this case. But the points of detail which they strove to observe were as nothing compared with the breach of order which they planned to condone. No trial by night could be valid in the eyes of the law; no court could be convened at all before the break of day. There would have been cause for scandal even in a civil law suit if that law were defied, but it would be unbearable in the case of a trial where the issues of life and death would be at stake. In no case was that law so much in point as in the case of one who had been seized and bound by night; it would prevent his trial before next day, and would give him time to arrange for his defense.[1] But the trial of Jesus would not permit delay! It was rushed on in the small hours of the morning.

The first attack by the prosecution broke down through the falsehood of the evidence: "And they that had laid hold on Jesus led him away to Caiaphas the high priest, where the scribes and the elders were assembled." The character of Caiaphas is drawn with strong, indelible colors in the gospel records; a man who was at once resolute, politic, sinister, merciless. Annas might be high priest *de jure,* in the eyes of Israel; Caiaphas was high priest *de facto* in the eyes of Caesar. He had replaced Annas on the order of Valerius Gratus in A.D. 14, and he retained his post until he was deposed by Vitellius in A.D. 36. Thus he was in office throughout the ten years of Pilate's tenure of power, and that alone proves how agile he was in that world of political unrest. He was a veteran enemy of the Lord Jesus, and had long since tried to compass His death. Two years before, at the pool of Bethesda, "the Jews (had) sought the more to kill him" (John 5:18); twelve months before, near the Temple in Jerusalem, Jesus Himself had asked: "Why go ye about to kill me?" (John 7:19). Twice they had set out to arrest Him (John 7:30; 10:39); twice they had taken up stones to stone Him (John 8: 59; 10:31). Then the Sanhedrin had been summoned to think out their line of action after Lazarus had been raised from the dead, and Caiaphas had come forward with his policy of murder (John 11:47-53). "Caiaphas was he, which gave counsel to the Jews, that it was expedient that one man should die for the people" (John 18:14). Since then this shrewd master of shrewd intrigue, ruled by implacable hatred, had kept but one purpose in mind: his one aim had been to contrive the death of Christ.

The first step on the part of the prosecution was to call those who could witness against the Lord Jesus: "And the chief

---

[1]A. Taylor Innes, *The Trial of Jesus Christ* (1899), pp. 33-35.

priests and all the council sought for witness against Jesus to put him to death; and found none" (Mark 14:55). The case had been prejudged by the members of that council; the verdict of guilty was their settled intent. But that would raise one most urgent question: what was the crime for which He was to be condemned? So far there had been no intimation on this subject, nor could there be up to this point, for no charge could be framed and no trial could be held at all until they had found at least two who would join in adverse witness at His expense. They had to find two men who would agree in a specific indictment of some word or action before the prisoner could be accused, tried, or condemned. But the priestly party had not had time to draw up their plans in detail or to school each witness for this trial in advance; they had to act on the spur of an hour or two, and their case was hastily improvised. Their sole anxiety was to trump up a clear enough line of witness to give legal authority for the fatal accusation, and it would seem that they tried to sweep up what they wanted through the underlings and the sycophants of the court and palace. But though they were ready enough to bear witness, their witness was useless; and though strenuous endeavors were made to find two whose witness would be of value, "they found none."

Were they then to be robbed of their prize, or were they to be balked of their prey? "For many bare false witness against him, but their witness agreed not together" (Mark 14:56). They could protest that He had frequently ignored the sanctities of the Sabbath; but what of the miracles? They could affirm that He had publicly disowned the traditions of the Rabbis; but what of the parables? There were many who had heard Him denounce both Pharisees and Sadducees with sternest woes; but to condemn Him on that ground would prove that His trial was due to private malice or party revenge. The fact was that a life so pure and so blameless had left scant room even for foes to fault or to accuse; He could indeed challenge the world to convict Him of sin. Yet to put Him to death was their avowed purpose, and they had few scruples. If they could not try Him on true witness, perhaps they could get Him on false! But it staggers the mind to think of the oath or adjuration which must have been imposed on those who came to speak against His life, for each witness had to be sworn in by the most solemn address that the law could devise. Caiaphas knew that perjury in a case which involved the death sentence meant that each false witness put his own life in dire peril. Yet while he sat in the seat of Moses he dared to look the Lord Jesus in the face, and to swear in those who came to bear false witness against His life![2] But so true was that life that no common falsehood was strong enough to stand its ground; they could not agree as to their witness, and for shame's sake they had to be dismissed.

The next attack by the prosecution broke down through the weakness of the evidence: "At the last came two false witnesses, and said, This fellow said, I am able to destroy the temple of God, and to build it in three days." Two men were found at last whose version of events had something in common; it looked as though they would agree on a point which could be construed into a momentous charge. They had heard Him three years before give voice to certain mystic words. "Destroy this temple," Jesus had said, "and in three days, I will raise it up" (John 2:19). That brief saying had been full of prophetic mystery, and had sorely perplexed the Jews; it had led to the first altercation between them and the Lord on the subject of His teaching. It had foretold the fact of the Resurrection in a poetical and mystical style, but their vulgar minds could see in it no more than a threat to the safety of the Temple structure. They did not recognize it as a reference to the far more sacred Temple of His human body, but thought that it implied some strange menace to the central shrine of Israel. This first misinterpretation of His words was strongly ingrained in the mind of the Jews, and was latent in the charge laid against Him now. But it came out still more clearly in the trial of Stephen not many months later: "We have heard him say, that this Jesus of Nazareth shall destroy this place, and shall change the customs which Moses delivered us" (Acts 6:14).

In substance, their witness was the same; but not in detail: "But neither so did their witness agree together (Mark 14:59). They were closely questioned on the text of what they alleged that they had heard; but each man had his own version, even although the degree of variation was only slight. They had

---

[2]A. Taylor Innes, *The Trial of Jesus Christ* (1899), p. 36; F. J. Powell, *The Trial of Jesus Christ* (1949), p. 67.

mingled with their report of what Jesus had said their own idea as to what He had meant, and Matthew gives the version of one of them: "This fellow said, I am able to destroy the temple of God, and to build it in three days." That cryptic reference to "three days" had troubled the Jews from the beginning: "Forty and six years was this temple in building, and wilt thou rear it up in three days?" (John 2:20).

Mark gives the version of the other witness: "We heard him say, I will destroy this temple that is made with hands, and within three days I will build another made without hands." The Lord Jesus had not used the words *made with hands* or *made without hands*, and it was His hearers who leaped to the view that He was speaking of things material. But the claim to destroy the Temple could be construed as sacrilege, and the claim to rebuild it in three days might be construed as sorcery.[3] The two were quite distinct, but not inconsistent, and each was strong enough to form the brief for a full-scale prosecution. But they were set aside on the ground that neither witness was in accord with the other!

At this point Caiaphas rose from his seat, and took a hand in the course of events: "And the high priest arose, and said unto him, Answerest thou nothing? what is it which these witness against thee?" The case for the prosecution ran the risk of collapse; it stood at the point of failure from sheer want of witness. It had now reached a stage when there was no accusation before the court at all, and the duty of the high priest in such a case was to discharge the prisoner.

But that was the one thing which he would not dream of doing; what he would try to do instead was to cross-examine the Lord Jesus. He had stood in silence all through that scene which had only served to mock the truth of law and justice; He had preserved His calm as though He heard not and cared not what the issue might be. It was more than the high priest of Israel could stand; he lost all sense of self-restraint. He sprang to his feet in desperation, and did all that he could do to extort just one damning remark. Had He nothing to say, and no comment to make? Would He not so much as hint that He was the Son of God? The whole court longed to hear some claim like that,

---

[3]F. J. Powell, *The Trial of Jesus Christ* (1949), pp. 67-68.

so that they could give a ruling on the point and denounce it
for ever!

The Lord Jesus returned look for look, but not a word passed
His lips: "He held his peace, and answered nothing" (Mark 14:
61). He was silent, for that challenge had been against the law;
no one could be asked to incriminate himself. Witness after
witness had filed before that court in an attempt to procure a
legal accusation, and it had been in vain. Clumsy men, brought
forward in haste, unversed in law, undrilled in the art of witness,
they all broke down in turn; the whole attempt had failed! No
charge could be drawn up; there was no case to try! Nothing
could have been more decisive or more impressive in its testimony to the perfection of His character; He had passed through
their midst like a sunbeam pure and golden. The most inveterate
and most unscrupulous of foes could find nothing on which they
could batten, neither word nor deed that lies or malice could
twist.

Thus He held His peace and answered nothing; but if we
would fill that silence with thoughts at all, we may suppose that
they would turn upon the scene before His eyes. He stood at
last face to face with the House of Israel, on the floor of their
Supreme Council; He had now come into the midst of His own,
and His own received Him not. Disowned, reviled, maligned,
He stood unmoved, composed, resolved; for though they knew
it not, this same Jesus stood there as the Judge of Israel![4]

---

[4]A. Taylor Innes, The Trial of Jesus Christ (1899), pp. 49-50.

Chapter 11

THE SOLEMN OATH

And the high priest answered and said unto him, I adjure thee by the living God, that thou tell us whether thou be the Christ, the Son of God. Jesus saith unto him, Thou hast said; nevertheless I say unto you, Hereafter shall ye see the Son of man sitting on the right hand of power, and coming in the clouds of heaven. Then the high priest rent his clothes, saying, He hath spoken blasphemy; what further need have we of witnesses? behold, now ye have heard his blasphemy. What think ye? They answered and said, He is guilty of death. — MATTHEW 26:63-66 (see MARK 14:61-64).

And the men that held Jesus mocked him, and smote him, And when they had blindfolded him, they struck him on the face, and asked him, saying, Prophesy, who is it that smote thee? And many other things blasphemously spake they against him. — LUKE 22:63-65 (see MATTHEW 26:67, 68; MARK 14:65).

CAIAPHAS had been as soundly beaten as his father-in-law in the attempt to bring the Son of Man to trial; the long train of false and futile witness had broken down in utter confusion. He was still on his feet, face to face with Jesus, who stood there serene, silent, deigning no word in reply; he was baffled, perplexed, perhaps angered, by the dignified bearing of that humble Prisoner. But he knew that the Lord Jesus had claimed to be the Christ, the Son of God.

It was two years since He had called God His Father, and had claimed to be His equal (John 5:18). Since then He had declared that He was one with the Father, and the Jews knew that this was a claim to Godhead (John 10:33). One great aim of the whole trial had been to nail down this claim by means of some witness; but no witness of this kind had emerged. Therefore he now resolved to put the Lord Jesus on oath in the set terms of a solemn adjuration, and so challenge Him to confess

His claims: "I adjure thee by the living God, that thou tell us whether thou be the Christ, the Son of God." If some kind of statement on this subject had been made in witness, it would have served as an accusation to which He would have had to reply; but this question was put to Him at a time when no such statement had come before the court, and there was in fact no case for Him to answer. The judge had no right to make up for the failure of the prosecution by this method; it was indeed the last drop in the cup of all that was wrong and unjust in the whole trial.[1] But it was one of the supreme moments in the life of the Son of Man, and He rose to meet it with words which take in the universe for an audience.

The first half of this paragraph from Matthew tells us how Jesus was charged with blasphemy. "Jesus saith unto him, Thou hast said" (Matthew 26:64); "And Jesus said, I am" (Mark 14: 62). He could not set aside that oath imposed by the judge at the head of the Supreme Court in Israel; further silence might be construed as the abandonment of all His claims and the dereliction of His Messiahship. He knew that an adjuration in the Name of God was meant to drive Him into a trap, and that a frank reply would spell His death. But He would not leave friend or foe in the slightest doubt with regard to His status as the appointed Messiah and as the Son of God now that He was charged to confess Himself on oath. Other voices would die away and all ruder sounds be hushed as the high priest made that great adjuration; it raised the one supreme question for whose answer men of Israel had been waiting so long. Therefore His calm clear voice rang out in the breathless silence: "Thou hast said, . . . I AM!" That would have been enough for them; but not for Him. He would state the truth and stake His claims in the boldest words and on the broadest scale. The whole crisis seemed to elevate His thoughts as it clarified His trial, and He went on to tell the high priest that an hour would come when all would be reversed. His words were framed in a glorious prophecy which that Council would soon connect with the sublime vision in Daniel: "Nevertheless I say unto you, Hereafter shall ye see the Son of Man sitting on the right hand

[1] F. J. Powell, *The Trial of Jesus Christ* (1949), p. 70.

of power, and coming in the clouds of heaven" (cf. Daniel 7:13).

It would take a moment or two for this astonishing claim to sink in; then came the reaction. "Then the high priest rent his clothes, saying, He hath spoken blasphemy; what further need have we of witnesses?" It seems quite clear that the high priest had felt certain that some kind of statement would be offered; he had imposed an oath which would have a binding force that nothing else was likely to have. But the full text of that reply went far beyond all his expectation, for the claims of the Lord Jesus had not faltered by a hair's breadth in that supreme moment. The Jews might not regard his claim to be the Son of God in the same sense in which we would today; it may have meant no more to them than a claim to hold some unique status in God's Kingdom. Such a status would fall short of the truth of the Incarnation, but to claim it at all would be like high treason on the part of a Jew.[2] It would constitute blasphemy, unless indeed the claim were true; and now the Lord Jesus had made that claim for Himself in the Name of God Himself. They might see Him now as the Son of God at the prisoner's bar; they would see Him yet as the Son of Man on the heavenly throne! That claim was so tremendous that the shock to Caiaphas may not have been entirely nominal. With an apparent reverence for the law which had been slighted beyond words in that trial, he now grasped his mantle and rent it in token of his abhorrence for such blasphemy; rent it downwards from the neck in two parts which might never again be sewn in one.[3]

The judge had thus summed up the case; now he asked his colleagues for a verdict. "Behold, now ye have heard his blasphemy. What think ye? " That claim to be the Son of God was like an act of high treason in the eyes of the law; it was as though He had blasphemed the Name of God in the hearing of all. But it was not until the end of the trial that such a charge had emerged, and then it was based on one great statement which had only been made under the seal of an adjuration. It was in fact based on something which had been said by the Accused Himself in the course of the trial, and not upon witness to an offense which had occurred before the court had been convened.

---

[2]F. J. Powell, *The Trial of Jesus Christ* (1949), p. 74.
[3]A. Taylor Innes, *The Trial of Jesus Christ* (1899), p. 55.

Nothing could be clearer than the Talmud that no one could be held to speak to his own hurt in a Hebrew law court. Maimonides had most plainly declared: "Our Law condemns no one to death upon his own confession."[4] But since other means had failed to provide a case for trial, the high priest was more than prepared for the flagrant violation of the law laid down by Maimonides which now ensued. He would call no further witness; he asked at once for a verdict on the ground of blasphemy. They had heard it; what did they think? But there was no calm vote by the members of that Council, taken one by one, as the law required, in a recognized succession. There was one wild tumultuous outcry as they all shrieked: "He is guilty of death!" (A.V.) "He is worthy to dye!" (Wycliffe).

The section in Luke tells us how He was hailed with mockery: "And the men that held Jesus mocked him, and smote him." That verdict of guilty and the sentence of death may have seemed right to some in that miscellaneous court; but all sympathy for the misguided, if such there were, is wrecked by the scandalous scene of misconduct which now took place. The churl who had struck Him in the hall of Annas was but the first to lay rough rude hands on the Son of Man. There was now a wicked outbreak of such unruly violence in the court of Caiaphas. Those who held Him, still bound with thongs, took their cue from the shout of death, and thought themselves free to molest Him as they wished. Luke says that they mocked Him and smote Him; Mark and Matthew say that they spat in His face and struck Him with the palms of their hands. Those smart slaps were grievous enough; they were meant to express the pent-up hatred and contempt of years. That vile rheum was far worse; it was meant to convey the utmost hatred and disgust of all. The whole scene was the worst conceivable combination of insolence and violence, of bitterness and resentment. Feeling was beyond control, and temper out of hand; hatred was without restraint, and passion in full storm.

But those open-handed, contemptuous blows were only like a signal for more definite forms of mockery: "And when they had blindfolded him, they struck him on the face, and asked him, saying, Prophesy, who is it that smote thee?" Things that pro-

---

[4]A. Taylor Innes, *The Trial of Jesus Christ* (1899), p. 56.

voke and wound may take more than one form, but both forms are found here. There was violence and injury done to the body; there was insolence and mockery done to the spirit. His was the most gentle spirit ever to be housed in the home of a human body, and the sensitive perfection of His nature would make the whole outrage more brutal in effect. They dragged something over His head so as to cover His face and bandage His eyes, for the plan was simply to blindfold and buffet Him on the floor of the courtroom. They would jostle Him and hustle Him right and left, would slap Him with their hands and beat Him in the face; and the word *to buffet* is an onomatopoeic word which almost makes us think that we hear the sound of those blows as they rained on Him from behind and before. But that rain of blows came to a head with the taunt of pure ridicule: "Prophesy unto us, *thou Christ,* Who is he that smote thee?" (Matthew 26:68.)

Those taunts, those blows, above all, that spittle, were all meant to set His feelings in a flame of helpless indignation: "And many other things blasphemously spake they against him." How long it all went on, we do not know; but they had to wait for daybreak, and the time was spent in making sport of Him Who was so meek and gentle. It was as if they felt that they could not go too far or do too badly, for the minions of that court felt free to follow where the masters of the law led the way. The Lord Jesus did not resist, would not reproach: "Who, when He was reviled, reviled not again; when he suffered, he threatened not" (I Peter 2:23). He had foreseen that the Gentiles would "mock him, and . . . spit upon him" (Mark 10:34), but the Jews proved to be first in the field with this pagan outrage.

Job had once long before suffered indignities like these, and his crowning sorrow had been that rude sign of contempt: "They . . . spare not to spit in my face" (Job 30:10). But the patriarch fell far behind his great Redeemer, both in suffering and in submission; for to Jesus alone could the words be applied, "I hid not my face from shame and spitting" (Isaiah 50:6). But this is a scene which we can only view with hushed and silent wonder; it leaves us speechless with awe and astonishment. There was but one in all that hall to look on with love and pity, and he never forgot that scene: "I John, who also am your brother and companion in tribulation, and in the . . . *patience of* Jesus Christ" (Revelation 1:9).

The whole scene in that court stands on a new plain in view of one great statement: "Hereafter shall ye see the Son of man sitting on the right hand of power, and coming in the clouds of heaven" (Matthew 26:64). Did not Stephen recall those words with an air of triumph when he was arraigned by that same Council? "Behold, I see the heavens opened, and the Son of man standing on the right hand of God" (Acts 7:56). They still reverberate down the corridors of time, and all who catch their sound in faith will breathe Amen! There are terrible things in human nature as this scene proves, infamies from which we shrink; there are some depths in our fallen humanity into which it is scarcely safe to probe. But all that is most tender and gracious filled the heart of Jesus, and His was the most superb patience and pity the world has ever seen. He had rallied all His love to bear that shame and spitting, for He had come to stand condemned that He might be for us the Death of Sin. If then we will behold Him with the eye of faith in that hall of scorn and sorrow — our Substitute, our Redeemer — we shall hail Him at the right hand of God with a voice and vision like those of the martyr — hail Him as King of kings and Lord of lords!

Chapter 12

THE LAST VERDICT

And as soon as it was day, the elders of the people and the chief priests and the scribes came together, and led him into their council, saying, Art thou the Christ? tell us. And he said unto them, If I tell you, ye will not believe: And if I also ask you, ye will not answer me, nor let me go. Hereafter shall the Son of man sit on the right hand of the power of God. Then said they all, Art thou then the Son of God? And he said unto them, Ye say that I am. And they said, What need we any further witness? for we ourselves have heard of his own mouth. — LUKE 22;66-71; (see MATTHEW 27:1, 2; MARK 15:1).

CAIAPHAS and the Sanhedrin had held the trial of Christ in the small hours of the morning, and had made sure of an adverse verdict by means of an unjust adjuration. But trial by night was not legal at all, for no Hebrew court could be held before daybreak. They had gone through the full procedure, but it was quite invalid in point of law. Therefore it was thought wise to hold a fresh session of that Council as soon as day should dawn; they would strictly observe all the forms of the law while they ignored it in substance and in spirit. The interval was occupied with that disgraceful scene of mockery; then as the first light of that Black Friday began to shine, the court resumed its work. Mark and Matthew, who had told the story of the trial by night in detail, merely hint at this new session: "And straightway in the morning the chief priests held a consultation with the elders and scribes and the whole council" (Mark 15:1). It is clear that the main purpose of this meeting was to endorse the verdict of guilty obtained at night, and to decide how to carry the grim sentence of death into effect.[1] The Sadducees and Pharisees,

---

[1]F. J. Powell, *The Trial of Jesus Christ* (1949), p. 81.

chief priests and scribes, had met with one common purpose: they "took counsel against Jesus, to put him to death" (Matthew 27:1). Then Luke, who had passed over the trial by night, records this fresh morning trial in detail, and shows how it was the third and final stage in His trial at the hands of the Jews. But his record makes it clear that it was little more in effect than a rehearsal of the decision which had been reached, carried out within the framework of an enlarged council, in the name and form of the law.

The first part of this scene dealt with His claim to be the Christ of God: "And as soon as it was day, the elders of the people and the chief priests and the scribes came together, and led him into their council." The Lord Jesus was thus once more arraigned before a court of men who were implacable, and He must have seemed a sorry Figure as He now stood before their gaze. All His garments would be dishevelled and in disarray from the ordeal in the palace of the high priest; His face would still tingle with the angry blows and sordid spittle with which He had been so defiled. He had passed through that dark hour of bloody sweat and anguish in the olive groves of Gethsemane; and the marks of mental storm and distress would now be stamped in new lines and furrows upon His face. He was fairer than all the children of men, the chief among ten thousand; yet His features were more marred than any man's, and His form more than the sons of men. But though He might stand with disordered appearance at the bar of hostile sinners, nothing even then could hide the dignity of His character or the majesty of His innocence.

But He was soon faced with the first abrupt question, asked no doubt by Caiaphas as the spokesman of the Sanhedrin: "Art thou the Christ? tell us." This scene had been so well planned and rehearsed that it was meant to be coldly formal. What they wanted was to get the verdict of guilty and sentence to death in strict legal form and fashion. Therefore they would re-apply the test which had proved so successful, and would examine Him as to His claim to be the Messiah. But He met that hostile question with a two-fold statement which would disown the whole competence of such a tribunal. "He said unto them, If I tell you, ye will not believe: and if I also ask you, ye will not answer me, nor let me go." Was He thinking sadly of their failure to weigh the words He had spoken daily in the Temple? (Matthew 26:55.) Had they ever answered Him when He had questioned them in public? (Mark 11:27-33.) They would not believe when He had spoken to them of David's Son and Lord; they would not answer when He had questioned them as to the origin of John's baptism.[2] Perhaps those words were once more a latent appeal to the Law of Witness, though framed in a way which would show that He knew them to be far past all care for the fairness of things. Their whole conduct proved that they were in quest neither of truth nor light; they had no real desire to know, and He would have them feel that He saw through all their hollow deceit.

But though He saw through their motives, He was ready once more to bear witness to His own real glory: "Hereafter shall the Son of man sit on the right hand of the power of God." As a prisoner at the tribunal of an unjust judge and jury, He had nothing further to say; yet He would speak once more in the capacity of one who claimed to be their Judge and King. He would repeat that great statement which He had made while on oath in the Name of God; they would hear Him speak this once, not in the character of a criminal, but in the majesty of a Sovereign.

Did they look on Him with bruised face and spittled brow in that court of sin? They would see Him yet as the Son of Man on the throne of glory, the Lord of all. Did they treat Him with the coarsest spite and crudest spleen in that hour of pain? They would see Him yet as the Son of God in the clouds of heaven, the Judge of all. Lofty as were the claims made in other days by the once despised Jesus, it was fitting that this supreme declaration of His true and peerless glory should have been reserved for the end!

The next part of this scene dealt with His claim to be the Son of God: "Then said they all, Art thou then the Son of God?" They had asked if He were the Christ, but His words in reply had gone even further. There had been various occasions when He had distinctly asserted that He had come to bear the Name and do the work of Him that should be called "The Christ"; but the Jews had never heard Him claim in plain terms to be

---

[2]A. Taylor Innes, *The Trial of Jesus Christ* (1899), p. 53.

"The Son of God" until that night when the high priest had put Him on oath to declare the truth. He had then gone beyond all their expectation in a deliberate statement that they would yet see Him in the place that belonged to God alone, and His voluntary repetition of that statement now in this scene seemed to sweep them right off their feet. He did not wait to be adjured, but voiced His claim once more in the words which had stirred Caiaphas to charge Him with blasphemy. The whole court now broke out in an uproar, and the voice of the high priest would be drowned in the sequel. Did they see in His face the light of that more than earthly renown, as they were to see in Stephen's face the light of an angel beauty (Acts 6:15.) They all rose up, flushed with anger, stirred to fury, and stormed as with one voice: "Art thou then the Son of God?" It was a frank outrage of all the laws of true justice; they flung down the challenge, knowing full well that death was in that gauntlet.

He was neither dismayed nor yet perturbed by that awful clamor, and He made His voice heard once more: "And he said unto them, Ye say that I am!" He would not flinch in that supreme crisis from the rude and stormy challenge to His Person, and He met that wild and shouting Council with a calm and emphatic assertion of His Divine Sonship. No words could ever be more in keeping with His glory than this simple, steadfast reply: Ye say the truth! I AM! He knew as they knew that this could only bear one meaning; it was a claim to the mystic Name by which God had made Himself known to Moses (Exodus 3:14). To the eye of sense, He stood there as the Man of Sorrows, the heir of all human griefs and burdens, despised and rejected; to the ear of faith, He spoke then as the Prince of Glory, the heir of all divine power and splendor, uncrowned but immortal. The Voice of the Baptismal Waters and the Transfiguration Glory still rang in the shrine of His soul: "This is my beloved Son, in whom I am well pleased" (Matthew 3: 17, 17:5.) Nothing could shake that pure inner witness that He was God's Peer and Fellow, Partner of His Throne and Equal in His glory, the Man of His right hand, the Son of His deep love; therefore He made reply in terms which would carry their minds back to holy ground, where the Voice that spake from the Burning Bush had startled Moses: "I AM THAT I AM!"

The trial had come to an end as far as the Lord Jesus was concerned: "And they said, What need we any further witness? for we ourselves have heard of his own mouth." They had secured all that they had designed; it was the same upshot as it had been before. They had no need to search for fresh witness; He stood in their midst self-condemned. There could only be a unanimous vote as they brought in their verdict; all were agreed on the sentence of guilt and the condemnation to death. Thus an unjust arrest, a trial by night contrary to the law, a long file of false and futile witness, an oath improperly administered, that grim verdict based on His own statement, and that willful sentence of death: all these were links in the chain of revolt against law and justice forged in the Name of God by men who sat in the seat of Moses. All that remained was for them to transmit the case to the imperial authorities, and the last task of that Council was to consult how they ought to bring it before Pilate. They knew that a charge of blasphemy would not be a capital offense in his judgment, but they knew well enough that a charge of sedition was an indictment worthy of death. Thus they agreed in that morning conclave to drop the great accusation that He had claimed to be the Son of God, and to "frame" Him before Pilate on the ground that He was a rival to Caesar. That would solve the problem of a warrant for His execution; Pilate could not refuse to have Him put to death! "And when they had bound him, they led him away, and delivered him to Pontius Pilate the governor" (Matthew 27:2).

Thus the whole trial in that Hebrew assize turned at last on one great question: "Art thou the Christ? . . . Art thou the Son of God?" The Lord Jesus knew quite well what meaning they would attach to a reply in the affirmative, but He did not falter for one moment as He answered in words which claimed equality with God. But if He were no more than a man with mortal limits, a son in the home of human parents, He was possessed by an audacity and an effrontery which have never been matched even by the blindest impostor or the wildest fanatic. There is only one way in which we can free His Name and clear His reputation from such a charge, whether of lunacy or vanity, and that is to bow in worship of Him as *God of God, Light of Light, Very God of Very God, Begotten Not Made.* Then we can turn from that scene of human shame and turpitude, and can ift our eyes to heights of sublime grace and majesty. We hear Him claim that great twofold title, *Son of God, Son of Man,* and t is as though He would blend humility with eternity, humanity with divinity. But all the time we bear in mind the fact that He tood there as our voluntary Saviour, on whose head the great God of heaven has made to meet the sins of us all. And Him we bless, we praise, we love, and we adore with the worship of heart and soul: for He only is holy; He only is the Lord; He only with the Holy Ghost is most high in the glory of God the Father!

AMEN!

PART TWO

THE CROWN
OF
THORNS

"In point of fact, when Pilate ultimately sent Jesus to the cross, it was as claiming to be a king, and on the original charge of acting adversus maiestatem populi Romani. The judgment was legal, though the unjust judge did not believe in it. For whatever Caesar's deputy may have thought, the claim of Jesus was truly inconsistent with the claim of the state which Caesar represented. And the world must judge between the two." —A. TAYLOR INNES: *The Trial of Jesus Christ* (1899), p. 122.

Chapter 13

HIMSELF A KING

Then led they Jesus from Caiaphas unto the hall of judgment: and it was early; and they themselves went not into the judgment hall, lest they should be defiled; but that they might eat the passover. Pilate then went out unto them, and said, What accusation bring ye against this man? They answered and said unto him, If he were not a malefactor, we would not have delivered him up unto thee. Then said Pilate unto them, Take ye him, and judge him according to your law. The Jews therefore said unto him, It is not lawful for us to put any man to death: that the saying of Jesus might be fulfilled, which he spake, signifying what death he should die. — JOHN 18:28-32 (see MATTHEW 27:2; MARK 15:1).

And the whole multitude of them arose, and led him unto Pilate. And they began to accuse him, saying, We found this fellow perverting the nation, and forbidding to give tribute to Caesar, saying that he himself is Christ a King. — LUKE 23:1, 2.

JERUSALEM was always a magnet for thousands of pilgrims at the paschal season, and the Roman procurator felt that it was imperative to be present at such times in case of riot. The six thousand legionaries who made up the normal garrison would be reinforced, and strong measures would be taken to prevent an outbreak of mob feeling. Pontius Pilate had come up from Caesarea for this reason and was quartered in the fortress of Antonia close to the temple; a great castle, built by Herod the Great partly as a tyrant stronghold, partly as a pleasure palace. Pilate had been procurator for some six years, and there was no love lost between him and the Jews. He had once slain a few Galileans while at worship in the temple and had mingled their blood with that of their sacrifices (Luke 13:1). Then there had been trouble with the effigies of Caesar and the aqueduct for Jerusalem, and the Jews were on the lookout for any pretext that would secure his recall.[1]

---

[1] F. J. Powell, *The Trial of Jesus Christ* (1949), pp. 96-7.

The supreme crisis of his life was at hand when they brought Christ before him for judgment. The trial before the Jews had come to an end at daybreak, with the verdict of guilt, and they had now adjourned to ask Pilate for his confirmation of the sentence of death. Then led they Jesus from Caiaphas unto the hall of judgment: and it was early. Consent for the execution must be obtained at once, for the Passover festival was to begin in the morning. No court of justice could be held while the feast was in progress, and they could not hope to keep Him in bonds until it was over. Thus they led Him through the gateway on to the broad pavement in front of the palace, and the trial would take place before the chair of state on an open platform where the procurator would sit in true Roman custom.

The first round in the trial of Christ before Pilate was placed on record by John alone: "Pilate then went out unto them, and said, What accusation bring ye against this man?" There were times when Jewish authorities chose to accuse a fellow Jew before a Roman court without a first hearing at their own bar at all (cf. Acts 18:12). There were also times when Roman authorities chose to arraign a fractious Jew before a Hebrew court without any judgment by their own law (cf. Acts 22:30). But the course of this trial makes it clear that Pilate had no idea that the Lord had already undergone a trial in the Jewish assize.

Since it was a charge of treason, he would naturally assume that the case had been brought direct to him. It would appear that at first he did not even know who it was who stood before him in those bonds. He must have heard reports of His sayings and His doings for three years past, and his wife's dream shows that Christ had been the theme of palace gossip. But, like Herod, he had never seen Him before that day when the Jewish leaders came to ask for His death. They came in the hope that he would take their statement on trust and would accede to their request at once. But the Valerian law tied his hands, and he would not condemn a man unheard. He met the Jews with the instinctive utterance of true Roman justice: "What accusation bring ye against this man?" It was in the spirit of the memorable dictum framed by Festus some years later: "It is not the manner of the Romans to deliver any man to die, before that he which is accused have the accusers face to face, and have license to answer for himself concerning the crime laid against him" (Acts 25:16).[2]

The Jews tried to evade this just demand and to force the issue in their proud and haughty reply: "They answered and said unto him, If he were not a malefactor, we would not have delivered him up unto thee." They were anxious to keep the trial in their own court out of Pilate's hearing; it had been held at night, and it was not legal even by the regulations of their own law. The charge on which the trial revolved was one of no account in the eyes of men like Pilate and would never win his consent for a sentence of death. He would dismiss it as something which had to do with the law of Moses, but which did not deserve either death or imprisonment (cf. Acts 23:29).

All this would flash before their minds as they heard him ask what accusation they meant to make, but they hoped to carry their point as a kind of favor without going into any details at all. If He were not a wrongdoer, would they have brought Him to Pilate? Would not their word suffice, if they declared that He deserved to die? They took a high tone in the hope that Pilate would yield, but he was not in the mood to comply. Their proud words were in fact just an insolent evasion of the question which he had put in his capacity as Procurator Caesaris, and they found that they had only stirred up a pride which was at least as strong as theirs.

Thus his reply was like gall and wormwood to the Jewish leaders: "Then said Pilate unto them, Take ye him, and judge him according to your law." Pilate had tried many, condemned many; and his practiced eye knew well the features which great guilt wears. But no criminal he had ever seen looked as this Prisoner now looked.[3] If, then, he were not to hear the accusation, he would neither judge nor punish the Man at all; he would not do what they asked him to do.

His words put the matter in its true light as he told them with calm contempt to take Him and judge Him after their law. He knew that their courts could do no more than pass a sentence of flagellation or imprisonment, and he knew that what they wanted was death! Thus he took a kind of malicious

---

[2]A. Taylor Innes, *The Trial of Jesus Christ* (1899), pp. 73-4.
[3]William Hanna, *Our Lord's Life on Earth* (1882), p. 487.

interest in extorting the confession which they were now forced to advance: "The Jews therefore said unto him, It is not lawful for us to put any man to death."

This was a most humbling acknowledgment of the hateful fact that they were under the heel of a foreign tyrant. They could not carry out their own sentence of death without consent from the Roman authorities. The words are as sullen as their former demand had been haughty; but John saw that they prepared the way for the unconscious fulfillment of an important prophecy. The Lord Jesus had more than once plainly foretold the kind of death that He would die; it would be death on the cross at the hands of the Gentiles.

The next round in the trial of Christ before Pilate was placed on record by Luke alone: "And they began to accuse him, saying, We found this fellow perverting the nation, and forbidding to give tribute to Caesar, saying that he himself is Christ a King!" The Jews were forced against their will to frame a charge, and were loud in accusation; but it was at this stage that their hypocrisy came out, for they did not dare to disclose the ground on which they had condemned the Lord Jesus. They would have been snubbed out of court if they had told Pilate that the charge was blasphemy; they would have shared the fate of the Jews in Corinth when they arraigned Paul before Gallio (Acts 18:14-16).

However, since they could not bring in the real charge they were in a difficult position. They had to fix on an offense of such a kind that the procurator would be compelled to take it up; and it had to be of sufficient magnitude to merit death. Therefore they dropped their own charge of blasphemy and brought in a charge of sedition; they said that He was out to pervert, to seduce, to revolutionize the nation! This was no doubt somewhat ambiguous, and Pilate might wonder if it were just a loose accusation. But it lingered in his mind with disturbing persistence, and he plainly referred to it at a later stage in the trial: "Ye have brought this man unto me, *as one that perverteth the people*: and, behold, I, having examined him before you, have found no fault in this man touching those things whereof ye accuse him" (Luke 23:14).

But the Jews knew that just one vague statement was not enough, and they went on to a detailed accusation: "We found this fellow . . . forbidding to give tribute to Caesar." They must have known that this was an outright falsehood, but it would lend deadly point to the first vague charge. The payment of tribute to Rome had been in full force since 63 B.C., when Pompey had imposed a fine of ten thousand talents upon the people of Judaea. It was the most unpopular of all the signs of their national subjection to a foreign tyrant, and no class in the whole Jewish community was so despised as the class of subordinate tax-gatherers.

Since it was well known that the Lord Jesus was on friendly terms with publicans such as Matthew and Zacchaeus, that was one major reason for the hostility of the Jewish leaders. They had even tried to embroil Him in hopeless conflict on this very problem by the subtle question: "Is it lawful to give tribute unto Caesar, or not?" (Matthew 22:17).

It was then that He made the great statement which was meant to declare His mind once and for all: "Render therefore unto Caesar the things which are Caesar's; and unto God the things that are God's" (Matthew 22:21). That was only two days before the Jews brought up this charge before Pilate that He forbade the payment of tribute. They knew that one of the Twelve was a Zealot, and they knew that Pilate would be aware that the Zealots refused to pay tribute. It was clever enough, even though it was false; but they little foresaw how a nation-wide refusal to pay tribute within a few years of this scene would lead to the fatal conflict with Rome in which Jerusalem would be destroyed.

Thus they denounced the Lord Jesus as an enemy to the State, and their last words sum up the whole accusation: "We found this fellow . . . saying that he himself is Christ a King." There was more truth and more color in this charge than in all that they had yet affirmed; yet it was just because He was not a king of Roman ideals that they despised Him. He had absolutely disowned all thought of a kingship which would be in any sense a rival to that of the Caesars, for the kingdom of which He so often spoke was the rule and reign of God in the heart of man.

That was why He had turned away from the Galilean crowds who would have taken Him by force and proclaimed Him as their king (John 6:15). But the implication in the charge now laid by the Jews was that He had in some sense set Himself up as a king who would defy Caesar.

There can be no doubt as to their motive; they meant to charge Him with the crime known as *crimen laesae maiestatis*. They meant to throw the blame for the death of such a prophet on to foreign shoulders, and they accused Him of treason as the greatest of all political crimes in the eyes of Rome. If He said that He were a king, it was equivalent to an attack upon the supreme majesty of the State.[4] Pilate could not afford to let it pass without the most scrupulous inquiry, and it was to remain the one supreme issue in Pilate's mind to the end of the trial and till His death on the cross itself.

Thus the Jewish rulers failed in their first object; they failed in their plan to induce Pilate to have Him put to death without trial or accusation. He had refused to treat the case as if it were of no account, as if he could condemn a man to death just to please the rulers. He had also refused to treat it as though it were the kind of offense which could be dealt with by mere police jurisdiction or by military warrant. His blunt conduct toward those who came to seek the death of Jesus meant that he bound himself before Jews and Gentiles alike to take up the case in virtue of his office as the supreme civil authority.

We will never know what Pilate would have done if they had told the truth when they "began to accuse" the Lord Jesus. The whole course of the trial might have been changed if their formal accusation had been in the same terms as their later outburst: "We have a law, and by our law he ought to die, because he made himself the Son of God" (John 19:7.) But as it was, Pilate's duty stood out in clear relief. He had put his jurisdiction between one who had been accused and the leading authorities of a subject nation, and his verdict would have to be given as a deliberate judgment in the name of Caesar.[5]

---

[4] A. Taylor Innes, *The Trial of Jesus Christ* (1899), pp. 84-5.
[5] A. Taylor Innes, *The Trial of Jesus Christ* (1899), pp. 81-2.

Chapter 14

NOT OF THIS WORLD

Then Pilate entered into the judgment hall again, and called Jesus, and said unto him, Art thou the King of the Jews? Jesus answered him, Sayest thou this thing of thyself, or did others tell it thee of me? Pilate answered, Am I a Jew? Thine own nation and the chief priests have delivered thee unto me: what hast thou done? Jesus answered, My kingdom is not of this world: if my kingdom were of this world, then would my servants fight, that I should not be delivered to the Jews: but now is my kingdom not from hence. Pilate therefore said unto him, Art thou a king then? Jesus answered, Thou sayest that I am a king. To this end was I born, and for this cause came I into the world, that I should bear witness unto the truth. Every one that is of the truth heareth my voice. Pilate saith unto him, What is truth? — JOHN 18:33-38 (see MATTHEW 27:11; MARK 15:2; LUKE 23:3).

ONCE the Jews had framed their formal accusation of high treason Pilate had no alternative but to take up the whole case in detail. The charge had been laid by the Jews before the chair of state on the open pavement, for they would not cross the palace threshold lest they should be defiled on the eve of the feast. But if Pilate were to interrogate the Man, if he were to sift what was false from what was true, the first and most reasonable step for him to take would be to withdraw from the crowd of vehement accusers into the quiet of the palace. He would know what to make of their sudden zeal for the payment of tribute; so, too, he would know what to think of their urgent care for the kingdom of Caesar.

Nothing could have been more telltale than the fact that such an accusation had come in from such a quarter. Pilate knew how much the Jews longed for a king of their own who would break the yoke of imperial authority and set up a Hebrew kingdom of splendor and renown. But how could he hope to find out the truth beneath the glare of so many cold and hostile eyes, or within the sound of so many loud and strident voices? Therefore he left the Jews outside on the pavement and strode into the interior judgment hall, calling upon Jesus as the accused to follow him within. The Lord Jesus had no fear or scruple about crossing Pilate's threshold, and He followed him in, almost as though He were turning from the Jews who scorned Him to at least one interested Gentile.

In the first part of this dialogue the main interest turns on Pilate. "Then Pilate entered into the judgment hall again, and called Jesus, and said unto him, Art thou the King of the Jews?" In the silence of the Praetorium, Pilate now found himself face to face with Jesus; alone with the Accused, the most momentous interview of his life was to begin. He was to address Him in person for the first time, and he began with an abrupt question. He passed by the first two accusations in an attempt to pin down the final statement: "Art thou the King of the Jews?"

It is remarkable that in each of the four gospels these words have been placed on record (Matthew 27:11; Mark 15:2; Luke 23:3). Westcott says that the form of the sentence suggests a mild sense of surprise on the part of Pilate: "Art Thou, poor, and bound, and wearied, the King of whom men have spoken?"[1] He could not fail to be surprised at the poor and lowly attire of the One who stood there in bonds; how could this Man be the King of the Jews? This plain title was in contrast with the theocratic title "King of Israel" (John 1:49) and had only been used on one previous occasion, when the wise men came from the east, saying, "Where is he that is born King of the Jews?" (Matthew 2:2).

Although the four gospels all record Pilate's first question, John alone proceeds to give details of the conversation to which it led. "Jesus answered him, Sayest thou this thing of thyself, or did others tell it thee of me?" The Lord waived a direct reply to ask a question of His own. This was the first time that He had spoken to the Roman ruler, and His words were undoubtedly meant to touch and stir his conscience. Pilate might be seated in the place of power and authority, while He stood in the chains of one who was accused. But it soon became clear that

---

[1]B. F. Westcott, *The Gospel According to St. John* (18th impr., 1937), p. 259.

he Prisoner was in moral command of the situation, while the governor was still groping for truth with a vague and restless uncertainty. Was there far down in the depths of Pilate's struggling conscience some faint glimmer of truth? And did not the Lord know that it was there when He tried to bring it into the light of day by means of His question?

The question nettled Pilate, and he replied in a tart and haughty spirit: "Am I a Jew? Thine own nation and the chief priests have delivered thee unto me. What hast thou done?" Far from yielding to that latent appeal, made with supreme kindness, Pilate flared up at the very idea that he should be thought to know the drift of Jewish superstition. Was he a Jew, that he should care about such things?

The depth of scorn which those words would convey can be measured by the tone of contempt for the Jews which marks the works of Horace and Tacitus, Pliny and Juvenal.[2] That proud disdain would be grievous enough to the Accused, but the sharp home thrust which followed would be still more painful; for was it not His own people who had given Him up in chains to the Gentiles? Yet while Pilate meant to voice his complete lack of concern in such Jewish affairs, his words seem to disclose the fact that in spite of himself he had begun to feel that there was more in this case than might meet the eye. It was men of His own nation, not some pagan informer, who had brought Him bound to Pilate; it was the high priest of Israel, not some Roman official, who had laid the accusation. What could it mean? "What hast thou done?" The Jews concerned themselves with dreams, but a Roman judge like Pilate asked for nothing but facts.

In the next part of this dialogue the main interest turns on Jesus: "Jesus answered, My kingdom is not of this world: if my kingdom were of this world, then would my servants fight, that I should not be delivered to the Jews: but now is my kingdom not from hence." These most memorable words were framed in substance, if not in form, as words of self-defense, and there is a rhythm and a balance in the Greek text of the sentence which is of great solemnity. He would confess that He did claim to be a king, and yet He would avoid the charge that He was

---

[2]J. C. Ryle, *Expository Thoughts on St. John's Gospel* (1897), vol. iii, p. 287

some kind of rival to the Caesars. To confess and avoid in this manner was quite common as a means of defense in a civil action.

He was a king and He had a kingdom; but it was not of this world, and it had nothing to do with force or arms. He was not out to wrest the crown from Caesar's brow, or His servants would have joined in constant battle for His defense. His words virtually agree that a kingdom of this world would have been ripe for attack by the Roman procurator, but they deny that the kingship which He claimed for Himself was of the kind which had just been alleged.[3] What He meant by saying that His kingdom was not of this world is explained by the words, "not from hence"; it was not a kingdom in the same sense as that kingdom of which Pilate was a servant and the Jews were subjects at all.

Thus He made His reply in words which met both the Roman and the Hebrew standpoint, and yet in words which were bound to lead to further questions: "Pilate therefore said unto him, Art thou a king then?" Pilate saw quite clearly that the critical words to which he had just listened would be meaningless, if they were not treated as an assertion of two separate spheres of authority.

Perhaps he saw too that there need be no necessary conflict between that strange kingdom of which Jesus spoke, and that great kingdom of this world which he now represented. And yet the Lord Jesus did speak of a kingdom, something that was in the world if not of the world. Therefore Pilate laid his finger on the exact point which stood in need of further explanation and asked again if He really were what His words implied — a king.

Pilate's question was half interrogative and half exclamatory; both the uncommon particle and the emphatic position of the pronoun lend a touch of ironic interest. He asked, not, as before, if He were the King of the Jews, but if He were a king at all; he asked, if He were not a king like the Caesars in Rome, nor yet like the Herods in His own land, in what real sense was He a king. "So then," he said, "thou art a king — thou, a helpless prisoner?"[4]

---

[3]A. Taylor Innes, *The Trial of Jesus Christ* (1899), p. 88.
[4]B. F. Westcott, *The Gospel According to St. John* (18th impr., 1937), p 260.

And to Pilate as the ambassador of the greatness of an earthly empire, He spoke the words that still mark a crisis in the world's history: "Jesus answered, Thou sayest that I am a king. To this end was I born, and for this cause came I into the world, that I should bear witness unto the truth. Every one that is of the truth heareth my voice." This was undoubtedly the great statement which Paul had in mind when he declared that the Son of Man had witnessed a good confession before Pontius Pilate (I Timothy 6:13). "Thou sayest," He replied. Thou dost speak but the truth; I am a king! He was not such a king as the kings of this world; and yet He was a king, and He had a kingdom! (cf. Matthew 26:64). He knew that such a claim before this man of the world was fraught with danger; it might mean that death on a cross would seal His fate.

That risk was in His thoughts as He went on to say that the one great end for which He was born was that He might proclaim the Truth. We cannot doubt that this testimony to Truth includes His great testimony of a moment before to a kingdom not of this world; but this supreme statement serves to light up the true nature of that kingdom with a touch of ageless beauty. His realm was the Kingdom of Truth, and His subjects were ruled by the scepter of Truth! He knew that Truth was as much the ideal of the noblest sons of Rome as Wisdom was for the sons of Greece, and He spoke in the hope that His words would make some hidden chord of longing in Pilate's heart vibrate again. All who follow the Truth, He had once told Nicodemus, come to the light (John 3:21); all who are of the Truth, so He now told Pilate, must hear His voice!

It was with the prophet's gift of insight and the Saviour's sense of mission that the Lord thus dealt with Pilate. He tried hard to reach his conscience, to see if there were some dormant feeling after truth in his soul. What if Pilate did long for a king and kingdom other than that which the Jews or Romans would own? What if he did set his heart on Truth as the crown and goal of all human aspiration? He had never heard words so royal as those words of truth and testimony from the lips of Jesus. But, alas for Pilate, he met those words of love with a cold and cynical rejection: "Pilate saith unto him, What is truth?" He may have felt that Truth was the thing of which men kept on saying, Lo! it is here; lo! it is there: and he may have come to think that neither here nor there, nor elsewhere, was the Truth to be found. That blank response, half in contempt, half in despair, wholly without awe, and even without serious interest, was his final gesture; for then at once he broke off that momentous interview, swung on his heel, and went outside.

In the midst of the sects and schools of the pagan philosophies, he was sick of so much arid speculation, and he asked his question about Truth much as a sceptic might ask for the secret of Faith. He could only think that the Realm of Truth must be some new kind of fairy kingdom; he had now come to treat all Truth as a phantom in the night or as a mirage in the desert. He did not speak sneeringly or scoffingly so much as bitterly and hopelessly; he did not wait for an answer because he had no faith that an answer could be given. What is Truth? Who could tell? Yet if he had but known, Truth was very close to him then; if he had but asked with a real desire to know, he might have heard words of matchless grace in reply. The Lord Jesus would have spoken, and this Roman judge might have heard Him say: "My word is truth!" (John 17:17); "I am the truth!" (John 14:6).

Chapter 15

NO FAULT AT ALL

And when he had said this, he went out again unto the Jews, and saith unto them, I find in him no fault at all. — JOHN 18:38 (cf. LUKE 23:4).

And the chief priests accused him of many things: but he answered nothing. And Pilate asked him again, saying, Answerest thou nothing? behold how many things they witness against thee. But Jesus yet answered nothing; so that Pilate marvelled. — MARK 15:3-5 (cf. MATTHEW 27:12-14).

And they were the more fierce, saying, He stirreth up the people, teaching throughout all Jewry, beginning from Galilee to this place. When Pilate heard of Galilee, he asked whether the man were a Galilaean. And as soon as he knew that he belonged unto Herod's jurisdiction, he sent him to Herod, who himself also was at Jerusalem at that time. — LUKE 23:5-7.

THAT brief but most impressive dialogue within the walls of the palace stands alone in human history and remains unique in human interest. But it turned out to be painfully abortive. It came to an abrupt termination when the procurator dismissed the whole subject with one careless last word about the Truth. But one thing at least had emerged from that conversation and stood out quite plainly in his line of mental vision. The Lord Jesus was not guilty of the charge of treason; He was just a guileless enthusiast from whom Rome had nothing to fear. Pilate felt that he had learned enough to know how to decide the case, and he meant to lose no time in making known his verdict.

"He went out again unto the Jews, and saith unto them, I find in him no fault at all!" This was his first utterance of a conviction which would increase in strength as time went on. It was made just at that point in the trial when he had heard both the accusation and the defense, and when he was convinced that the Accused had done no wrong. No doubt it would prove a shock to the Jews who had laid the accusation, but his next step ought to have been quite plain. Now it was his duty to set the Lord Jesus free and to shield Him if necessary from mob outrage. But he was no match for the Jews who had set their hearts on His death, and they were in no mood to treat such a verdict as if it were final. A fresh agitation at once broke out, and dark passions were called into play with a force which he knew not how to resist.

We owe to Mark's account of this scene an illustration of the perfect dignity which ruled the Prisoner: "and the chief priests accused him of many things: but he answered nothing." The blunt assertion of His innocence made the Jews more vehement than ever, for they could not afford to recognize failure or even to tolerate delay. They were quick to employ the same tactics as when they had first faced Pilate, and they met his formal verdict with a storm of hot and angry statement. We are not told what the "many things" were with which they now charged Him, and the text may, in fact, refer to the number of their reckless allegations rather than the number of His supposed misdemeanors.[1]

No doubt they would accuse Him in the same terms as before, but it would be hard to catch the drift or detail of their accusations in the noise and hubbub which had now been provoked. But the storm which had thus burst round Pilate's head found the Lord Jesus altogether at peace. He heard as though He did not hear, or, if hearing, as though He did not mind. He faced that storm of wild accusation in the spirit of strict silence, as He had done when false testimony was called for in the court of Caiaphas. Not by one word in self-defense would He give His sanction to an uproar which now threatened to turn the whole cause of Roman justice into a farce.

Pilate was flustered and irresolute, for this calm self-restraint was quite outside the range of his experience: "And Pilate asked him again, saying, Answerest thou nothing? behold how many things they witness against thee." He had spoken freely and frankly to Pilate alone in the palace, out of sight and hearing as far as the Jews were concerned; and yet now that He was assailed by so many voices He had nothing to say. Pilate could not account for that unruffled composure or that majestic at-

---

[1] James Morison, *St. Mark* (1887), p. 420.

titude. He stood so calm and so unmoved that it almost seemed as if He were not conscious of it at all.

Pilate was so perplexed that he tried to provoke Him to make some remark in self-defense, for that sustained silence was so unlike what a Roman judge would expect. The truth was that Pilate had not the moral strength to resist that fierce Jewish clamor; yet he knew that Christ was guiltless, and he longed to find some way of escape. If the Accused would but break His silence and speak, a way out might appear! It was uncanny for a prisoner to hold his peace when he could so convincingly refute all these accusations!

In the midst of so much uproar the Lord Jesus alone was really calm: "But Jesus yet answered nothing; so that Pilate marvelled." The Lord had no reply for His accusers; and no reply for the governor either. He had done all that He meant to do — for Himself; said all that He meant to say — for Pilate. He had convinced him of His own absolute innocence; He had also made a fruitless appeal to his conscience. Now He would do no more.

His silence was so strange that Pilate could not hide his surprise, and this is most clearly expressed in Matthew's narrative: "And He answered him to never a word; insomuch that the governor marvelled greatly" (Matthew 27:14). He who had spoken without reserve before Annas in private had also spoken without reserve before Pilate in private; but He who had held His peace when He stood in the Hebrew council also held His peace while He stood on the Gentile pavement. False testimony, plain contradiction, and all accusations of an inferior kind He ignored; those were issues which broke down and failed of themselves. He had confessed His divine Sonship in the Hebrew court, and His divine kingdom to the Roman judge; and for that charge alone would He consent to His trial or condemnation.

We owe to Luke's account of this scene an illustration of the painful dilemma which faced the governor: "And they were the more fierce, saying, He stirreth up the people, teaching throughout all Jewry, beginning from Galilee to this place." The Jews were not likely to stand and let Pilate muse and ponder in the presence of that strangely silent Figure. They grew the more urgent when they saw that he took things so lightly, and they released a fresh flood of accusation. The vague uproar began to take on a definite character, and their one main charge was repeated and amplified again and again. They saw plainly that the one way to force Pilate into action was to drive home the first charge of treason, and they began this new attack on the ground that He was rightly suspect for His political activities.

They said that He was the prophet of revolt throughout all Jewry, and that He had tried to foment trouble both in Galilee and in Judaea. The reference to Galilee may have been meant merely to show how widely the movement had spread, or it may have had in mind the northern pilgrims who had been His escort less than a week before for His regal entry into Jerusalem. At all events, Galilee was a name that would fan suspicion, for it was a hotbed of revolt and insurrection. Pilate knew well enough how that spirit was always ready to erupt; and the Jews knew that no other charge could ever make the imperial authorities half so alert.

In the midst of that outcry Pilate saw a way through his own embarrassment: "When Pilate heard of Galilee, he asked whether the man were a Galilaean." Pilate was in sore straits; he did not know how to extricate himself from the case. Never before had he been so hard pressed, though he was no stranger to the importunate cries of the Jews. Never before had he seen them so set on a thing as they were now on Christ's death.

It would have been easy enough just to accede to their request and give up the Accused to death; it would only cost the life of a Jew, and he had done as much before! But Pilate could not escape from the feeling that this strange and silent Figure was free from guilt; and His whole look, His bearing and conduct made him want to resist their will. That is why he was so anxious to find something that would release him from responsibility, and the chance reference to Galilee seemed to offer what he wanted. The Jews had meant to shock Pilate with this remark about the chief haunt of popular resistance, but it only served to start up a new train of thought in his mind.

Pilate's plan of action was clear enough once he knew that Jesus was a Galilaean: "And as soon as he knew that he belonged unto Herod's jurisdiction, he sent him to Herod, who himself also was at Jerusalem at that time." Pilate's slaughter of the Galilaean pilgrims may have estranged him from Herod, for the tetrarch would look on them as his subjects and might resent their death as a breach of his own jurisdiction (Luke 13:1).

Perhaps this fact would flash before Pilate when he heard that Jesus was a Galilaean, for he knew that Herod had come up to Jerusalem for the Passover festival. Would he repeat an old offense by trying this Galilaean, whether or not the trial were to end in condemnation? He might, of course, refer the case to Herod Antipas for advice, much as Festus was to refer Paul's case to Herod Agrippa. But could he not remit the whole case to Herod's judgment, as an act of appeasement no less than as a way out of his own dilemma?[2]

It would be in line with Roman custom if he were to transfer a man from the province of his arrest to that of his native jurisdiction. If he were to suspend his own verdict and to remit the case to the tetrarch he would offend neither Jews nor Herod.[3] He would wash his own hands of the whole case and would patch up an old quarrel by his recognition of a neighbor's authority. The thought was no sooner conceived than a soldier escort was called to march Him off.

One great fact had emerged from this initial appearance before Pilate, and that was the governor's conviction that He was not guilty! Pilate had told the Jews what he thought of the case in that memorable verdict: "I find in him no fault at all!" He could not understand His bearing, but he felt and confessed His innocence; he could not comprehend His kingdom, but he read and revered His character. But the recognition of that faultless spirit was a challenge both to conscience and to manhood, and his confession is still one of the most momentous in all history. The most hostile advocates, the most searching scrutiny, could show up no blemish. Both the Hebrew court and the Roman judge had failed to find in Him the least hint of the blight of sin.

Friend and foe were to join in this testimony, for to Him bear all the prophets witness. "He did no sin!" So Peter could affirm (I Peter 2:22). "He knew no sin!" So Paul could say (II Corinthians 5:21). "He had no sin!" So John could write (I John 3:5). It was not just that He was free from sins of life and speech, of habit and conduct; there was no stain on His

---

[2]F. J. Powell, *The Trial of Jesus Christ* (1949), p. 98.
[3]*Ibid.*, p. 118.

inner spirit at all. His calm unruffled composure in the midst of many accusations was due to His majestic innocence, and our hearts must still stand in awe at the moral perfection of His unique character. "For such an high priest became us, Who is holy, harmless, undefiled, separate from sinners, and made higher than the heavens" (Hebrews 7:26).

Chapter 16

SET AT NOUGHT

And when Herod saw Jesus, he was exceeding glad: for he was desirous to see him of a long season, because he had heard many things of him; and he hoped to have seen some miracle done by him. Then he questioned with him in many words; but he answered him nothing. And the chief priests and scribes stood and vehemently accused him. And Herod with his men of war set him at nought, and mocked him, and arrayed him in a gorgeous robe, and sent him again to Pilate. And the same day, Pilate and Herod were made friends together: for before they were at enmity between themselves. — LUKE 23:8-12.

PILATE thought, no doubt, that if it were to come to Herod's knowledge that he had let Jesus go though he knew that he had been accused of some crime in Galilee as well as in Judaea, the breach between them would have been gravely widened. It would be a friendly gesture to make the case over to the jurisdiction of the Galilaean tetrarch, and it would rid Pilate of all responsibility for a trial which he had found most irksome. Therefore an armed escort led Him down from Pilate's hall to Herod's court in recognition of his authority. But it was a strange turn in the wheel of fortune which thus brought Him before Herod.

This was Herod the Fox who had divorced his own wife so as to carry on an intrigue with his sister-in-law, and that fatal affair was the ugly background for his character as well as his history in the gospel records. But his better aspirations had not even then been wholly smothered, for he was soon deeply impressed by the court preaching of John the Baptist. There was a strange fascination for the guilty monarch about this desert seer, and he heard John gladly until the day when John rebuked him in public for his life of adultery. He had John thrown into prison, where he lay while eighteen months dragged by in drab and cheerless monotony; and then Herodias prevailed on him by means of a drunken oath to have off his head. Eighteen months more had passed away since that wanton murder, and now Herod was to stand face to face with John's divine Friend and Master.

The first part of Luke's narrative illustrates the attitude of Herod towards the Accused: "And when Herod saw Jesus, he was exceeding glad." Herod's mind and conscience had been hardened with the passage of time since John's execution. This was a slow process; it took place by degrees. Herod himself would hardly be aware of the subtle change in his own feelings, and it would need some fresh crisis to bring it out in its sordid contrast. At first, indeed, he found himself a prey to the horrid specters of a selfish remorse. He had often seen that trunkless head in his dreams, framed as it were in the light of setting suns and blood-red skies. It would haunt his nights and fill his days with anxiety, while that prior sin of adultery brought its own harsh revenge in terms of war. Herod sustained both disgrace and defeat when the father of his aggrieved wife marched into his realm to fight for her honor, and his subjects believed that this was a divine retribution. But the wrong was never righted, and the fires of remorse slowly died out. New dread and new superstition crept in and took hold of his mind; and it found a center, not in John the Baptist, but in Jesus the Nazarene.

All this perhaps makes it seem strange that we should now read what Luke records: "For he was desirous to see him of a long season, because he had heard many things of him." Reports had reached him that men were flocking to hear Jesus just as they had flocked to hear John, and the fact was that when he first heard of Jesus he was filled with terror. Some said that He was John who had come back to life; others said that He was one of the prophets who had returned to earth. But the conscience-stricken king could only think in one direction. He was caught in the grip of a feverish excitement lest he should be brought face to face with the murdered prophet.

"It is John whom I beheaded!" he cried; "he is risen from the dead!" (Mark 6:16). That sense of awe would make him shun rather than court any kind of meeting at first. Thus when Jesus was on His way through the cities in his domains, he tried to play on His fears and so to frighten Him off. He sent certain Jews to warn Him that he meant to kill Him, hoping that He would take fright and depart. But the Son of Man saw through the artful device and sent His own scathing message back to Herod, whom He scarified as "that fox!" (Luke 13:31-33).

There had been a change since then, however, and now he wished to see Him for himself: "And he hoped to have seen some miracle done by him." There had been a grievous work of decay in the stronghold of Herod's conscience, and its unseen moral ramparts had been gravely weakened. He had begun to turn more and more to amusement or to sensation to while away his life, and the appearance of Christ before him in criminal guise was a real excitement for the jaded mind of a royal profligate.

His gladness was more awful and much sadder than his former alarm had been, for his state of mind was now such that he felt no rebuke of conscience and no desire for teaching. Many a bad man would have been abashed to see John's Friend where John had stood. Herod himself had once been moved with awe at the name of Jesus; but that was a thing of the past. Remorse was now so dead that he could eye the Lord without concern; he could look Him up and down with no thought at all for the bloody head of John the Baptist. He thought of Him as a kind of juggler, a master of magic, and with eager, idle, prurient curiosity he hoped to see some miracle done.[1]

The next part of Luke's narrative illustrates the attitude of Jesus to the tetrarch: "Then he questioned with him in many words; but he answered him nothing." John had wrought no miracles, but the country rang with stories of the miracles wrought by the Lord Jesus. Herod seems to have looked on Him as a dabbler in the occult, and he thought to treat Him much as He would a new artist in dance or song.

The Lord had never used His miraculous powers merely to gratify the wish of the multitude, however, still less would He do so now to please a man like Herod. Nevertheless Herod spoke up at length, with friendly show and many words. Had he theories to ventilate, and problems to propound, and comments to offer? Perhaps he had many questions to ply, and he

---

[1]William Hanna, *Our Lord's Life on Earth* (1882), p. 499.

rambled on like a man who could not stop until he had poured out all that he had to pour. But then at last he paused to wait for a reply, and no reply was heard.[2] He tried time and again to get Jesus to speak, but not a word fell from His lips. No word was spoken, no sign was given, not a finger was raised to suit the king's fancy.

Herod's questions were all miserably irrelevant, but not so the other voices that were now heard: "And the chief priests and scribes stood, and vehemently accused him." Herod had more or less ignored the real reason for His presence; he had calmly shouldered aside the fact that He was there for trial. The chief priests had remained silent while the king was speaking, but the points at issue had not been touched by his questions. Now they could no longer contain themselves, and they burst out into angry accusation.

Though their vehement earnestness seems out of place in that frivolous atmosphere, the Lord was as calm in His silence as they were fierce in their anger. What could He say to a man like Herod? What could He do in a palace like this? The trial before Annas had been a farce, and yet not such a farce as this. For if He had chosen to speak He might have made His voice heard in words which would have electrified the king with fear; and if He had chosen to act He might have made His power felt in ways which would have revived his sense of guilt. John had once said: "It is not lawful for thee to have thy brother's wife!" (Mark 6:18). Jesus might now have said: "It was not lawful for thee to take the Baptist's head!"

That deep death-like silence grew till Herod could bear it no longer: "And Herod with his men of war set him at nought, and mocked him, and arrayed him in a gorgeous robe, and sent him again to Pilate." The Lord's silence made Herod feel foolish and awkward; perhaps he was flushed and angry. He could get nothing out of that Figure who stood before him in chains, remote as He was serene, aloof as He was silent. His mind was rasped with a sense of irritation; the keen irritation of a mortified vanity. He was galled and riled by failure, and he chose to treat the whole case as though His claims were false; as though He would not speak because He could not speak, and as though His powers had all gone now that He was in bonds. He would

---

dismiss the case with a master stroke of wit and ridicule; he would take a despicable revenge in the form of a court pantomime.

He called out his guard of honor and had Jesus clothed with a robe in imitation of the imperial purple. The Greek participles have a dominant emphasis as the first word in each new clause; they build up the final picture of that splendid raiment which was meant to mock Him as a pseudo-monarch who could vie with Tiberius in royal renown.[3] Then he was sent back to Pilate, with the scoffing innuendo that such a man was the dreaded rival of the Caesars!

Herod thus drove Him away with peals of laughter; but that mocking laughter was in awful contrast with His utter silence. Herod alone was met by Christ with this continued, resolute, unbending refusal to speak. Annas had heard Him speak; Caiaphas had broken through the wall of silence; Pilate had talked with Him at length; but not Herod! If He were silent, surely Herod should have been left speechless! For Jesus was silent so that the voice of the murdered seer, John the Baptist, might at last be heard. Had there been a spark of conscience or a trace of manhood still left in the guilty tetrarch, those eyes looking him through and through would have made his sins rise up from the grave.[4] The whole scene is a dark illustration of the downward course of unrepented evil; a heart dead to reproof, hardened in sin, beyond true fear, doomed to face a silent Master.

Faith was no more than a religious diversion, a plaything, for Herod; and to such a man, whose conscience had been wronged and ruined, the Lord must be silent. Yet what could be worse than to have all the voices that speak of God and of duty — the voice of conscience, the voice of Jesus — hushed in awful stillness! Yet there was a sense in which that very silence was a last and telling appeal. It was meant to warn him that he stood in danger of that worst of ills, the fate of spiritual insensibility. There is but one message to suit a man in such a case: "The Holy Ghost saith, To day if ye will hear his voice, harden not your hearts!" (Hebrews 3:7, 8).

---

[3]Alfred Plummer, *St. Luke* (1922), p. 523.

[4]James Stalker, *The Trial and Death of Jesus Christ* (1894), p. 69.

Chapter 17

WHOM THEY WOULD

And Pilate, when he had called together the chief priests and the rulers and the people, said unto them, Ye have brought this man unto me as one that perverteth the people: and, behold, I, having examined him before you, have found no fault in this man touching those things whereof ye accuse him: No, nor yet Herod: for I sent you to him; and, lo, nothing worthy of death is done unto him. I will therefore chastise him and release him. (For of necessity he must release one unto them at the feast.) — LUKE 23:13-17.

Now at that feast the governor was wont to release unto the people a prisoner, whom they would. And they had then a notable prisoner, called Barabbas. Therefore when they were gathered together, Pilate said unto them, Whom will ye that I release unto you? Barabbas, or Jesus which is called Christ? For he knew that for envy they had delivered him. — MATTHEW 27:15-18 (cf. MARK 15:6-10).

HEROD had dared to treat the Son of Man and His claims for kingship with rude disdain, and had then sent Him back to the Praetorium with an air of careless boredom. Perhaps Pilate had not plainly informed him that he had found no fault in the Lord Jesus and was willing for Him to be set free if the tetrarch failed to find Him guilty. Perhaps Herod had been rather anxious not to embroil himself with the Galilaean pilgrims and would not risk a fresh murder of one whom the people all hailed as a prophet.[1] Pilate's hope that Herod would take the case out of his hands had thus collapsed, and the only gain to accrue was that the old quarrel over rights of jurisdiction had now been healed. Thus the soldier escort stood once more in Pilate's presence on the palace pavement, and the procurator found that he was compelled to start afresh.

---

[1] F. J. Powell, *The Trial of Jesus Christ* (1949), p. 120.

A picked group of priests and scribes had gone to accuse Him in Herod's hearing, but it would seem that the lesser members of the Jewish council had been dispersed in the meantime. Pilate therefore had to summon them back from the temple or its precincts; but he also called some of the common people in the hope that they would be more kindly disposed: "And Pilate . . . called together the chief priests and the rulers and the people." He was, in fact, genuinely irritated when the case was thrown back to his court for trial and judgment, and he began to cast in strange waters in search of some way out of the predicament which now seemed to haunt him.

The third gospel is our clearest guide with regard to the verdict on the Accused: "Ye have brought this man unto me as one that perverteth the people: and, behold, I, having examined him before you, have found no fault in this man touching those things whereof ye accuse him." Pilate's words go back to the first vociferous assault when He had been accused as a would-be rebel: "We found this fellow perverting the nation, and forbidding to give tribute to Caesar, saying that he himself is Christ a king" (Luke 23:2). That had been a direct charge of treason, and these words sum it up in a single clear-cut statement. Pilate had found Him "not guilty" on the charge of treason, but the Jews had thundered back in reply: "He stirreth up the people, teaching throughout all Jewry, beginning from Galilee to this place" (Luke 23:5).

Pilate had clutched at the rumor that He was a Galilaean and had ordered him away to Herod; but that door of escape closed in his face, and he had been left to act for himself. Thus at last he took his courage in his hands and informed the Jews that he had tried Him on all the points at issue; and his verdict was that he could find in Him no fault or failure at all in those things of which He had been accused. This was Pilate's second affirmation of his belief in His freedom from guilt or blame. Nothing was to efface from his mind that first clear insight into the true integrity of the Accused.

Pilate felt that he could argue that the rightness of his verdict had been upheld in an independent quarter: "No, nor yet Herod: for he sent him back unto us; and behold, nothing worthy of death hath been done by him" (R.V.). Herod had tried by all the means in his power to induce the Lord to speak, and he had failed. He had sent Him back to Pilate with neither judgment nor verdict, but with a clear indication that he had found in Him no real proof of the charge of high treason. He had merely made light of His kingly honor and had held it up for jest and ridicule. It was clear that Herod's judgment was in line with Pilate's verdict; both men thought that His claims as a king were chimerical, visionary, even fanatical, but not treasonable, and not worthy of death.

Herod had been balked and beaten by His silence, but he had found no fault in Him; and he was not the man to let a state rebel escape to stir up fresh revolt in his domains. Pilate saw it all with painful clearness; he was just as anxious as the tetrarch not to imbrue his hands in blood by the sacrifice of the innocent. There was something so out of the common in the Accused that both rulers were loath to have Him put to death.

It is because Pilate's verdict was so plain and honest that his sentence leaves us shocked and surprised: "I will therefore chastise him and release him." Pilate was a Roman who knew little about Jewish law and custom, and it may have been wise not to release a man such as Jesus until he had appeared before Herod. But since Herod had now confirmed his own judgment there should have been no thought of fresh delay. His plain duty was to acquit and protect the Accused; but he announced instead that he would now chastise Him and then let Him go.

The word which spoke of this ordeal was the lightest that he could choose, as though he would make the sentence sound as soft as he could. He would scourge Him, as a sop to their fury; he would loose Him, as a sop to his conscience. "For of necessity," we are told in parenthesis, "he must release one unto them at the feast." This was undoubtedly meant to mark the end of the trial.

The verdict and the sentence fail to square as they should. For why should he chastise Him at all? Why did he not release Him at once? Why did he not send Him away absolved at the bar of Roman justice? Pilate did not intend his words in the spirit of some needless cruelty; they were meant to be an escape from yet darker penalties. He would have Him chastised as a warning to be more circumspect in the future, and he hoped that such a flagellation would be enough to satisfy His accusers and reconcile His enemies.

The first gospel is our clearest guide with regard to the appeal to the people: "Now at that feast the governor was wont to release unto the people a prisoner, whom they would." Nothing is known of this custom apart from the gospels, but an early procurator may have instituted it in imitation of the Roman practice.[2] One act of this kind would ripen into a claim almost at once, and it had come into vogue as part of the shrewd Roman system of rule in a subject country. It was meant as a sop to the common people in an attempt to keep them in more or less good humor, and that was why they were allowed to ask for the release of a popular favorite of their own choice. It would appear that just at the moment when the trial of Christ was near a climax the mob poured through the gates of the palace courtyard, shouting for this annual amnesty.

"And the multitude," Mark's narrative tells us, "crying aloud, began to desire him to do as he had ever done unto them" (Mark 15:8). It is clear that they had no thought of the trial which was in progress; it seems from the course of events that they did not even know that Jesus had been arraigned before the bar of Rome. They were simply intent on their own rights at the Paschal season. But their arrival was to introduce a new element at the decisive point in the trial of Christ.

The mob, knowing nothing of the case which was then before Pilate, had quite another favorite in mind: "And they had then a notable prisoner, called Barabbas." The pronoun "they" refers to the multitude, not the governor, and there is something odd in its usage. But it perfectly indicates the fact that the man in question belonged to the crowd like themselves, was of that class of which the mob would be made up.[3]

Nothing is known about this man apart from the gospels; even his name is a patronymic.[4] He was "a notable prisoner," a criminal character, half bandit, half rebel, who had shed blood in some recent foray hard by the walls of the city against the might of Rome. "There was one named Barabbas," Mark tells us, "which lay bound with them that had made insurrection with him, who had committed murder in the insurrection" (Mark 15:7). He had been flung into prison with his comrades-in-arms on the double charge of faction and of murder.

---

[2]Alfred Plummer, *St. Luke* (1922), p. 525.

[3]James Morison, *St. Matthew* (1885), p. 577.

[4]H. B. Swete, *The Gospel According to St. Mark* (1913), p. 370.

Perhaps he was waiting to stand his trial; perhaps he was under sentence of death. But he was an outlaw whose life of crime wore the cloak of patriotic fervor (cf. Acts 21:38), and his conflict with the Roman authorities would make a strong appeal to the national sentiment of the crowds in Jerusalem. Thus in the eyes of the multitude Barabbas was the man of the hour.

Pilate at once construed the cry of the mob as a new way of escape out of his own difficulties: "Therefore when they were gathered together, Pilate said unto them, Whom will ye that I release unto you? Barabbas, or Jesus which is called Christ?" Pilate interrupted the trial on hand while the sentence was still fresh on his lips, for he now thought that he could see a still better way to release the Lord Jesus. He would not even have Him scourged; he would arrange things so deftly that the people would ask for His release! He would get the trial off his hands and would meet the wish of the mob by a single effort! He would appeal over the head of the priestly party to the good will and the humanity of the common people! "For he knew," we are told in parenthesis, "that for envy they had delivered him"!

He did not wait to ask who it was that they had in mind; he threw out the names of Jesus and Barabbas as though the choice could lie only between the two. Pilate thought of Jesus as a visionary whose dreams could do no harm; they would know Him as a prophet who had told of grace and judgment. It was only a few days since He had been the hero of a triumphal procession; could they fail to ask now for His release? It was adroit enough as a move by Pilate to find a way out of further trouble; it was shrewd, but it was unjust! It was to treat Jesus as if He were condemned, as if in fact His life were now forfeit. It was to stake that life on fancy or caprice; it was the policy of compromise and maneuver. But it was too good a chance for Pilate to lose!

Pilate had now broken away from the course of justice for the sake of weak and dishonest concession. It was the mark of a faltering character. It is not as though he were the first or the last to choose that course, but it was his sinister distinction to do so in the one case where it was to be most fully exposed. The first wrong step was the threat to scourge Him before he let Him go; the next false move was the plan to free Him if the mob would agree to His release. He thought that thus he could guide his craft through the rocks and shoals of that sacerdotal envy which he could not ignore and yet dared not defy.

He knew not that this was to steer straight for total loss and shipwreck. Those lynx-eyed Jews had seen at once that he could still be made to yield, because they saw that he was not prepared to stand firmly on the ground of his own verdict of not guilty. If he had gone so far out of regard for them, would he not go further? If he had been willing to have Him scourged, would he not yet condemn Him to the cross? Pilate had twice tampered with the sluice-gates of compromise, and the first tiny trickles were soon to become one vast and mighty torrent. He thought that he was in control as far as the trial had yet gone, but he would soon be swept away by the flood which he had himself released. Hands would be stretched out to reach him, to save him if they could; but the terrible momentum of his own first politic surrender to what was so unjust bore him on to final ruin.[5]

---

[5]James Stalker, *The Trial and Death of Jesus Christ* (1894), p. 76.

Chapter 18

THAT JUST MAN

> When he was set down on the judgment seat, his wife sent unto him, saying, Have thou nothing to do with that just man: for I have suffered many things this day in a dream because of him. But the chief priests and elders persuaded the multitude that they should ask Barabbas, and destroy Jesus. The governor answered and said unto them, Whether of the twain will ye that I release unto you? They said, Barabbas. Pilate saith unto them, What shall I do then with Jesus which is called Christ? They all say unto him, Let him be crucified. And the governor said, Why, what evil hath he done? But they cried out the more, saying, Let him be crucified. — MATTHEW 27:19-23 (cf. MARK 15:11-14; LUKE 23:18-23; JOHN 18:39-40).

PILATE was now on the judgment seat, faced with the gravest crisis of his career. But at least one loving hand was held out to save him from the doom which lured him on. It was held out in the spirit of an uncommon entreaty which he now received from his wife: "Have thou nothing to do with that just man: for I have suffered many things this day in a dream because of him." Perhaps, while the Son of Man was away in the court of Herod, Pilate had joined his wife in the Praetorium and had told her something of this strange trial. On his return to the seat of judgment she had fallen asleep and dreamed of it. Her dream had been such that she was filled with awe and alarm, and the message to her husband would be conceived in a strain of the most urgent authority. There was all the anxiety of a woman that no harm should befall one who was innocent, and there was the solicitude of a loving wife to save her husband from a deed of shame.

A dream! There was an uncanny element in such things, and they were not to be ignored. Did not Shakespeare's Caesar meet

112

his fate on the Ides of March in 44 B.C. because he had ignored his wife's dreams of the night before?[1] Roman soldiers feared dreams such as this as portents of ill to come, and a man like Pilate might well recoil from so dark an omen. But the hand of God was in it, and its warning knell would ring in curious harmony with the somber peal of that still nameless fear at work in his soul.

The first movement in the drama that now took place has its center in the choice by the crowd: "But the chief priests and elders persuaded the multitude that they should ask Barabbas, and destroy Jesus." Pilate had staked the trial on his appeal to the people; surely he could trust them to ask for Christ rather than Barabbas. They had stood there, tongue-tied for the moment. Perhaps they would split up into groups to discuss for which of the twain they would ask. The whole course of events was thus in the balance when the trial was interrupted. The message for Pilate had come in from his wife at a fateful moment, and the effect of his appeal stood in suspense while he pondered that strange warning. But this unexpected pause gave the priests and the elders a chance which they were quick to seize.

They had marked the momentary hesitation of the mob when Pilate had named Jesus and Barabbas. Therefore they joined the crowd and used all their persuasive faculties to prompt the right reply. Their most effective argument may have been to whisper that since Jesus was so plainly Pilate's first choice, He could hardly be theirs. Let them choose their own man and make away with this Jesus!

It was not long before Pilate had recovered his composure and had turned back to the Jews: "The governor answered and said unto them, Whether of the twain will ye that I release unto you?" Perhaps the word "answered" implies that the voice of the crowd could be heard from many quarters; perhaps there was already in the air a cry for Barabbas. Pilate would be as surprised and annoyed by this warning shout as he had been disturbed and alarmed by the warning dream. But he was still willing to hope that there was some mistake, and he silenced all stray voices while he put the appeal to them again.[2]

---

[1] *Julius Caesar*, Act II, Scene ii, lines 1-3.
[2] James Morison, *St. Matthew* (1885), p. 580.

He phrased it now in a slightly new form; there was no need this time to name the two. One was a bandit and a rebel; his hands were red with the stains of murder. And one was a Prophet and a Saviour; His eyes were bright with the light of mercy. Pilate pinned his faith to the hope that they would choose one who stood for mercy, one whose appeal would touch the things which make the whole earth kin. But he had not taken the priests into account; he had not seen them with the crowd. It would only require one brief moment before their cry rang out: "Not this man, but Barabbas!" (John 18:40). That shout was as sudden and spontaneous as a thunderclap: "They cried out all at once, saying, Away with this man, and release unto us Barabbas!" (Luke 23:18).

That cry went up from a thousand throats as if it were the cry of one man: "They say, Barabbas!" It left Pilate in no doubt at all as to the mood of the mob or the man of their choice. But it was far worse than a shock or a surprise for the procurator. It was staggering in its vehemence, for it had smashed all his plans to outwit the Jews. He had been rash enough to stake the life of Christ on what was no better than a gambler's appeal, and he could not retreat although he knew that he was in the wrong.

If it were a blow to Pilate, who can tell what it must have been to Jesus? These were the sons of Zion; He was the heir of David; and had it come to this? He had often longed to gather them under the shadow of His mercy; but they would not, and now they had chosen to vouch for a robber! This was the grand proof that, though He had come unto His own, His own received Him not. It was never put more plainly than by Simon Peter in after days: "Ye denied the Holy One and the Just, and desired a murderer to be granted unto you" (Acts 3:14).

The next movement in the drama that now took place has its center in the choice of the judge: "Pilate saith unto them, What shall I do then with Jesus which is called Christ?" Pilate was in sore straits. He had lost the gambler's throw and was now badly frightened. He was more than ever anxious to find some chance loophole by means of which he could escape, and his next move was to test the public feeling with regard to Jesus. Luke's record is in somewhat vague terms: "Pilate therefore, willing to release Jesus, spake again to them" (Luke 23:20).

Mark's version gives us Pilate's words with some slight varia-
ion from Matthew's narrative: "What will ye then that I shall
do unto him whom ye call the King of the Jews?" (Mark 15:12).
Mark twice speaks of Him in this passage as the King of the
Jews where Matthew speaks of Him as Jesus the Christ (cf.
Mark 15:9; Matthew 27:17), and he ascribes it to Pilate in a
way which suggests that he designedly threw the choice of the
royal title back on the Jews.

His question was weak, almost pitiable, however, with its latent
appeal; it could only have one final outcome. The judge had
now begun to cringe to the vulgar passions of the excited
multitude, casting the fate of the Accused on their fickle mercies.
He had resigned his own right of judgment to them, and this
only made them more confident in their outcry, more insistent
in their demands. They now had the whip in their hands, and
they would make him do their will. Their shouts rang out again,
and yet again, with fresh and fierce demand: "Crucify Him,
crucify Him!" (Luke 23:21).

Pilate was more shocked by this wild outburst than by all
that had yet occured: "And the governor said, Why, what evil
hath he done?" Pilate knew that the chief priests were inspired
by motives of envy; but the priests were not the people. Had
he heard them aright? Could they really mean what they said?
"Crucified!" It was the first time that this dread word had been
voiced in his hearing, the first time that they had plainly told
him what they really wanted done with Jesus. *Crucified!* Give
Him up to that worst and most shameful of deaths? Deal with
Him as he would have dealt with Barabbas? Pilate's fancied
loophole had turned out to be a death-noose, and it left him
aghast.

Sir John Cheke has rendered that cry with stark simplicity:
"Let Him be crossed!"[3] And yet, had they proved Him guilty
of a single offense for which He ought to die a felon's death?
"And he said unto them the third time, Why, what evil hath
He done?" (Luke 23:22).

The Greek text gives us the word "for" where the English
version has the word "why"; it is a word which looks back to
the shout for crucifixion and asks for an explanation. It would
imply some word or words which he did not utter aloud: "Im-

---

[3]James Morison, St. *Matthew* (1885), p. 581.

possible! For what evil hath this man done?"[4] Pilate had twice affirmed that he could find no fault in Him (Luke 23:4, 14) and he would still insist that He had done nothing worthy of death, even if there were some offense in the background. He would therefore echo Herod's judgment (Luke 23:15), and then repeat his own sentence (Luke 23:16): "I have found no cause of death in him; I will therefore chastise him, and let him go" (Luke 23:22).

The mob had no reason to give apart from its own will, and the only answer was a louder outburst.[5] "But they cried out the more, saying, Let him be crucified!" Pilate had tried to tell them that he would take his own way and would act on his own previous decision. But the crowd was now far beyond the point where they would still bandy words with Pilate. The mere thought of letting Him go only provoked them to tenfold frenzy: "And they were instant with loud voices," so Luke says, "requiring that he might be crucified" (Luke 23:23). "And they cried out the more exceedingly," Mark has it, "Crucify him!" (Mark 15:14).

The tense of the verb in Matthew's narrative makes it clear that they kept up this savage outcry until they were sure of success. The man who was afraid to do what he ought to have done simply could not defy that fierce storm of angry uproar. Pilate had trifled with conscience and gambled with justice; and this was the result. The trial had slipped from his nerveless fingers until he found himself at their mercy. The case was now beyond control, and he could hold out no longer. "And the voices of them and of the chief priests prevailed" (Luke 23:23).

One question shows up Pilate as the representative of many thousands down the ages: "What shall I do then with Jesus, which is called Christ?" There may be few today who would take part in that merciless shout, "Crucify him!" But are there not thousands who stand irresolute, as if they ask themselves what they will do with Jesus? They must give a verdict; but they waver. They must pass a sentence; but they falter. They would rather stand on one side; they would rather leave the problem alone.

They are just like Pilate in that they shrink from the necessity

---

[4]Alfred Plummer, St. Luke (1922), p. 526.
[5]H. B. Swete, The Gospel According to St. Mark (1913), p. 373.

for decision; yet it was not that he did not know what he ought to do with Jesus. Had not his wife warned him? It were better to have nothing to do with Him than to do ill. Had not conscience told him? One in whom he could find no fault at all ought to go free. Pilate's verdict at last was to let the voice of others prevail; but he little thought that this would condemn his own soul to the night of an endless darkness. For the day will come when he will stand at the bar of yet another tribunal, and the answer which he found for his own never-to-be-forgotten words will determine his eternal destiny. You can no more escape that duty to decide than could Pilate. What then will you do with Jesus, which is called Christ?

Chapter 19

SEE YE TO IT

> When Pilate saw that he could prevail nothing, but that rather a tumult was made, he took water, and washed his hands before the multitude, saying, I am innocent of the blood of this just person: see ye to it. Then answered all the people, and said, His blood be on us, and on our children. — MATTHEW 27:24, 25.

THE trial of Christ had passed beyond the point where right and wrong were at issue. It had even lost its aspect as a simple conflict between Pilate's will and the will of the people. The judge had been convinced that the Accused was quite guiltless on the score of treason, but he lacked the moral fiber which was necessary to resist the outcry and release the captive. He had ordered Him away to Herod, but the tetrarch had been baffled by Him. He had proposed Him to the crowd, but the crowd had clamored for a robber.

The mob had been maddened by the subtle propaganda of the priests and elders, and the uproar which had burst round Pilate's head soon bordered on the worst kind of mob riot. It was like the riot which took place when Stephen was dragged outside Jerusalem and stoned to death (Acts 7:57, 58), or when Paul was almost lynched by the mob in the precincts of the temple (Acts 21:30, 32).

The angry cries of passionate men and the ugly shouts for innocent blood may remind us of the red Reign of Terror in the streets of Paris when nothing but falling heads could appease the mob. It was Pilate's failure to act firmly in the early stage of the trial which had left him helpless at this crisis. He had passed through a whole cycle of attitudes and emotions, but there was no stability in his feelings. Weakness and bluster, caution and protest, argument and evasion, compromise and surrender: all played their part in turn until this last scene in which his moral features have been caught in photograph for ever.

The first element in the narrative of this crisis was the symbolic gesture on the part of the judge: "When Pilate saw that he could prevail nothing, but that rather a tumult was made." Pilate had not done the one thing which he knew he ought to have done; he had not set Jesus free when he had pronounced Him clear of guilt. But he had tried after his own fashion to pave the way for His release, and he was slow enough to see that these efforts were all doomed to failure.

Now at last he had been forced to face the fact that to resist the mob further would be fraught with peril. It would provoke a grave riot at a time when Jerusalem was crowded with pilgrims, and it might cost many lives to suppress such an affray. But the bloodshed which this would involve would leave him exposed to new accusations of tyranny and massacre, and he hardly dared to risk his future career in such circumstances to the whims of Tiberius Caesar. If he were to resist the mob, who could tell what the end might be? To yield would mean no more than the loss of one life, the life of an obscure Jew, which could not involve him in danger.

But he could not feel at ease and he longed to do something which would clear his conscience: "He took water, and washed his hands before the multitude." There was an old Hebrew law which would throw a flood of light on his conduct for the Jewish rabble. It laid down a certain course of action which was to be taken when a man was found dead in the open country and there was no clue as to his slayer. All the city elders were to wash their hands over the head of a slain heifer, while they made a solemn declaration of their freedom from guilt. "Our hands have not shed this blood," they were to say, "neither have our eyes seen it" (Deuteronomy 21:7).

We cannot tell whether or not Pilate would be aware of this ancient custom, but there can be no doubt that it would lend significance to his actions in the eyes of the mob. He called for a bowl of water and rinsed his hands as a public gesture. This was as uncommon and surprising as it was symbolic and impressive. It was one last attempt to throw off all responsibility for the trial of the Lord Jesus. But it was too theatrical; water could not cleanse from the stains of blood.

His words provide one more testimony to the moral glory of the Accused: "I am innocent of the blood of this just person: see ye to it." Pilate himself could scarce tell why, but he felt as he had never felt before. He had never before seen the man whose blood he cared so little to shed, and he was still deeply troubled. He had resolved to let Him go to the cross in spite of conscience and in spite of justice; yet he could not do it until he had staged some demonstration of his disapproval. He claimed that he was not responsible for the blood of the just, that he was not answerable for the death that was planned. But that very claim was like a judicial confession that the crucifixion would be murder.

Pilate told them to see to it, as if that were enough to free him from blame or blunder — as if indeed he could transfer to them the guilt of what he knew to be willful murder. But he forgot that an abnegation of all responsibility was out of the question. In things moral, men cannot clear or cleanse themselves by a mere act of will. Pilate washed his hands of the deed; but the guilt of sinful action is not so easily removed. The blood of Jesus was left on Pilate's conscience; he and his have suffered for it.

The next element in the narrative of this crisis was the dramatic outburst on the part of the crowd: "Then answered all the people!" The mob had no patience with the Roman procurator and his qualms of conscience. They were deeper in the mire of that wrong-doing, but they could see through his hollow pretense. Pilate had told them three times at least that he could find no fault in the Accused; he had asked them with an air of pain and surprise what He had done amiss.

His last words had declared Jesus an innocent character, not a criminal renegade, and yet he was yielding to their demands for His death by crucifixion. Pilate meant that washing of his hands to be a solemn disavowal of guilt, and they had no qualms in taking up the responsibility which he disowned. But they despised the judge who would not bear his share of blame, and their shout in reply was in tones most defiant. That shout came back as with one voice, and it was like the bay of hounds with the taste of blood on their tongues.

It was as much as to say that Pilate might be afraid of guilt but they were not: "His blood be on us, and on our children!"

They were willing, with blind and rash bravado, to clear the magistrate whom they so despised. "See ye to it," he had exclaimed in deep chagrin. "Give thyself no concern," they now thundered in hoarse reply. They were maddened with rage, reckless with guilt, and they gave no thought to the words which they employed. Their eye would not pity, nor their voice spare; their one master passion was to hurry Jesus to His death on the cross.

No more dreadful imprecation could have fallen from the lips of humanity — least of all from those of Israel. That shout was a shout for deicide, for they knew what Pilate did not yet know; they would dip their hands in the blood of God,[1] for they knew that He made Himself equal with God. It was just as He had foreseen; they that slew the prophets would slay the Son Himself, "that upon you may come all the righteous blood shed upon the earth" (Matthew 23:35). But that wild and reckless cry was so dark and so profane that we tremble when we reflect on it. The curse which they invoked was the curse of bloodguiltiness for the death of the Son of God, and that curse was to haunt Jerusalem like a specter in the dark years at hand.

It was not long before that dread malediction was to descend on the guilty nation: "Then answered all the people, and said, His blood be on us, and on our children." The whole scene is like a mirror in which we can clearly trace the features of magistrate and populace, and those features tell us so plainly what dark and dreadful paths lie before those who resign themselves to wrongdoing at the will of others. Public men often bow to the force of a vocal mob, and a vocal mob often yields to the force of a hidden few. But the hidden few in this case were fast steering the ship of state to the shoals of ruin.

Within a few years they were to accuse those who proclaimed the name of this Jesus in terms strangely reminiscent of this very outcry: "Behold, ye have filled Jerusalem with your doctrine, and intend to bring this man's blood upon us!" (Acts 5:28). That savage demand for the blood of Jesus must have returned to the minds of many when at length the Roman legions laid siege to the Holy City. The soldiers of Titus had no pity for age or sex in their frightful slaughter; the mountains of Zion were covered with crosses, and looked like one vast

---

[1]See Acts 20:28.

field of blood. The sons of Israel are still shadowed by that wanton imprecation; they are scattered like wrecks, unwanted, derelict, on the shores of many countries. The mob took the blame for the crime, and the curse has not yet spent all its force. The blood of Jesus was left on Israel's spirit; they and theirs still suffer for it.

Shakespeare's *Macbeth* contains one scene which no one can ever forget who knows the play. It was some time after the murder of Banquo, a crime which had been thought out by Lady Macbeth. Macbeth himself had been haunted by the ghost of the man he had murdered; but things grew worse when a troubled conscience drove his wife to walk in her sleep. She was like a woman whose mind had been drugged with stupor, while rest for her spirit had forever vanished. Thus in the trance of sleep she came slowly, slowly down the stairway by the light of one dim candle. Then she began to wring her hands, rubbing them again and again. Her voice was heard in a hollow whisper as she wrung them, talking in low tones with herself: "Yet here's a spot. Out, damned spot! Out, I say! . . . What! Will these hands ne'er be clean?" This wringing her hands at the midnight hour could not wash away the stains of blood, however; those murder stains only seemed to grow more crimson as she rubbed them.[2]

Pilate might wash his hands ever so clean, yet the guilt of Christ's blood would leave its stain on his conscience in a way that water could not efface. There was only one way for him as for those who took and slew the Prince of Glory, and that was to turn the words of the curse into the words of prayer; conscience-stricken, guilty, to cry with new meaning, "His blood be on us!" Then, though their sins were as scarlet, they should be white as snow; and though they were red like crimson, they should be white like wool.

---

[2]William Shakespeare, *Macbeth*, Act V, Scene i, lines 21-70.

Chapter 20

WITH HIS STRIPES

And Pilate gave sentence that it should be as they required. — LUKE 23:24.

And so Pilate, willing to content the people, released Barabbas unto them. — MARK 15:15.

Then Pilate therefore took Jesus, and scourged him. — JOHN 19:1.

And when he had scourged Jesus, he delivered him to be crucified. — MATTHEW 27:26.

PILATE had been beaten at each twist and turn of the trial, driven from this corner to that corner, until he had lost the power to resist the wrong or to uphold the right. His vacillation and indecision had made him the prey of crafty-minded priests and rulers, and he had let others dictate to him in a matter which he should have kept in his own control. His choice was made at last for no reason at all apart from his desire to keep the mob at bay: "And Pilate gave sentence that it should be as they required."

There is some doubt whether these words mark a formal sentence or not. Swete and Westcott argue that he did not pronounce such a sentence, but just let the mob have their way.[1] At all events, it meant that his original verdict was quite ignored and his original sentence was now reversed. He had said that he would chastise Him and let Him go; but now he would chastise Him and put Him to death. It was in line with this anxiety to please the crowd that he now gave Barabbas his freedom: "And so Pilate, willing to content the people, released Barabbas unto them."

---

[1] H. B. Swete, *The Gospel According to St. Mark* (1913), p. 373; B. F. Westcott, *The Gospel According to St. John* (18th impr., 1937), p. 273.

It was ironical that Pilate should find himself forced to release a man who was guilty of the very crime which the priests had tried so hard to nail to Christ. Thus one who was guilty went free, while One who was sinless went to the cross. But the harshness of the law had yet to appear, for the regular overture to the pains of crucifixion was the frightful ordeal by scourge.

We may think first of this experience as an ordeal imposed on Jesus by Pilate: "Then Pilate therefore took Jesus and scourged him." There is only the most fleeting mention of this ordeal in the first two gospels, and it is passed by in silence in Luke. But it found a record in John's narrative in words of stark simplicity, words most dignified, words most reticent. This was not the first time that the scourge had been named, for the worried judge had had it in view as a means of escape from worse calamity.

He had pronounced both verdict and sentence after His return from Herod with that unfortunate mixture of what was right and what was wrong: "Behold, nothing worthy of death hath been done by him; I will therefore chastise him, and release him" (Luke 23:15, 16 R.V.). But the hostile rabble had cried out in angry clamor for the cross, not the scourge, and the conflict went on until Pilate had his back to the wall. Then he tried once more to assert himself; he would do as he had said he would do! "I have found no cause of death in him; I will therefore chastise him, and let him go" (Luke 23:22). Surely the sight of such crimson weals would appease their rage for blood! But no; no blood would suit their cry save the blood of the cross.

Thus the scourge which he had at first proposed as an escape from death was now ordered as a preface to death. This cruel flagellation had been foretold in the pages of the ancient prophet as part of His redemptive sufferings: "I gave my back to the smiters, and my cheeks to them that plucked off the hair" (Isaiah 50:6). The Lord Himself had seen as it were from afar that this flagellation would play its part in His Passion: "The Son of man . . . shall be delivered unto the Gentiles, and shall be . . . spitefully entreated. . . . And they shall scourge him, and put him to death" (Luke 18:31-33).

Ancient writers like Horace and Livy have told enough for us to know that this was a frightful experience. The scourge itself was a lash or cat-o'-nine tails, composed of leather thongs and designed to inflict the utmost pain. The tail of each thong was loaded with bits of bone or balls of iron, so that each blow would raise a weal or break the skin. The shock as well as the laceration was so severe that it sometimes led to fatal results. There were many who died beneath the lash before ever they came to the torment of a death on the cross.[2]

What was now done must have been done at the direct command of the procurator. The Lord Jesus was led away by six Roman lictors and was scourged in military fashion. It ought to have taken place in semi-private in the palace guardroom where the soldiers had their quarters; but it seems to have been carried out in public on the tessellated pavement where the trial had been held.

The Lord Jesus must have been stripped and bound to a post or pillar, while His hands would be tied so that He could not shield Himself. Hebrew law laid down the regulation that no more than forty stripes should be inflicted, but there was no merciful provision of this kind to curb a Roman flogging. It can only fill us with a sense of absolute nausea to think of the scene which must have taken place at Pilate's bidding. It was as though all that was most callous in feeling had joined hands with all that was most brutal in conduct to do despite to the Man of Sorrows. Those Roman soldiers, cold, implacable, stood by and plied the scourge; and that scourge flayed the form of One who was fairer than the children of men.

We may think next of this experience as an ordeal endured by Jesus for sinners: "Then Pilate therefore took Jesus and scourged him." It is better to throw a veil over the more ghastly facts of this scene, and that is in fact what John has done. We would only wish to lift that veil in so far as this may be necessary to give a true insight into the real nature of His Passion. But we ought to observe that there was a slowly increasing momentum in the character of His sufferings as the *via crucis* came more clearly into men's view.

There had been the terrible agony of the Garden, when the beads of sweat had stood out on His brow like great drops of blood. There were the bonds which had been laid on Him at His arrest, and the blow in His face while He was still before

---

[2]H. B. Swete, *The Gospel According to St. Mark* (1913), p. 374.

Annas. There had been the scene of mockery and of violence in the presence of the high priest, when some had spat in His face and ridiculed Him, and some had struck at His head and buffeted Him. Thus His flagellation by these Roman soldiers was not the first assault which He had to endure; but it was the first of physical injuries which He had to sustain at the hands of Gentiles, and it would far exceed all that had yet transpired in the way of violent suffering.

Men have sometimes liked to suppose that this scourging was less severe in His case than in the case of others. Would not Pilate seek to minimize the blows, to moderate their severity? But there is no valid reason why we should think that this was in fact what happened. There seem indeed to be other facts which suggest that He must have sustained the full ordeal. Pilate still hoped against hope that by this frightful experience he could appease the Jews; and his appeal to the crowd would depend on the terrible character of this ordeal.

The Lord Jesus was in the flower of a perfect manhood, sensitive to pain in all its forms, and the procurator cherished the hope that when the crowd saw Him, beaten, bleeding, torn and lacerated, they would agree to let Him go. This is confirmed by the fact that He could not bear His cross when He went forth at length to the hill of execution, and this must have been due to the double burden of violence and exhaustion which He had been forced to sustain. These hints are a better indication of the truth than uncertain conjecture. We must believe that the full weight of that dreadful scourge was laid on Jesus.

It may be less trying to bear in mind what this must have entailed if we think of what it meant in the case of one who trod as a servant in the Master's footsteps. Thus we can turn to the life of Paul for an illustration of its severity, for he tells us how he had to bear "stripes above measure." "Of the Jews," he tells us, "five times received I forty stripes save one; thrice was I beaten with rods" (II Corinthians 11:24, 25). There is no account of the five floggings which he suffered at the hands of the Jews, but the frail and sensitive apostle may well have felt beaten almost to death.

We know only of one castigation, though there were three, at the hands of Gentiles, but we do know how he shrank from the scourge a fourth time in Jerusalem (Acts 22:25). We can never forget how both Paul and Silas had "many stripes" laid on them in Philippi; and then, bleeding, lacerated, with ugly weals, and swollen wounds, they were placed in the stocks in a common prison. Nevertheless they joined voices and sang praises to their God at midnight (Acts 16:25). May we not say that they were in some real measure partners in the sorrows of Him who bared His back to lash and scourge as part of His redemptive suffering?

Pilate's sentence that it should be as they desired was meant to mark the end of the long trial. Willing to content them, he let Barabbas go; anxious to appease them, he had Jesus scourged. All that remained was to arrange for the formalities of His execution, and Matthew's narrative sums up the trial with an air of finality: "And when he had scourged Jesus, he delivered him to be crucified."

There was a strange movement in the Middle Ages which called forth bands of men known as Flagellantes. Hordes of these curious penitents poured out of Italy and spread through Germany. Naked down to the waist, they roamed through country lanes and crowded cities for weeks on end, singing penitential hymns like *Dies Irae* and flogging each other with the fanatical zeal of untaught enthusiasts.[3]

They knew not the comfort of the gospel message of Christ for us; they knew nothing of the deeper values of that ordeal in which He was flayed with the scourge on our behalf. But we who were like sheep astray on the mountains and have returned to the Shepherd of Souls, we know why it was that He so suffered in His sacred human body. We know, and we rejoice in the testimony of old: "The chastisement of our peace was upon him, and with his stripes we are healed" (Isaiah 53:5; cf. I Peter 2:24).

---

[3] J. C. Ryle, *Expository Thoughts on St. John's Gospel* (popular ed., 1897), vol. iii, p. 303.

Chapter 21

A CROWN OF THORNS

> Then the soldiers of the governor took Jesus into the common hall, and gathered unto him the whole band of soldiers. And they stripped him, and put on him a scarlet robe. And when they had platted a crown of thorns, they put it upon his head, and a reed in his right hand: and they bowed the knee before him, and mocked him, saying, Hail, King of the Jews! And they spit upon Him, and took the reed, and smote him on the head. — MATTHEW 27:27-30; (cf. MARK 15:16-19; JOHN 19:2-3).

THE Lord Jesus had been stripped and scourged in public as a felon marked for the cross. But worse was to follow, for the violence which had thus been sustained was mild enough compared with the scene of ridicule which now took place. It was a mark of the harsh and pagan spirit in which the world was ruled from Rome that a man who had been condemned to die was first made an object of rude and brutal burlesque.

Thus was Jesus, condemned and scourged, handed over to the Roman soldiers, much as a fox, ridden down by careless huntsmen, is then flung to the dogs: "Then the soldiers of the governor took Jesus into the common hall, and gathered unto him the whole band of soldiers." The Jews who still thronged the open pavement would watch them march Him off, content to think that it was to prepare Him for crucifixion. They would conduct Him to their own guardroom, and would summon all who were at hand or who were not on duty for an hour of horseplay. There would be the lictors who had carried out the flagellation; there would be the centurion and his quaternion who would carry out the execution.

We may think it almost incredible that men should join hands for such a purpose: to gloat over human suffering, to turn His pain and shame into brutal mockery. But these were men

128

who had long been inured to the sight of bloodshed on the field of battle, and who found a sadistic attraction in the life-and-death encounters of the Roman circus.[1]

The first round in this rude horseplay was a pantomime of ridicule, with all the mock regalia of kingship. This scene took place in an immense courtyard which was situated within the walls of the palace-castle of the Antonia. It was paved with flagstones which still exist and cover almost its entire surface. Many of them are more than three feet square, and from twelve to eighteen inches in thickness. They are held in a bed of thick cement and show no sign of dislocation or repair.

We can still trace the belt that ran between the entrance gates and the palace by the striation of the stones with close-cut grooves to guard a slipping horsehoof. Games were marked out on the flagstones, just as in the camps and forums of all Roman cities, and they are grouped in front of the stairway which led from the courtyard to the guardroom. The most complex design was stamped with a capital beta, the first letter of the Greek word for king, and was spread out over several flagstones. There was a rough prickly crown at the head and a naked sabre at the bottom of this design. This was well known as the Game of the King, a game derived from the Saturnalia and common throughout the Roman army.[2]

To play this game the guards would choose a man under sentence of death and would stand him on the flagstones. Then they buffeted him, jostling him to and fro, until at last he stood on crown or sword. If the end of the game found him standing over the sword he would be put to death at once; but if it were his fate to stand upon the crown he would be hailed as a mock king.

This gives us a vivid explanation of the scene which took place in the case of the Lord Jesus. He was chosen as a victim for the Game of the King, with the added zest of derisive pantomine. Perhaps a few idle soldiers had been in the guardroom when the scourging took place. It soon occured to them that they could now play the old game with a realism that was

---

[1] James Stalker, *The Trial and Death of Jesus Christ* (1894), pp. 88-9.

[2] These details are published in a small and anonymous booklet on the Lithostrotos, bought at the Basilica of the Ecce Homo in the Convent of Notre Dame de Sion in 1938.

seldom available; they could turn the monotony of mere make-believe into the merriment of a living farce.

They had gleaned a hint from the trial before Herod, when He had been arrayed in a bright robe. They had caught the drift of the trial before Pilate, when He had been accused as a false king. Thus when Jesus was led into their midst they were more than ready to make Him an object of sport. They would treat His claims as a king to the caricature of a bloody burlesque.[3]

There is something infinitely sad and somber in the very reading of this tale of callous pantomime: "And they stripped him, and put on him a scarlet robe. And when they had platted a crown of thorns, they put it upon his head, and a reed in his right hand." Someone brought an old and faded tunic with just a tinge of the imperial color, and that they flung over His now torn and bleeding shoulders as if He were born to wear the purple. Then they brought a bunch of jagged thorn-bush from the palace garden, and that they had twisted into a wreath of thorns and crammed like a garland upon His brow. The last thing they chose was a reed, and that they thrust into His hand.

A reed shaken in the wind was the emblem of weakness, and it mocked a scepter which was the emblem of royal power. The crown of thorns was a shameful caricature of the laurel wreath worn by the victorious Imperator and seen upon his arms. And the blood-soaked garment was meant to mock the robe of a kingly victor as he returned from his wars in triumph.

The next round in this rude horseplay was a masquerade of violence, with all the sham insignia of homage. Strange that He should have thus been mocked, first by the Jews and then by the Gentiles! In the palace of the high priest He had been found guilty on the ground that He claimed to be the Son of God, and the minions of the court had made Him taste the gall and wormwood of taunt and jibe. "Then did they spit in his face, and buffeted him; and others smote him with the palms of their hands" (Matthew 26:67).

Had He said that He would sit as the Son of Man at the right hand of power? They spat out their contempt, and spat

---

[3] I have not been able to find any independent confirmation for this reconstruction of the gospel narrative; it is simply based upon the details contained in the booklet on the Lithostrotos.

t in His fair and sacred face. Had He said that they would
ee Him as the Son of God on the clouds of heaven? They
mote Him in disgust, and smote Him with a free and vicious
and. They could hardly do more to mark their coarse disdain
or Him and all His claims. They had chosen that rough and
vulgar kind of abuse which would hurt most of all.

But this ordeal was more or less mild in comparison with what
Ie was now to endure at the hands of Roman legionaries. Jews
nd Gentiles followed much the same form of violence, but there
vas a change in the tone of mockery. The Jews had seized
ipon His claim as a prophet and had held it up to scornful
panter: "Prophesy unto us, thou Christ; who is he that smote
hee?" (Matthew 26:68). Now the soldiers caught at the talk
of His kingship and made it the butt of ribald laughter.

They meant to scoff at the Jews as well as Jesus when they
hailed Him as king, and their words were just a mocking echo
of the words which they had heard Pilate use. Did He say that
He was a king, even though His kingdom might not be of this
world? There was a half-amused smile of scorn at the thought
of such a rival to the Caesars. Did He say that He owned a
realm, even though His scepter may have been one of truth?
There was an ill-concealed scowl of spleen at the hint of such
a menace to the empire. Thus they brought out the tattered
robe, and jagged wreath, and worthless reed, and they bowed
the knee to Him in hollow contempt for the Jews as well as
their king.

But this vulgar coronation was pressed one stage further with
all the marks of a savage masquerade: "And they bowed the
knee before him, and mocked him, saying, Hail, King of the
Jews! And they spit upon him, and took the reed, and smote
him on the head." They had often seen how Caesar's servants
knelt in homage and said, *Ave Imperator!* So now they came
forward to bend the knee and to cry in scoffing imitation, "Hail,
thou King of the Jews!"

John's record employs a tense which adds one more vivid
detail to our understanding of what took place. They filed past
Him in a long queue, so that each one could make his own
formal act of homage.[4] But that alone would soon prove much

B. F. Westcott, *The Gospel According to St. John* (18th impr., 1937),
p. 268.

too tame; men would grow tired of this childish pageant. They would soon add brutal insult to this mimic homage, and they did it in ways which the world still finds it hard to forgive.

Each man would turn when he had made his bow of sham respect and would laugh in His face with the scorn of heartless hilarity. He could not put off the robe or garland of thorns but He had let the reed drop from His hand; but they snatched it up as they filed by and smote His thorn-crowned brow again and again. And last, and worst indignity of all, they soiled His blood-stained face with the spittle of a shameless contempt.

There stood Jesus, scourged and lacerated, robed in scarlet, mocked by pagan soldiers; but the one thing which has always caught the imagination of the world was the crown of thorns. We may never know in our own bodies the pain and horror of the scourge; but we have all felt the sudden wound of a thorn, and that garland of thorns seems to make His pain and passion real to us in one form which we have felt and known.

Thorns were a sign of the curse brought upon man by sin when he was driven out of Eden; He now took that curse upon His own head, and so lifted it off the heart of our sin-worn humanity. Thus Godfrey of Bouillon refused to wear a crown at his coronation as the mediaeval king of Jerusalem: for was it right, he asked, for him to wear a crown of gold in that city where his Saviour had worn the crown of thorns? So too John Huss refused to make any complaint when he was led out to die at the stake, his head covered with a cap on which three devils were scrawled: for had not Christ, he asked, for his sake worn the crown of thorns, and would not he for Christ's sake wear this cap of shame?[6]

We know that He who once was wreathed with thorns will come again, crowned with many crowns and clothed in blood-red raiment for His kingly triumph (Revelation 19:12, 13). But if He were to stand before us now, the crown of thorns wreathed round His head, who would not wish to put forth his hand and lift that crown from His sacred brow? Who would not most gladly come to bow at His feet and hail Him, King of kings, and Lord of lords?

[5]H. B. Swete, *The Gospel According to St. Mark* (1913), p. 376.

[6]J. C. Ryle, *Expository Thoughts on St. John's Gospel* (popular ed., 1897) vol. iii, p. 304.

Chapter 22

BEHOLD THE MAN

Pilate therefore went forth again, and saith unto them, Behold I bring him forth to you, that ye may know that I find no fault in him. Then came Jesus forth, wearing the crown of thorns, and the purple robe. And Pilate saith unto them, Behold the man! When the chief priests therefore and officers saw him, they cried out saying, Crucify him, crucify him. Pilate saith unto them, Take ye him, and crucify him: for I find no fault in him. The Jews answered him, We have a law, and by our law he ought to die, because he made himself the Son of God. — John 19:4-7.

WE might have thought that the trial of Christ would come to an end with His condemnation. There had been no word of appeal when the sentence was made known by Pilate, and He had been transferred without ado to the guard for execution. He had been scourged; He had been mocked; and it would seem as if nothing could save Him from the cross. Flagellation was the customary herald of death, and the Jews had no fear now of a stay in the course of events. But this passage opens up a new and unexpected scene in the long drama of His Passion; unexpected, because it turns on the sudden intervention of the Roman procurator.

His work as judge was now over, and there was no need for him to preside at the execution. Wearied with conflict, troubled by conscience, he would, we might have thought, be glad to retire. Why then did he remain when he could have withdrawn? Or if he did withdraw, why did he then return? A singular fascination seemed to compel him to linger by the scene of events. No doubt he did retire to the palace while the horseplay took place in that interior courtyard. Perhaps his wife would make further efforts to secure the release of "that just man." Thus he returned with the hidden desire to do some-

133

thing for His rescue, and his secret hope was that he might now act on his first resolution. He would let the Jews see how He had been chastised, and then would let Him go.

The first step in this fresh drama was when Pilate put his case to the Jews: "Pilate therefore went forth again, and saith unto them, Behold, I bring him forth to you, that ye may know that I find no fault in him." It would seem that Pilate at first went out alone and faced the Jews once more while they were still waiting on the pavement. He meant to tell them what he had in mind; then he would bring Christ out on view. The crowd believed that the trial was over; they were merely waiting for the Victim. But his few words would let them know that the case was not yet finished. He hoped that they would be content once they saw Him as He was now, and he proposed to bring Him forth as one in whom he found no fault at all.

This had been his verdict from the very outset of the whole case; neither accusation on the part of the Jews nor yet discovery on his own part had led him to vary that first judgment in a single detail. The Lord Jesus was obviously not the kind of felon that they claimed Him to be. Yet he had had Him scourged as if He were at least partly guilty in an attempt to placate the prosecution. But now he would assert that the Lord had suffered enough for one who was faultless in the eyes of the law.

Thus He was led out to be a spectacle for the clamorous multitude: "Then came Jesus forth, wearing the crown of thorns, and the purple robe." Pilate had been lost in wonder in the presence of this vilified Nazarene: His patience, His silence, His gentleness, His forbearance, left him amazed. He could sense no guilt in that calm dignity, and no weakness in that grave composure. He saw only a strength of character, a rock-like rectitude, such as he had not seen before. And that impressive character had lost none of its force now that He had been shamed and scourged.

This was the most remarkable feature of all; disgrace and pain only seemed to add more to His essential dignity. It was a sight which stirred Pilate's heart and Pilate's conscience, in spite of his judicial aloofness. It would, he thought, touch any heart; it might even soften the Jews outside. It might appease their wild thirst for revenge, and he would at least see if he could now appeal to their better nature. Therefore Jesus was led forth to appear once more before the hostile crowd, His temples crowned with the garland of thorns, His shoulders clothed with the garment of scorn.

Then as Jesus came forth Pilate turned and pointed to Him: "And Pilate saith unto them, Behold the man!" *Ecce homo!* What lies behind that phrase is more or less inarticulate, is left to the imagination. For did Pilate speak in contempt? He wore a crown and was robed in scarlet. Was this their king? Could they not see what a weak and helpless creature He was? Or did Pilate speak in pity? He bore on His face and figure the marks of pain. Would they kill Him? Did they not feel that He had been punished enough?

The Jews may have stared with looks of contempt, and Pilate may have looked with eyes of pity. But may we not say that there was admiration as well as pity in his voice? "Behold, the man!" Pilate for once dropped the jibe of calling Him the King of the Jews, and spoke of Him in terms of His manhood. He had never seen so singular or so impressive a man before, and the cruelty of His sufferings was in such stark contrast with the majesty of His appearance. *Ecce homo!* This was the half-conscious cry of admiration on the part of one who was more than a little moved and impressed by His bearing. Would the Jews still press their demand for His crucifixion? Behold Him, and suffer me to let Him go!

The next step in this strange drama was when they threw the case back to Pilate: "When the chief priests therefore and officers saw him, they cried out, saying, "Crucify him! Crucify him!" The plain people might have felt the force of Pilate's appeal, and might have been ready to yield; there was neither rhyme nor reason in the demand for still further indignities. But the chief priests would not relent. Their hearts were hard as the nether-millstone. They saw Him well enough, but it was a sight which only inflamed their worst passions.

Fanatical hatred had crushed every kinder impulse in their human nature, and their hearts were hardened in the savage resolve to have His blood. *Therefore* they stirred up a fresh cry, the loud shouts and frightful clamor of wild, reckless frenzy. The same word was used to describe the wild outcry against Paul on the castle stairway: "They cried out, and cast off their clothes, and threw dust into the air" (Acts 22:23). John gives the very idea of the fierce roar, like that of wild beasts for their prey, in a sharp, short exclamation which leaves out the pronoun: "Crucify! Crucify!" (see Mark 15:13, 14: "Crucify Him!"). And the theme of that shout was the darkest that men could frame. It was worse than the cry for heads in the streets of Paris; it was a shout for the death of God!

Pilate was in no mood to take kindly to that outburst, and his reply was as cold as theirs was angry: "Pilate saith unto them, Take ye him, and crucify him: for I find no fault in him!" He was seriously disappointed to find himself baffled and beaten yet again. He was at his wits' end — vexed, impatient, and irritated by failure. Did they ask for crucifixion, and was his voice not to be heard? Then let them take Him and do the bloody deed themselves! They were not to trouble him, nor ask him to sign the death-warrant!

It is hard to tell how far this was a threat to renounce authority, or how far it was meant as an angry sarcasm. Pilate may have meant that he would only yield Him up if they made themselves responsible for the execution — if indeed his angry words had any meaning at all apart from their expression of sheer annoyance.[1] He knew that they could not put Him to death with their own hands; he knew that the foul deed would have to be done, if done at all, in the name of Rome. For the third time, in identical words, John records his fixed judgment; Pilate could find no fault in Him at all (John 18:38, 19:4, 19:6; cf. Luke 23:4, 23:14). The most searching analysis of His conduct had shown that there was no ground for reproach.

The judge had found no fault in Him, and he refused to be their tool! They were words of vexation, irony, bitterness, yet words full of unconscious testimony to the absolute righteousness of Christ.

But the Jews caught up the challenge, and their reply took him by storm: "The Jews answered him, We have a law, and by our law he ought to die, because he made himself the Son of God!" At last the truth was out! They had kept it in reserve as long as they could, but the crucial hour had now come. They had to speak at once, or not at all; and so the real reason why they were so intent on His execution came out. They had accused Him of treason under the law of Rome; now they fell

---

[1]James Stalker, *The Trial and Death of Jesus Christ* (1894), p. 101.

back on their own law with a charge of blasphemy (see Leviticus 24:16). They let Pilate know that their demand was not so groundless as he averred. They had found Him guilty because He made Himself the Son of God, and the phrase which is used was meant to hint that He had staked His claim both in word and action (cf. John 19:12).

Pilate had said, "Behold, the Man!" with a notable emphasis on the word "Man"; and their reaction to this emphasis was to accuse Him as *the Son of God!* (see John 5:18; 10:33). It was useless for the procurator to tell them to take Him and nail Him to the cross; for that would not accord with the law of Moses, while it would be against the law of Rome. But let Pilate put Him to death, for one point was quite clear: He was guilty of an offense against their law, and by that law He ought to die!

Pilate's tactics had been fraught with danger, for they were the tactics of false delay. Good can seldom come from wrongful delay, and it only gave the Jews more time to assail. He did indeed resist; he fought them round by round with all his strength. But his mistake was that he had ever let them have the first chance, and he succumbed at last. Meanwhile they were so bent on His execution that they could think of nothing else, and they were quite beyond that last appeal, "Behold, the man!" But this is an exclamation which has become famous in the Latin of the Vulgate: *Ecce Homo!*

It is still a phrase which ought to stir the chords of all our truest feelings: "Behold, the man!" Scorned and reviled, scourged and disowned, in scarlet robe, with thorn-crowned brow! Pilate was plainly moved; but the chief priests were as hard as ever. Who would not now rather stand with Pilate than with the Jews, hushed with wonder, perhaps rather than with pity? "Is it nothing to you, all ye that pass by? Behold, and see if there be any sorrow like unto my sorrow!" (Lamentations 1:12).

Chapter 23

THE GREATER SIN

When Pilate therefore heard that saying, he was the more afraid; and went again into the judgment hall, and saith unto Jesus, Whence art thou? But Jesus gave him no answer. Then saith Pilate unto him, Speakest thou not unto me? knowest thou not that I have power to crucify thee, and have power to release thee? Jesus answered, Thou couldest have no power at all against me, except it were given thee from above: therefore he that delivered me unto thee hath the greater sin. And from thenceforth Pilate sought to release him, but the Jews cried out, saying, If thou let this man go, thou art not Caesar's friend: whosoever maketh himself a king speaketh against Caesar! — JOHN 19:8-12.

THE Jews had thrown a new ingredient into the trial with the charge that He was the Son of God, for this was an accusation which shed fresh light on the restless feelings in Pilate's soul. He had not felt easy from the outset; this Man Jesus was no ordinary person! The more he saw of Him, the more did he dislike the part he had to play. His calm and majestic demeanor; His frank and evident innocence; the fierce malice and deep envy of the Jews whom Pilate knew all too well: facts like these would combine to produce an effect which could not be denied. The first charge had been that He was a plain malefactor (John 18:30); then the Jews had made Him out to be a rival king to Caesar (John 18:33). Now they said that He was the Son of God, and this disturbed Pilate still more gravely (John 19:7).

Even before this last accusation he had felt most anxious to set Him free, and this unexpected statement only deepened the sense of awe which had slowly taken hold of his mind. He had had fears before, but now those fears took on definite proportions and alarming qualities. "When Pilate therefore heard that saying, he was the more afraid." It was the whole saying which made up the accusation, not the title alone, which filled him with alarm. We ought not to miss the force of that one word *more* — "the *more* afraid." He was seized with salutary apprehension like Gamaliel lest haply he should turn out to be engaged in a conflict with God.

The first emphasis in this paragraph falls on the figure of Pilate. He ". . . went again into the judgment hall." The Jews were left outside while he once more took Christ aside. "The Son of God" was a phrase which could not fail to awaken memories of both Greek and Roman legend.

There were many stories of gods, or sons of gods, who had at times appeared on the earth in disguise. He had very likely thrown off all faith in their divinity, as so many Romans had done; yet there may have lingered within some kind of faith that there were still beings higher than our humanity. What then if this Galilaean were one of these? What if he had before him a god in human disguise? What if this strange Man were a Son of God who had come down to earth from some vague and misty heaven?

Never had he met a man in the least like Him — so mysterious, so inscrutable, one so kinglike, one so godlike, even though He stood there clad in scarlet robe and wreathed with jagged thorns. Never in kingly dress, never with imperial crown, had he seen a sceptred sovereign stand so serene, so far above lesser men all around.[1] And this Man he had put to the frightful ordeal of the scourge!

The charge was so grave that he would not deal with it until he was alone with Christ: "He . . . saith unto Jesus, Whence art thou?" He was once more face to face with Jesus. In the earlier interview the Lord Jesus had told him that His kingdom was not of this world. But what Pilate would fain now ask was this: What of Thyself, rather than Thy kingdom? Who art Thou? Whence art Thou? Art Thou of this earth like other men, or art Thou other than what Thou seemest? Comest Thou indeed from heaven? Art Thou one of the gods come down to earth?

Pilate wanted to know about His origin, His history, His nature, His person; and he wanted to know now, in private, so that he could decide how to deal with the case. It looks as though he

---

[1] William Hanna, *Our Lord's Life on Earth* (1882), p. 508.

were clutching at the hope that some new fact might emerge, which would help him to take up a bold line with the Jews so as to save Him out of their hands.[2] One who had a kingdom not of this world — could He be of this world? And if not of this world, could He not tell Pilate something that would guide him?

Thus the Governor and the Prisoner stood face to face, that proud Roman, that strange Hebrew: "But Jesus gave him no answer." He had spoken freely enough before, but now He was silent. He had withdrawn into that same sublime silence which had more than once marked His trial. But of all the silent moments which had occurred that day, this is the most difficult for us now to understand.

It is easy to say that the reason for that silence was the state of Pilate's own soul; he had been told so much without effect that he deserved to hear no more! He had been told of the nature of His kingdom, the purpose of His coming, and the secret of truth. Yet he had thrown aside what he had learnt and had gone off with the careless saying, "What is truth?" He had confessed five times in all that he could find no fault in Him; yet with all this light and knowledge he had allowed Him to be scourged and mocked. But the truest explanation of that silence may have been that Jesus would not offer any comment as to whether He was the Son of God. For He did not wish to be set free as the Son of God, but as Man not guilty; and His silence was meant to call Pilate once more to his sense of duty.[3]

The next emphasis in this paragraph falls on the Person of Jesus. "Then saith Pilate unto him, Speakest thou not unto me? Knowest thou not that I have power to crucify thee, and have power to release thee?" No doubt Pilate would feel nonplussed at this silence and more than a little nettled. He knew how to deal with men who cringed and fawned for favors, but this Man baffled and stirred his pride.

Silence before others might have been intelligible, but Pilate was supreme; his word was the final voice, not of a party, but of the law of Rome.[4] He was annoyed by that air of apparent nonchalance, and it awoke the old haughty imperious temper

---

[2]J. C. Ryle, *Expository Thoughts on St. John's Gospel* (popular ed., 1897), vol. iii, p. 312.

[3]James Stalker, *The Trial and Death of Jesus Christ* (1894), p. 103.

[4]B. F. Westcott, *The Gospel According to St. John* (18th impr., 1937), p. 270.

which could so easily quench all deeper thought and feeling. Thus just at the time when he found himself inwardly "more afraid," the pride of an offended dignity flashed out in this question.

His words were a futile attempt to work on the selfish fears of the Lord Jesus. Did He not know that it was in his power to put Him to death or to set Him free? Alas for him! It would soon be seen how little power he had to do what he would! He spoke indeed as if he had arbitrary authority to do just what he liked. But no just judge would have made such a claim; justice itself would prevent it. Pilate's vision of what was just had been blurred since he had begun to yield to that wrongful pressure.

The Lord broke His silence with dignity and sympathy to put him in mind of this fact: "Jesus answered, Thou couldest have no power at all against me, except it were given thee from above." That power of his, to put to death or to release, was not what Pilate thought it was. It was neither original nor independent authority; it was derived from God, permitted by God. There was but one Absolute Origin for all authority; that was neither Pilate nor Caesar. They might hold great power in their hands, but it came as He had come from heaven.

Pilate was no more and no less than a human agent in the hand of Divine Omnipotence, for it was God who had brought the Roman eagles to the walls and precincts of the Holy City. Pilate's authority had been *given* him from above; it was delegated authority, for the powers that be were ordained of God. Even if he were the servant of an earthly kingdom, he ought to know that the kingdoms of this world were in some sense from above. Therefore his power ought not to be used at his own caprice, but in the cause of truth and right. Pilate held an office in which he was compelled to try the case, but it would be only by the determinate counsel of God that a verdict could be pronounced.

On the other hand, the Jewish leaders, unlike Pilate, were in the case by their own choice: "Therefore he that delivered me unto thee hath the greater sin." The Lord's latent idea was to make him see how ignorantly he was acting, and how little he knew what he was now about, compared with those others.[5]

[5] J. C. Ryle, *Expository Thoughts on St. John's Gospel* (popular ed., 1897), vol. iii, p. 315.

Caiaphas, who had delivered Him into Pilate's hands, knew that authority is from heaven alone. He knew quite well what he did, and whose death he sought. He had lodged an appeal with a heathen judge to carry out an unjust sentence on the King of Israel.

Pilate was not without excuse, but more ample knowledge made the chief priests and his fellow Jews more guilty by far. Theirs had been sin against the light, and so they were deeper in guilt. There is something remarkable in this statement. Even at this crisis He was the true Judge of mankind. Though He were the Accused, He was better able to judge rightly than the official magistrate himself. Despite His own sorrows, He could calmly weigh the comparative guilt of Pilate and the Jewish rulers.

He was ready to make every allowance for Pilate, and to excuse him as far as He could right to the end. Could the world wish to see a more complete triumph over resentment and irritation?[6]

This was the last word that Jesus spoke in His trial; henceforth, as a sheep in the hands of its shearers, so He was dumb. If His bearing had been sublime, no less sublime were the occasional statements which He had made. They had not been without effect upon Pilate; he could not get away from their tone of magnanimous authority. He sensed the true greatness of the Accused, and his training as a judge told him that He was guiltless. Thus he went back once more, resolved at all hazards to secure His release: "And from thenceforth, Pilate sought to release him."

He left the Lord in the palace, while he went out alone to tell the Jews that he would let Him go. How he sought to arrange matters, we do not know; but the Jews saw it in his face, and at once brought out their final accusation. "But the Jews cried out, saying, If thou let this man go, thou art not Caesar's friend: whosoever maketh himself a king speaketh against Caesar!" In that last, loud, angry outburst they dropped all their early, formal, considered objections and put themselves forward as the pretended guardians of the rights of Tiberius.[7]

---

[6]James Stalker, *The Trial and Death of Jesus Christ* (1894), p. 104.

[7]B. F. Westcott, *The Gospel According to St. John* (18th impr., 1937), p. 271.

Thus if Pilate were now to let Him go he would be no friend to Caesar! If he dared to follow his own line of action they would accuse him as against Caesar! This was desperately unscrupulous, but decisive. Pilate knew the cold, cruel, suspicious character of his master. He would rather connive at the murder of Christ than run the risk of an accusation before Tiberius. He would choose the path of safety and try to save himself, rather than the path of duty which might have saved the Son of Man. And yet had I stood in his place, with the same light, but no more, to guide me, am I sure that I would have done better or more bravely?

Chapter 24

AWAY WITH HIM

> When Pilate therefore heard that saying, he brought Jesus forth, and sat down in the judgment seat in a place that is called the Pavement, but in the Hebrew, Gabbatha. And it was the preparation of the passover, and about the sixth hour; and he saith unto the Jews, Behold, your King! But they cried out, Away with him! Away with him! Crucify him! Pilate saith unto them, Shall I crucify your King? The chief priests answered, We have no king but Caesar! Then delivered he him therefore unto them to be crucified. And they took Jesus, and led him away. — JOHN 19:13-16.

PILATE had been a prey to so many alarms on that day while Christ stood His trial. Twice he had been lost in mental turmoil when the Jews made some new statement, and twice the same phrase is used to denote the new crisis. "When Pilate therefore heard that saying" (19:8): the saying that He was the Son of God. "When Pilate therefore heard that saying" (19:13): the saying that He had spoken against Caesar. But it was the second saying which led to the final collapse of his authority: "If thou let this man go, thou art not Caesar's friend: whosoever maketh himself a king speaketh against Caesar" (19:12).

There was much more in this than the bare fact that his rule could not bear the light of an official inquiry. There was nothing which a provincial governor would dread more than such a complaint. Tiberius was a ruler who took a morose and savage delight in the disgrace of his subordinates. At the close of his reign he was harassed by a diseased body and a mental gloom akin to insanity. He grew still more taciturn and more suspicious with the fall of Sejanus in A.D. 31, and the repercussions of this fall would be grave enough for a man like Pilate since he had been Pilate's patron.

The one title which a provincial governor would most desire would be that of Amicus Caesaris, Friend of Caesar, and no charge would be so likely to bring vengeance upon Pilate as that which the Jews had threatened.

Pilate was now forced to arraign the Lord Jesus at the bar of judgment. "When Pilate therefore heard that saying, he brought Jesus forth." Pilate had left Jesus within the hall while he went out to face the Jews. He was convinced that Jesus was guiltless, and he was still anxious to secure His release. But just when he meant to take a humane and righteous step, his foot was stayed. The Jews threw up a threat which the dead weight of past sins would make all too real. He could never explain to a man like Tiberius that this Jesus was not a king in the sense that the Jews alleged.

A pagan emperor would never understand such an explanation. He would have no excuse and no defense, and he was not equal to so great a challenge. He should have stood his ground and risked his own career; but he would not. That obscure and friendless Galilaean, however innocent, however impressive, was not worth it. Pilate was a man of the world whose fashion and favor were his rule and reward. Therefore he turned on his heel, went inside once more, and then brought Him out for judgment.[1]

Pilate now took his seat on the throne of judgment in the courtyard: "He . . . sat down in the judgment seat in a place that is called the Pavement, but in the Hebrew, Gabbatha." This was the fifth time that Pilate had gone outside to meet the Jews. But he could hold out no longer, and he assumed his seat for the formal act of judgment. It was customary for the procurator to have his chair placed out in the open for this purpose. So it was that Festus took the chair of judgment to hear the case against Paul at Caesarea (Acts 25:6). This tribunal or judgment-seat would be set up in a conspicuous situation, in a courtyard which would be known in Greek as the Lithostrotos, or in Aramaic as Gabbatha. It was a kind of floor, paved with marble or mosaic, on which the chair was placed.

Julius Caesar had a portable mosaic floor which could be carried about for this purpose. But since the courts of the temple were paved (II Chronicles 7:3) there may have been a paved platform at the head of the steps leading from the temple to the

---

[1] James Stalker, *The Trial and Death of Jesus Christ* (1894), pp. 106-107.

castle (Acts 21:40). This was no doubt the place where the throne of judgment would be set up.[2] Pilate therefore would sit in the very shadow of the temple itself to give judgment against the One who was King of the Jews.

The trial now moved to a close with swift and terrible suddenness: "And it was the preparation of the passover, and about the sixth hour: and he saith unto the Jews, Behold, your king!" It was now six o'clock in the morning; the next day would be the paschal Sabbath; hence the anxiety of the Jewish leaders. This marks the day and the hour in a way that for ever fixes attention on this as the central crisis of all human history.

Pilate's heart was sore and savage. He was about to do something which he knew that he could never defend, and he would feel glad to humiliate the Jews if he could see how to do it. That was no doubt why he pointed to Him from the throne of judgment and said: "Behold, your king!" It was only a short time since he had brought Him out and made an appeal to their sense of pity in almost identical words: "Behold, the man!" But the mob had refused that first appeal to their humanity, and he spoke now in a kind of scornful anger, with irony and bitterness. Behold! This meek, mishandled Prisoner, this Man, mocked and bleeding, whom you accuse as a rival king to Caesar. You wish your king to die! Look at Him now, and say![3]

Pilate was now forced to condemn the Lord Jesus to the fate of crucifixion: "But they cried out, Away with him! Away with him! Crucify him!" Pilate had scored a mild revenge; his thrust had sunk right home and made them smart with pain. They cried out at once in reply, and the pronoun *they* is meant to isolate them as those who were His enemies. They were marked off from Him with an emphatic precision as they disclaimed Him as their king. It was as though one loud universal cry burst from the throat of the mob, "Away, away with him!"[4]

The French Revolution and the Reign of Terror brought to

---

[2]B. F. Westcott, *The Gospel According to St. John* (18th impr., 1937), p. 272.

[3]J. C. Ryle, *Expository Thoughts on St. John's Gospel* (popular ed., 1897), vol. iii, p. 322.

[4]B. F. Westcott, *The Gospel According to St. John* (18th impr., 1937), p. 272.

ight the savage spirit which may infect a city mob even in
modern times. It was just so that the Jews raised this fierce,
relentless, obstinate shout once again. It was the last, decisive
rejection of Him whom God had sealed as Lord and Christ.
They would despise Him for apparent helplessness when He
had raised their hopes so high, and they would now reject Him
as another Messiah who was false to the name. And that
ultimate rejection was so complete that they shrieked for His
death.

But the procurator had not done yet; once more he would
drive home that bitter taunt. "Pilate saith unto them, Shall I
crucify your King?" The real barb in this last question was the
accent on its last words: "Your king!" Must I, Roman that I
am, crucify your king? Is that your wish? It was this thought of
His kingship which had run through the whole trial for Pilate.

Pilate could not rid his mind of the original accusation that
He was a rival to the Caesars. If he were to let Him go, the
Jews would accuse him of the crime of high treason. They
would turn the tables with the keenest malice, and he would be
exposed to the very charge for which this Jesus was now on
trial! And yet he was more than ever convinced that He was
not a king in the sense of this world, and he flung the Jewish
accusation back in their face with a feeling of helpless scorn.

He would adhere to this point to the end: "Jesus of Nazareth,
the King of the Jews" (John 19:19). He nailed that name above
His head when He had been placed on the cross, and he would
not have it removed. The Jews could not bear it and begged
him to have it altered. But his only answer was the sardonic
refusal: "What I have written, I have written!" (John 19:22).

There is singular interest in the precise definition of those who
joined in the final outburst: "The chief priests answered, We
have no king but Caesar." Those words reflect indelible disgrace
on those who were the chief agents of the theocracy. They
serve to stamp the Jews as a fallen, perjured, God-forsaken, God-
forsaking people. Pilate knew well what it would cost their pride
thus to forswear the faith of their fathers. To have made them
swallow that draught was some compensation for the cup which
they had forced him to drink.[5] It was Israel to whom pertained
the adoption, and the glory, and the covenants; but the chief

---

James Stalker, *The Trial and Death of Jesus Christ* (1894), p. 109.

priests had now renounced their own birthright and forsaken their destiny.

It was shameful enough to see Pilate trampling on his conscience so as not to run the risk of recall, disgrace, exile, and perhaps death. It was infinitely worse to find the sons of Aaron standing for the rights of Caesar, as though they had no king but him! The word "Ichabod" could not have been better framed than for this hour of history, for the glory had fled from Mount Zion.

Pilate at last gave Him up to their will and let them have their way: "Then delivered he him therefore unto them to be crucified. And they took Jesus, and led him away." But was it not the judge who was in fact on trial throughout this long drama? And do not the gospel memoirs leave wide latitude and large allowance for his many hesitations? There was neither contempt of justice nor yet absence of feeling in his treatment of the case as a whole. It was marked by certain notes of subdued pity, respect, courtesy, gentleness, that excite our wonder.

No king and no ruler with whom the Lord Jesus or His servants ever had to do was half so considerate. Not Herod, nor Felix, nor Gallio, nor Agrippa: Pilate was far above them all. He had struggled hard to evade the Jews and to find a way of escape for Christ and for himself, and we feel that there was something in his compunctions, his relentings, his vacillation, his embarrassment, that was very human.[6]

The Lord Jesus Himself declared that "he that delivered me unto thee hath the greater sin" (John 19:11). Peter was to accuse the Jews plainly: "Ye denied him in the presence of Pilate, when he was determined to let him go" (Acts 3:13). Yet in the end Pilate took sides with Herod and the people against the Lord's Anointed (Acts 4:27). Pilate never recalled his first verdict of not guilty, yet "he delivered Jesus to their will' (Luke 23:25).

The great irony of his compromise was that very soon he met his own fate, and it was the very fate which he had striven to stave off by that base condemnation. The Jews lodged a complaint against him soon after the death of Christ, and the jealous Tiberius brought him back to end his days in disgrace and to die at last by his own hand in despair.

---

[6]William Hanna, *Our Lord's Life on Earth* (1882), p. 510.

"In both trials, the judges were unjust, and the trial was unfair; yet in both, the right issue was substantially raised. Even the form which that issue took was in a sense the same in both. Jesus Christ was arraigned on a double charge of treason: the treason in the Theocratic court being a (constructive) speaking against God, while in the Imperial court it was a (constructive) speaking against Caesar. But under these tortuous traditions of a twofold law, the real historical question was twice-over reached, and the true claim of the accused was made truly known. He died because in the ecclesiastical council He claimed to be the Son of God and the Messiah of Israel, and because before the world-wide tribunal He claimed to be Christ a King."
—A. Taylor Innes,. *The Trial of Jesus Christ*, (1899), p. 123.

PART THREE

THE PRINCE

OF

LIFE

"In Passion Week, as I was reading Bishop Wilson on the Lord's Supper, I met with an expression to this effect: 'That the Jews knew what they did when they transferred their sin to the head of their offering.' The thought came into my mind, 'What, may I transfer all my guilt to another? Has God provided an Offering for me that I may lay my sins on His head? Then, God willing, I will not bear them on my own soul one moment longer.' Accordingly I sought to lay my sins upon the sacred head of Jesus; and on the Wednesday began to have a hope of mercy; on the Thursday that hope increased; on the Friday and Saturday it became more strong; and on the Sunday morning, Easter Day, April 4th, I awoke early with those words upon my heart and lips, 'Jesus Christ is risen today! Hallelujah! Hallelujah!' From that hour peace flowed in rich abundance into my soul; and at the Lord's Table in our chapel I had the sweetest access to God through my blessed Saviour."

CHARLES SIMEON

Chapter 25

THE RIVEN SIDE

The Jews therefore, because it was the preparation, that the bodies should not remain upon the cross on the sabbath day, (for that sabbath day was an high day,) besought Pilate that their legs might be broken, and that they might be taken away. Then came the soldiers, and brake the legs of the first, and of the other which was crucified with him. But when they came to Jesus, and saw that he was dead already, they brake not his legs: But one of the soldiers with a spear pierced his side, and forthwith came there out blood and water. And he that saw it bare record, and his record is true: and he knoweth that he saith true, that ye might believe. For these things were done that the scripture should be fulfilled, A bone of him shall not be broken. And again another scripture saith, They shall look on him whom they pierced.
— JOHN 19:31-37.

IT WAS mid-afternoon when the Lord Jesus bowed His head in the silence of death, and three hours at most would bring the day to an end with sunset and nightfall. This made the Jews bethink themselves of an ancient law which forbade them to leave a body on gallows or gibbet once the sun had gone down: "His body shall not remain all night upon the tree, but thou shalt in any wise bury him that day . . . that thy land be not defiled, which the Lord thy God giveth thee for an inheritance" (Deuteronomy 21:22, 23).

It is doubtful whether the Jews could often carry out this law under Roman rule, for it was Roman custom to let the corpse hang on the cross until birds of prey had torn it to pieces or wind and rain had rotted it away. But there was a special motive which would induce them to make the strictest efforts to keep the law on this notable occasion, for the setting sun would usher in the Sabbath, and that Sabbath was "an high day." The crucifixion had taken place on the eve of the Paschal Sabbath,

153

and they wanted to avoid the desecration of such a day which would occur if three bodies were left to hang in full view from the Temple gates or city walls. But if they were to break through the Roman custom they must get leave from their Roman masters. This was the need which drove them to make their suit to Pilate.

"The Jews therefore, because it was the preparation, that the bodies should not remain upon the cross on the sabbath day, (for that sabbath day was an high day,) besought Pilate that their legs might be broken, and that they might be taken away." This was a blunt request for the terrible punishment known as the crurifragium, something almost as brutal and barbarous as crucifixion itself. It meant that the victim was clubbed to death, for clubs were used to smash the bones of his body. In the case of one who had been nailed to the cross it would be quite enough to break his legs; other bones might be left intact, for no one on the cross could have survived such a cumulative assault of pain and shock. Thus the Jewish rulers thought to accelerate His death by an act of revolting cruelty. They were ready to lay this fresh indignity on the Son of Man in order to save that high day from desecration. It was one more appalling example of the self-deception which can sometimes fool the human conscience. Men who were fresh from the murder of God's own Son, without remorse for such a crime, were yet full of solicitude lest the Sabbath should be defiled. But God, who can turn man's wrath to His praise, overruled it all in the interest of that great love wherewith He loves us still.

The first three verses in this paragraph tell us what John saw: "Then came the soldiers, and brake the legs of the first, and of the other which was crucified with him." These words make it clear that Pilate had given his consent to the callous request of the Jewish leaders: they were to have their wish. Thus orders were issued to the centurion in charge of the guard at the cross, and his four rough henchmen would take the gruesome work in hand. We are not told why the thieves who hung on each side of Christ should have been the first to suffer, but the cross in the midst was the last which the four legionaries thought to approach. Perhaps two of them were sent from each end to deal with the two thieves, and the four would then meet in front of the cross in the midst. Nor are we told how the legs were to be broken; but the common practice was to make use of a heavy mallet. Limbs would be cold and nerveless after six long hours of horror, and a simple fracture would be enough to speed the swift approach of death. But the object in view makes it likely that the men would carry out their task in rough and ruthless fashion.

The root meaning of the Greek word in this passage conveys the idea of something shivered into pieces, and it may be feared that this was in fact what did take place. They smashed the legs of the two thieves and left them to their fate. It was little more than the last act of brutal indignity in the case of one of the two; for the other, it would be like knocking off the fetters to let him soar aloft in freedom of spirit to keep his tryst with the Son of Man in glory. He was not spared when the soldiers stood before him, but they were no more than heedless agents who were employed to fulfill the promise: "Verily, I say unto thee, To day shalt thou be with me in paradise" (Luke 23:42).

"But when they came to Jesus, and saw that he was dead already, they brake not his legs." A few rough rude blows had shattered the limbs of the two thieves, and the soldiers had then moved on to stand before the cross of Christ. But when they saw Him they forbore. One curt look would show them that they could do nothing to speed the work of death — He was already dead. Soldiers they were, hardened by trade, pagans roughened by greed, and they had thought little enough of His execution. They had nailed His limbs to the cross when He came forth to die, and had pinned the placard above His head to mock Him as a king. They had sat down to take their ease and to look on with cool cold stare while He poured out His soul in death. They had shared His raiment beneath His eyes and had gambled for His seamless vesture. They had heard the jibes which were coined at His expense and had caught up the taunts which fell from the lips of others. But now there was a change. Now they had seen how the events on the cross through those six long hours had made known the drama of a love that was stronger than death. A change had been wrought in their minds which they knew not how to explain, but it was a change so real and profound that they could not act in wanton haste or unconcern. They could not break His legs when they saw His pallid face and drooping figure. His limbs were spared because they knew that death had been before them, and their thoughts were summed up in the words of the centurion himself: "Truly this man was the Son of God" (Mark 15:39; cf. Matthew 27:54).

"But one of the soldiers with a spear pierced his side, and forthwith came there out blood and water." This was the last clear sign that life had fled, that He had sunk into the cold embrace of death. Wounds of every kind and death in every form were common enough in the experience of the Roman soldiers. They were trained to take life away, and of all men they were the least likely to make a mistake in such a matter. And yet, as if to make things sure once and for all, one of the four poised his spear and plunged it into His side. This was perhaps the means by which he used to prove if the bodies of the fallen on the field of battle were dead or yet alive.

The Greek word which describes the wound is used both of a light touch and of a deep gash, but the weapon and the object in view leave no doubt in this case.[1] It would be a strong shrewd thrust, in itself enough to kill, and it would cause a broad deep wound which would leave no mean scar behind. What that gash was like we may glean from the fact that Thomas was asked to thrust his hand rather than his finger into the hole which it had made (John 20:27). No doubt the spear was aimed upward toward the heart, for this would best assure the fact of death. Then, as it was withdrawn, the wound released a large stream of blood and water. This meant that there was a flow of solid blood clots in a stream of liquid serum, but John spoke of it just as it would appear to an unskilled layman.

The spear had been guided by the unseen hand of God in heaven, and that flow of blood and water was the final proof that His heart had been pierced beyond repair. The Lord Jesus was dead; and it was the real death of a real man. No one who trusts the voice of the disciple whom Jesus loved can ever doubt it. He who had been born of Mary was now in the place of death for mankind, and the blood and water which flowed from that open wound had unsealed the long-promised fountain "for sin and uncleanness" (Zechariah 13:1).

The next three verses in this paragraph tell us what John thought: "And he that saw it bare record, and his record is true: and he knoweth that he saith true, that ye might believe."

---

[1] B. F. Westcott, *The Gospel According to St. John* (1908), p. 279.

Plummer notes that the use of the perfect participle rather than the aorist is an added indication that the person who saw and bare record was the author himself.[2] He would have his readers to know that what he had written was neither more nor less than bare and naked truth. He wrote of things which he had seen with his own eyes, and he would have us to rely on his witness when we read what he wrote. The Greek text is quite free from the tautology which the Authorized Version seems to contain. John makes a double statement: his evidence was adequate, and the contents of the statement were true.[3]

It is clear that he saw more than would have met the outward eye in that scene. He first took time to describe what he saw, and then took pains to comment on it all; and his comment is fraught with an impressive emphasis as well as a tremendous conviction. It seems to pass right out of the general sphere of history into the more personal realm of reverie, and it makes us feel that we should pause and linger on ground where he paused and lingered while he framed this deliberate testimony. It is clear that what he had seen was stamped on his mind as something of strange and deep significance, though he might not fully perceive all that it meant. But the fact that caught and held his mind with surpassing interest was the fact that this scene on the cross rang so true to the prophetic utterance of the seers of Israel. The four soldiers had gone about their work in the spirit of rude indifference; but John, who saw what they did and who knew what had been foretold, could trace in that scene the divine finger, pointing out the Son of Man as the One whom God had sent.[4]

"For these things were done, that the scripture should be fulfilled, A bone of him shall not be broken." Was it pure chance that the soldiers had refrained from breaking the legs of the crucified Nazarene? John recalled how the psalmist had said: "He keepeth all his bones: not one of them is broken" (Psalm 34:20). But he also looked back to the ancient charge with regard to the Paschal lamb: it was to die in a way that would shed its blood, yet not a bone of its body might be

---

[2]Alfred Plummer, *St. John* (Cambridge Greek Testament for Schools, 1882), p. 334.

[3]*Ibid.*

[4]James Stalker, *The Trial and Death of Jesus Christ* (1894), p. 289.

broken (Exodus 12:46). It was this great Passover offering year by year which had done more than all else to keep the history of redemption alive and green in the mind of Israel. It spoke of the blood of the lamb which had once been shed to save them from the angel of death; it spoke as well of the blood of a lamb yet to be shed that would save them from the burden of guilt.

John had now grasped the fact that in this scene on the cross it was the Lamb of God who had thus been slain. The plan to break his legs would have made it impossible to think of Him as the Passover sacrifice. But when John saw how His limbs were spared and yet His blood was shed, it was as though a flash of light had caused the truth to gleam and shine within his soul. He called to mind the words of that other John beside the Jordan and he saw the Man of the cross as the Lamb of God slain for the sin of the world (John 1:29, 36). The Lord Jesus had been preserved in the terms of Hebrew type and prophet, and the words of David were true of Him in His latest moment: "I may tell all my bones: they look and stare upon me" (Psalm 22:17).

"And again another scripture saith, They shall look on him whom they pierced." Was it sheer chance that the soldier should lift up his spear and drive it through the body of the crucified Nazarene? John recalled words of the psalmist: "The assembly of the wicked have inclosed me: they pierced my hands and my feet" (Psalm 22:16). But he also looked back to the solemn phrase with regard to the wounded Man: "And they shall look upon me whom they have pierced, and they shall mourn for him, as one mourneth for his only son" (Zechariah 12:10). John's primary reference would be to this prophetic utterance in which He had spoken as one who was pierced with pain and sorrow, while He spoke of Israel as those who would look on the work of their hands with shame and horror.

John had now grasped the fact that in this scene on the cross it was the Son of God who had thus been pierced. His hands and feet had been nailed with brutal force to the tree, and the spear had been thrust with deadly strength through His side. It would seem that John thought of this as the act of the Jewish people rather than the Roman soldiers, and Luke told how that very day sorrow and mourning filled the hearts of many in Israel: "And all the people that came together to that sight, beholding the things which were done, smote their breasts, and returned" (Luke 23:48). But it was an act in which the Jewish people and the Roman soldiers would together represent all mankind, for it was the sin of the world which drove the nails through those gentle hands and which forced the spear through that naked body.

We must all look on Him as One whom we have pierced, and we must own that our hand was in that dark deed. The Lord Jesus had been transfixed in the terms of Hebrew type and prophet, and the Seer of Patmos could say of Him in His coming glory: "Every eye shall see him, and they also which pierced him: and all kindreds of the earth shall wail because of him" (Revelation 1:7).

So John bore witness to what he had seen, and he bore it that we might believe. He had seen the Prince of Life in the sleep of death, and he would have it known that such a death was real. He had seen how His limbs were spared from the fate that befell the thieves, and he would have it known that He died as the Lamb of God. He had seen how the spear was thrust home to His heart, and he would have us look on Him as the One who was pierced. He had seen how blood and water had poured from that wound in His side, and he would have us come to Him as the fount where sins are washed away.

But there was more in that scene than he could absorb; the element of mystery clings to it still. He had passed through a world of awe and woe from the first beads of sweat in the Garden to the cry of utter desolation in the darkness. Speechless sorrow had placed a strain on the walls of His heart which was almost too great to bear. Some have thought that they were rent and torn in hopeless rupture. The blood was then discharged into the sac in which His heart was sheathed. Crimson blood clots would then congeal in a pool of liquid serum so that blood and water would be released when the spear pierced His side. This would proclaim the fact that His heart had been tried and taxed beyond its power to bear, and when it broke He died.

That stream of blood and water from His broken heart and riven side may be seen as an omen of life and peace for all who will look in faith to Him who was pierced. It is the sign that He can cleanse the guilt of all who will wash and be clean. It was Moody who once pictured the scene as though it were the Lord who was saying: "Search for the man that drove the spear into My side, and tell him there is a nearer way to My heart than that." And as Henry Drummond remarked: "Prepared or impromptu, what could surpass that touch? Tell him there is a nearer way to My heart than that!"[5]

---

[5]W. R. Moody, *The Life of D. L. Moody*, p. 378.

Chapter 26

THE BURIED LORD

And after this Joseph of Arimathaea, being a disciple of Jesus, but secretly for fear of the Jews, besought Pilate that he might take away the body of Jesus: and Pilate gave him leave. He came therefore, and took the body of Jesus. And there came also Nicodemus, which at the first came to Jesus by night, and brought a mixture of myrrh and aloes, about an hundred pound weight. Then took they the body of Jesus, and wound it in linen clothes with the spices, as the manner of the Jews is to bury. Now in the place where he was crucified there was a garden; and in the garden a new sepulchre, wherein was never man yet laid. There laid they Jesus therefore because of the Jews' preparation day; for the sepulchre was nigh at hand. — JOHN 19:38-42.

THE SUN was far down in the west before steps were taken to remove the bodies from the gallows on Calvary. This is clear from Mark's brief note: "And now when the even was come" (Mark 15:42). An hour before nightfall would be relatively late when sunset would bring in the Paschal Sabbath. The thieves would no doubt be taken down by the four soldiers and their bodies would be cast into some mean ditch in final obscurity and disgrace (cf. Jeremiah 26:23). This would also have been the fate in store for the Son of Man but for the overruling purpose of God. He had been put to death side by side with evildoers, but He was to be laid at rest by the hands of loving servants.

All four gospels tell the story of His reverent burial by Joseph of Arimathaea, and each gospel adds some detail to our knowledge of the manner of man he was. But John stands alone in his account of the role of Nicodemus, and his record is an essential supplement to the burial narrative of the first three gospels. These men were both members of the Jewish Council which was responsible for His trial and condemnation (Luke

23:51; John 3:1), but it does not follow that they had been summoned to that special meeting which had pronounced His doom (Luke 22:66-71; Matthew 26:63-68). The summons was ignored if it ever reached them, for we cannot believe that they were in the hall when that shout for His death went up (Luke 23:50, 51; John 7:51). Joseph was a secret disciple (John 19:38), while Nicodemus was known for his sympathy with the Nazarene (John 7:52). There was no room for them in a conclave which was intent on the murder of One who stood in their midst as the Christ. But they may have joined the crowd which saw Him die, for it was His death which put their fears to flight.

The malice and hatred of the Jews had gone too far; the silence and patience of His friends could bear no more. Are we to think that they were not aware of each other's feelings? Was it by chance that they were brought into contact beneath the cross? Their design was carried out so promptly that each must have known the other's intent. They were impelled by the common ties of love to act in concert for the honor of the sacred body of the crucified Redeemer.

John directs our attention first to Joseph of Arimathaea: "And after this Joseph of Arimathaea, being a disciple of Jesus, but secretly for fear of the Jews." There is singular interest in the fact that Joseph is not mentioned in the gospels at all apart from the burial narrative, yet some new trait of character or circumstance is brought to light in each record of this event. He was a native of Arimathaea, a village which nestled somewhere in the fruitful hill country of Judah (Luke 23:51); he was also "a rich man," who owned an estate in the environs of Jerusalem (Matthew 27:57). Wealth and social standing would no doubt assist him in his approach to the Roman Procurator and would attract notice in his tribute to the crucified Nazarene.

Then we are told that he was "an honorable counsellor which also waited for the kingdom of God" (Mark 15:43; cf. Luke 23:51). This was a phrase which had found its place in the New Testament as a recognized term to describe men like Simeon and Nathanael: it summed up the devout spirit which ruled their life with a wholesome simplicity (see Luke 2:25; John 1:47). It was among such as these that John the Baptist and the Son of Man had enrolled their most willing auditors and most eager disciples, although many of them remained in doubt as to whether the Son of Man was He that should come or whether they should look for another. Joseph himself was "a good man and a just," who had no part in "the counsel and deed" of those who had put Him to death (Luke 23:50, 51). He was, in fact, a true disciple, "but secretly for fear of the Jews" (John 19:38; Matthew 27:57). He had waited long in sober patience for the Kingdom; the time had now come to declare himself for Christ the King.

"And after this Joseph of Arimathaea . . . besought Pilate that he might take away the body of Jesus." Plummer notes that the Greek particle marks a contrast between the hostile attitude of the Jews (see John 19:31) and the devout petition by Joseph.[1] The phrase as a whole should be read in the plural number: "And after these things." This shows that it does not refer to one special event on the day of the cross but to the whole result of the crucifixion. The words do not mean that Joseph's action was a direct sequel to the action of the soldiers which had just been described; the sequence was indefinite.[2] Joseph may have been stirred to act as soon as he knew that Jesus was dead; there was little enough time to do all that he planned to do. He knew that the Jews meant to have the three bodies removed before nightfall, and he could not bear to think that rude and careless hands should consign the Son of Man to a grave like the Valley of Hinnom.

Therefore he would do as the Jews had done; he would ask for Pilate's consent to "take away the body of Jesus" (John 19:38), just as they had asked for consent to have the three bodies "taken away" (John 19:31). He would honor the Son of Man when they would have done Him despite; and this he would do while it was full of hazard to be known as His friend. But there was a decision and a promptitude in his movements which had not been displayed before. He who had treasured his faith in secret "for fear of the Jews" now "went in boldly unto Pilate, and craved the body of Jesus" (Mark 15:43). He

---

[1] Alfred Plummer, St. John (Cambridge Greek Testament for Schools, 1882), p. 335.

[2] B. F. Westcott, The Gospel According to St. John (1908), p. 81 (note on 5:1).

dared to act with a courage that was foreign to his native
spirit, and it won him a rich reward.

"And Pilate gave him leave. He came therefore and took the
body of Jesus." It was common enough for an avaricious ruler
to sell the privilege of burial in the case of a state execution;
but the name of Pilate is free from that disgrace.[3] He was indeed surprised to hear that Christ was dead, but he was not
loath to grant the request. He sent for the centurion to ask
how long it was since His death had occurred; "and when he
knew it of the centurion, he gave the body to Joseph"
(Mark 15:45).

Mark employs a fresh word for "body," and this new word
was the word for a corpse (Mark 15:43). It would convey the
idea of contempt when it was used of a human body, and it
never occurs elsewhere as a term to describe the body of Jesus.
But the language in this verse has the ring of an official utterance, and that was how Pilate would regard the body.[4]

Joseph could thus act with authority and do for the body of
Jesus what others had done in the case of John the Baptist
(Matthew 14:12; cf. Acts 8:2). He would return at once, for
there would be no time to lose. Evening was near (Matthew
27:57), and "the Sabbath drew on" (Luke 23:54). He would
come to the cross where that body was still outstretched in
death; "and he took it down" while the thieves, though dead,
were yet on their gallows (Luke 23:53). It was all in accord
with the Scripture, which had foretold that the dignity of His
burial would be in sharp contrast with the shame of His death:
"And he made his grave with the wicked, and with the rich
in his death: because He had done no violence, neither was any
deceit in his mouth" (Isaiah 53:9). The poor estate of the
Joseph whose task was to cradle the body of Jesus at the
manger of Bethlehem was now more than matched by the rich
estate of the Joseph whose task was to bury the body of Jesus
in the garden near Calvary.

John's next words direct our attention to Nicodemus: "And
there came also Nicodemus, which at the first came to Jesus by

[3] B. F. Westcott, *The Gospel According to St. John* (1908), p. 281.
[4] H. B. Swete, *St. Mark* (3rd ed., 1913), p. 392.

night." There is evident interest in the fact that Nicodemus is not once named in the first three gospels, yet John makes mention of him on three separate occasions. He had risked his reputation as a ruler of the Jews when he had sought a personal interview with the Lord on His first visit to Jerusalem. He had come to Jesus by night as one who was afraid lest his approach should be observed (John 3:2). But he had come in the spirit of an earnest seeker, and he was the only ruler in Jerusalem who ever came thus at all. And the Lord, who was not wont to commit Himself to men, gave him a clear picture of the work which He had come to do and the death which He had come to die.

"Christ must have seen good soil in that man's heart to have scattered there so much of the good seed.[5] That seed took long to germinate and fructify, but it bore fruit at last. His heart had gone out to the Son of Man that night, although he did not take his stand as a committed disciple. But once at least he dared reproach from the chief priests and Pharisees when they began to speak with scorn of those who had failed to carry out an arrest. "Are ye also deceived?" they had exclaimed. "Have any of the rulers or of the Pharisees believed on him?" (John 7:47, 48). Nicodemus could not repress his first shy and reasonable protest: "Doth our law judge any man before it hear him, and know what he doeth?" (John 7:51). He was snubbed and silenced with their contemptuous reply: "Art thou also of Galilee? Search, and look: for out of Galilee ariseth no prophet" (John 7:52). But he who "at the first came to Jesus by night" was now ready to act in broad daylight, and John's phrase points the contrast between that first cautious approach and this open act of reverence on the hill of Calvary.

"And . . . Nicodemus . . . brought a mixture of myrrh and aloes, about an hundred pound weight." Nicodemus would have had time to bring out this gift of spices while Joseph was engaged in his suit to Pilate. He was a true partner in devotion and sacrifice, for the myrrh and aloes were a costly tribute to the crucified Nazarene. They may have been either in the form of a compact roll or in the form of dry aromatic powder, and they would be crumbled or sprinkled between the folds of the linen which was used for a shroud. Nicodemus no doubt meant

---

[5]William Hanna, *Our Lord's Life on Earth* (1882), p. 574.

to cover the whole body with this aromatic mixture (see II Chronicles 16:14), and this accounts for the fact that it weighed some twelve hundred Roman ounces. This may seem an enormous quantity to us, but a body which had been so torn and lacerated would need a large amount. It would act as a strong antiseptic in that sultry climate, and a lavish supply would be the more valuable since there was not enough time to embalm the whole body.

Myrrh and aloes in that linen shroud might remind Nicodemus of the picture of the Messianic King in other circumstances. "All thy garments smell of myrrh, and aloes, and cassia, out of the ivory palaces, whereby they have made thee glad" (Psalm 45:8). It was the gift of a rich man, prompted by the love and sorrow of true discipleship. It meant that the despised Nazarene was thus treated with the kind of honor that the proudest Pharisee might have desired. He who had not where to lay His head while He dwelt in their midst would now be laid to rest with all the fragrance that would accrue from that gift of myrrh and aloes.

"Then took they the body of Jesus, and wound it in linen clothes with the spices, as the manner of the Jews is to bury." No pains have been spared to etch this scene with all the skill that art can afford, but the gospel records are bare and brief. Joseph and Nicodemus appear to have taken down the sacred body with their own hands, and their gentle treatment would be in contrast with the careless handling which the bodies of the thieves would sustain. To touch a dead body would make a Jew unclean, and this was the eve of the Paschal Sabbath, when no Jew would care to be defiled (cf. John 18:28). But they thought not of that as they prized out the nails and laid the now lifeless limbs on the ground.

The crowds had now melted away, and there were few who still remained to watch as these rites were performed. Mary Magdalene and Mary the mother of Joses were there (Matthew 27:61; Mark 15:47; Luke 23:55); and, though his name is not mentioned, we may safely conclude that John was there (John 19:35). But they would be strangers to Joseph and Nicodemus, and they do not appear to have joined them in the arrangements for the burial. Perhaps they stood at a little distance and watched them at work with growing wonder.

The long roll of clean white linen brought by Joseph as a

shroud lay nearby (Mark 15:46), and the myrrh and aloes brought by Nicodemus were close at hand. There may have been no time to wash His limbs from the stains of the cross (cf. Acts 9:37); they would simply wrap the body in the long fine folds of linen (cf. John 11:44). The rich spices were strewn between the folds, and a linen turban was wound about the thorn-scarred brow. It was all in accord with the Scripture, which had foretold that the body in which He would come to death would yet be preserved from death's decay: "For thou wilt not leave my soul in hell; neither wilt thou suffer thine Holy One to see corruption" (Psalm 16:10). The myrrh and frankincense which wise men from the east had once brought in honor of His birth at Bethlehem were now more than matched by the myrrh and aloes which this son of Israel had been moved to bring in sorrow for His death on Calvary.

The Lord Jesus was dead; they could not be deceived. But His body had been prepared for its burial with all the reverence of their race for the dead. The one duty which still remained was to bear that sacred burden to its last place of rest: but where would they lay Him? In a garden nearby there was a new tomb in which no one had ever reposed; and that new tomb belonged to Joseph (Matthew 27:60). John alone refers to the garden as he alone records the fact that there was a garden in the place called Gethsemane (John 18:1), and he combines the statements in Matthew and Luke about the tomb with marked effect. That tomb had been hewn out of the cliff by Joseph as a vault in which his body might be laid as in the very shadow of the City of God. But he was now ready to use it as a tomb for Him who was to have redeemed Israel, and John rounds off the burial narrative accordingly: "Now in the place where he was crucified there was a garden; and in the garden a new sepulchre, wherein was never man yet laid. There laid they Jesus therefore because of the Jews' preparation day; for the sepulchre was nigh at hand."

Thus Joseph and Nicodemus bore His wounded body to that new tomb, and in silent sorrow placed it in its linen shroud on the cold rock bed. He who had once ridden on a colt whereon no other man had ever sat (Luke 19:30) was now buried in a tomb wherein no other man was ever laid (Luke 23:53). It was fitting that He should rest in that undefiled sepulchre, for

His body was thus preserved from contact with decay even when it had been placed in the tomb. We should retain the same order which the Greek text observes as it builds up the deep sense of pathos in the last phrase: "There therefore, on account of the preparation of the Jews, for the tomb was nigh at hand, laid they Jesus."[6]

Joseph and Nicodemus then withdrew; they rolled a stone to the mouth of the grave, and went their way (Matthew 27:60; Mark 15:46). They had waited long to confess their faith, but now they had dared to avow the Lord just when to do so would be to share His reproach. They had come with more faith and love than the recognized disciples seemed to possess, and they had carried out the last service which His human body would receive or require at the hands of others. Shall we not hold them in honor for this? "Yes, verily, wherever this Gospel of the Kingdom shall be made known, what they thus did shall be told for a memorial of them."[7]

---

[6]Alfred Plummer, *St. John* (Cambridge Greek Testament for Schools, 1882), p. 336.

[7]William Hanna, *Our Lord's Life on Earth* (1882), pp. 577, 578.

Chapter 27

THE TEMPLE GUARD

Now the next day, that followed the day of the preparation, the chief priests and Pharisees came together unto Pilate, saying, Sir, we remember that that deceiver said, while he was yet alive, After three days I will rise again. Command therefore that the sepulchre be made sure until the third day, lest his disciples come by night, and steal him away, and say unto the people, He is risen from the dead: so the last error shall be worse than the first. Pilate said unto them, Ye have a watch: go your way, make it as sure as ye can. So they went, and made the sepuchre sure, sealing the stone, and setting a watch. — MATTHEW 27:62-66.

THE SUN must have been low in the sky when Joseph and Nicodemus turned away from the great stone which they had rolled to the door of the tomb. But there were two who still lingered in the garden as the shadows began to fall: "And Mary Magdalene and Mary the mother of Joses beheld where He was laid " (Mark 15:47). They were the last of that loving band of women who had followed Him to the end (Matthew 27:56; Mark 15:40; Luke 23:49). Four of them are mentioned by name: Mary His mother and Mary's sister, Salome, the mother of Zebedee's children; Mary Magdalene and the other Mary, the wife of Cleophas, the mother of James and Joses (John 19:25; Matthew 27:56; Mark 15:40).

We can account for the absence of His mother from the garden at the close of that day; but where was Salome? Mark tells us that she was one of those who went out to the tomb on the Resurrection morning (Mark 16:1); yet she was not with them when they followed Him to the grave (Mark 15:47). But her absence was not without design. She was clearly acting in the closest concert with Mary Magdalene and the other Mary, and they must have felt the gravest concern for the

stricken mother in her hour of sorrow. Thus when John led
her away from the hill of the cross they may have felt that
an understanding woman ought to be at her side. Would not
Salome volunteer — for John was her son and Mary was her
sister? And her presence must have released John so that he
was able to turn back in time to see the last rites on the cross
and in the garden (cf. John 19:35). It was just like John to
have referred to Salome as Mary's sister and not to have mentioned her name: he would withhold her name since she was
his mother, just as he had withheld his own (see John 19:25).
But this explains why there were two women only to keep vigil
by the tomb as night was falling: "And there was Mary Magdalene, and the other Mary, sitting over against the sepulchre"
(Matthew 27:61). There they lingered until the sun's last
ray told them that the Sabbath had come. Then "they returned
. . . and rested the Sabbath day according to the commandment"
(Luke 23:56). The Sabbath was observed by the disciples of
the Nazarene; it was otherwise with His enemies.

Matthew first records the request of the Jews: "Now the next
day, that followed the day of the preparation, the chief priests
and Pharisees came together unto Pilate." The first gospel alone
has an account of this event, and it is the only event of which
we read between nightfall on the Friday and daybreak on Sunday. The time is fixed by an indirect reference to the Sabbath,
for Matthew could not forget that the preparation for that
Paschal season had been the dread day of the cross. Then he
refers to the Jewish rulers who had been so anxious lest that
Sabbath should be defiled: what did they do? They had pursued the Lord to death, yet they could not dismiss Him from
their minds. They knew that His lifeless body lay in its tomb,
but they were now vexed with a new problem. They would
have been content if His body could have remained in the
nominal custody of the Roman Procurator: it would then have
been thrown into a pit like that of the two thieves.

It must have been to their intense chagrin when they found
that Joseph had gone to Pilate and begged the body for a
dignified burial. He was one of their own Council, but his private
action had changed the whole question of the legal control of
the body. Pilate had ceased to be responsible for what happened after it was taken down from the cross. He had washed

his hands of the whole affair far more effectively than in his first attempt. He had transferred the care of that body from himself to Joseph, so that its fate would now be a strictly Jewish concern.[1] The Jews may not have been aware of this situation at first, but the truth forced itself on their minds with the fear that some mysterious event might yet take place. It was still the Sabbath, but they met in secret to discuss the problem. These were the men who had refused to cross Pilate's threshold the day before lest they should be defiled (John 18:28) and who would not permit the dead to hang on their gallows lest the Sabbath should be disturbed (John 19:31): yet they did not scruple to meet on the Sabbath and to approach Pilate with a fresh plan.

"Sir, we remember that that deceiver said, while he was yet alive, After three days I will rise again." Their scheme was to imply that they had now come to Pilate because they had been fortunate enough to recollect certain facts just in time. They had suddenly remembered that "that deceiver," a term of fierce contempt, "that vagabond, that impostor," whom they had put to death, had made the claim that on the third day He would rise again. They may have thought of that mysterious saying which had baffled them all along: "Destroy this temple, and in three days I will raise it up" (John 2:18-22). They may have thought of that other cryptic saying which had angered them just as much: "For as Jonas was three days and three nights in the whale's belly, so shall the Son of man be three days and three nights in the heart of the earth" (Matthew 12:38-41). Perhaps they had heard of His thrice-repeated prophecy that though He would be put to death He would rise from the dead on the third day (Matthew 16:21; 17:22, 23; 20:18, 19).

All this had caused so much gossip that the whole case against Him at His trial hinged on a charge which was based on those words: "In three days (Matthew 26:61; Mark 14:58). It had been dropped when the men whom they had suborned and who were to bear false witness failed to agree in their testimony. But the fact which stands out in bold relief was the power of that phrase to provoke and annoy. Thus it became one of the taunts which were levelled against Him on the cross (Matthew 27:40), and it lived on to haunt their minds

[1]Frank Morison, *Who Moved the Stone?* (1st ed., 1930), pp. 240-242.

when He was dead (Matthew 27:63). The Pharisees still remembered when disciples had forgotten; His foes began to fear just when His friends had ceased to hope.

"Command therefore that the sepulchre be made sure until the third day, lest his disciples come by night, and steal him away, and say unto the people, He is risen from the dead: so the last error shall be worse than the first." This request was designed to make Pilate suppose that their only concern was lest the tomb should be rifled and false rumor should be started. It would conceal their own secret trepidation lest the saying should be fulfilled that He would rise again. If they were to furnish a guard outside the tomb it would keep the body under their own control; but if they were to leave the tomb without a guard it would expose them to certain trouble. So they reasoned, and they believed that they were still in time. They knew that the body would be secure on the Sabbath, for it was not until the third day that He was supposed to rise again. The sanctity of the Sabbath would prevent any design on the part of His friends to rob the tomb before sunset; the character of the saying would preclude any anxiety on the part of the Jews lest He should rise before nightfall.

The Pharisees also knew that the critical period would be confined to the twenty-four hours from the Sabbath sunset to the Sunday nightfall: that would comprise the third day in which it would be vital to guard the tomb. They would not have felt so concerned had the body remained in the control of the Roman authorities, but the entire situation had been altered once it had been consigned to Joseph of Arimathaea. It was this fact which had placed them in the immediate difficulty from which they hardly knew how to escape. The most obvious way out of the dilemma would have been to employ their own Temple police (cf. John 7:32; 18:3), but it would be far more congenial if they could have an armed guard of Roman soldiers. That would reverse the whole situation and make Pilate responsible once more. Therefore they asked him to concede the point and to provide military supervision until the third day had come to an end.

Matthew's next words record the rebuff by Pilate: "Pilate said unto them, Ye have a watch: go your way, make it as sure as ye can." This was the third time that Pilate had been confronted with a petition from the Jews since he had condemned the Son of Man at their behest. The chief priests had come to protest against the words of superscription which had been nailed above His head. But he was not in the humor to yield the point, and the real man had come out in his blunt reply: "What I have written I have written" (John 19:19-22). Their next errand took place as the day of the cross drew to a close. They wanted to accelerate the work of death so that the three bodies might be removed, and their request was that Pilate should instruct the centurion to have their legs broken. Pilate agreed; but the truculence in his attitude seems clear from his cordial surrender of one body to Joseph of Arimathaea (John 19:31-38). He knew that the superscription over His head and the reverent burial of His body would insult and disturb the Jews, and it gave him a sweet taste of minor revenge.

It was improbable in such circumstances that the Jews would have made this third approach if they had not been spurred by a sense of the most urgent necessity. But they framed their request in words which would represent it as in the interest of the Procurator himself. Thus they explained that His friends might steal the body and then claim that He was alive. That would revive the hope of the common people and make them think that He was what He had professed to be. This would be as injurious to the cause of Caesar as it would be erroneous in the eyes of the Jews. It would create political disaffection, and would result in worse touble than at the first. It was the same kind of argument which had overcome Pilate's scruples when they had first tried to secure a death warrant (Luke 23:2). Pilate had seen through that stratagem; he knew that they had come to seek their own advantage (Matthew 27:18). But where he had been forced to yield before, he now refused to stir.

"So they went, and made the sepulchre sure, sealing the stone and setting a watch." Commentators used to think that the Jews had gained their point and that Pilate's reply gave them authority to guard the tomb with men from the Roman barracks. This was largely based on the fact that his words may be read as an imperative: "Take a guard" (R.V.M.). But it is most improbable that this is a correct reconstruction of the course of events. It is far more likely that he met the request with a flash of the scorn which had revealed itself before (John 18:31). Not for them the Roman Eagles! They had their own Temple police and could order out a guard for the tomb just as they had furnished a guard for His arrest. Thus he dismissed them with a curt rebuff, and they had to return without a guard.

This meant that the Pharisees had no alternative but to fall back on the Temple police and an armed band would be called out for the purpose. Then they left the city and went to the garden where the body had been interred. Their first task was to seal the stone at the mouth of the tomb so that they could protect it from undiscovered interference. A cord was drawn across the stone at the door of the tomb and was fastened at each end to the rock from which the tomb was cut. The seals would be impressed on wax or clay at both ends and in the center, so that they would break up at once if the stone were displaced. The whole project reminds us of the scene in which the prophet Daniel was cast into the den of lions while the stone at its mouth was sealed by his relentless enemies (Daniel 6:17). The last step was taken when the guard was mounted as watch and ward for the security of the place where the Lord lay.

Thus the restless hostility of the Jewish leaders could not sleep even when that scarred body had been laid in welcome repose in that newly cut tomb. The men who had displayed so much haste and anxiety to have the dead removed before sunset on the Friday now showed the same haste and solicitude to have the tomb patrolled before nightfall on the Sabbath. The day of rest would end with the evening shadows and the city would soon return to its normal activity as a new week began. There were sentries pacing to and fro in Joseph's garden, and the Jews would think the hours of darkness safe from alarm. They had pursued the Lord with the malice of fear even when His body lay in the tomb, but they little knew how all their measures were to work out.

They were scheming against the Son of Man, and knew not that they were unconscious instruments in the purpose of God. The most famous sign that He had ever proposed was that He would lie in the grave for three days and then rise again, and this action on the part of the Jews would soon help to confirm the sign which they meant to prevent. They had spared no pains to see that the tomb and body were as secure as the hands of men could make them. They had done all that man could do to rule out all thought of interference, for they themselves had sealed the stone and placed the guard. It seemed as though they had mastered the whole situation; but "vain the stone, the watch, the seal!"

The guard was on duty throughout the night and was still at the tomb when the first grey streaks of dawn began to appear. Then came a great earthquake which shook the ground beneath their feet, and the descent of an angel, who rolled away the stone from the mouth of the tomb. Temple police had been stricken to the ground in mortal terror at the arrest of the Son of Man in that other garden (John 18:6). Now they were seized with awed alarm in the presence of an angel: "And for fear of him the keepers did shake, and became as dead men" (Matthew 28:4). They shook and quaked in the grip of panic, and were flung to the earth as men who had lost self-control. They fled as soon as they could find strength to get on their feet and told the priests what had happened: "Behold, some of the watch came into the city, and shewed unto the chief priests all the things that were done" (Matthew 28:11).

The Jews were so disturbed that a hasty meeting was held and a course of action was planned. Those who had bribed Judas to betray his Master would now bribe the police to deny the Resurrection; but whereas a paltry sum had sufficed to tempt Judas, a large amount was required to induce the guard to tell the lie. "They gave large money unto the soldiers, saying, Say ye, His disciples came by night, and stole him away while we slept" (Matthew 28:12, 13). The priests also gave a solemn pledge to protect them should Pilate hear the report and show concern: "And if this come to the governor's ears, we will persuade him, and secure you" (Matthew 28:14). This would have been impossible if the guard had been a Roman unit, captained by a centurion and responsible to Pilate. Roman soldiers who slept at their posts would be put to death, and no Jewish intercession could have saved them. Nothing would have induced them to incriminate themselves by such a lie if they had been Roman soldiers; nothing was less likely than that Pilate should take notice of the report if they were the Temple police.

"So they took the money, and did as they were taught: and this saying is commonly reported among the Jews until this day" (Matthew 28:15). The lie was well paid for, but few would be deceived. How could they say what had taken place if they were so fast asleep that they slept right through the events which they claimed to describe.[2] The lie involved the Jews in a new and awkward disadvantage: they were forced to admit that the tomb had been found vacant. They did not know where to find the body, and its absence was fatal to falsehood.

---

[2]Alfred Plummer, *St. Matthew* (n.d.), pp. 423, 424.

Chapter 28

THE OPEN DOOR

The first day of the week cometh Mary Magdalene early, when it was yet dark, unto the sepulchre, and seeth the stone taken away from the sepulchre. Then she runneth and cometh to Simon Peter, and to the other disciple, whom Jesus loved, and saith unto them, They have taken away the Lord out of the sepulchre, and we know not where they have laid him. — JOHN 20:1, 2.

IT MUST have been after midnight when the silent drama of the Resurrection took place within the tomb. This was in strict accord with the lapse of three days which had more than once been foretold. "The third day," as He had once said of Himself, "He shall rise again" (Matthew 20:19). "After three days," so the Jews declared that He had said, "I will rise again" (Matthew 27:63). "The third day" and "after three days" were more or less general expressions which could refer either to a period of time totally occupied by three complete days or to a period of time partially occupied by three distinct days (cf. I Kings 12:5, 12). This meant that the letter of His promise would have allowed Him to return as soon as the Sabbath sunset announced the first moments of a new day, because the full course of twenty-four hours could be represented by the smallest fraction of the whole day.

However we know that the great transformation must have occurred in the early morning, not long before daybreak, but while it was yet dark. Mark plainly says that He rose *early the first day of the week*" (Mark 16:9). No eye beheld the change nor saw behind the stone; neither man nor angel was there to see Him rise or to tell the process. But the corruptible put on incorruption and the mortal was clothed with immortality. The Lord arose in His human body and passed through the

graveclothes which were left in perfect order; then He went forth
from that closed tomb and passed through the great stone which
was left in solid reality. Who now should fear the grave when
he reflects that it was once "the place where the Lord lay"
(Matthew 28:6)?

The first point of interest lies in Mary's visit to the tomb.
"The first day of the week cometh Mary Magdalene early, when
it was yet dark, unto the sepulchre." Mary was not alone in
this venture; there were other women with whom she had
shared the crisis of His cross and passion. They had honored
Him at the height of His fame in Galilee (Luke 8:1-3) and
had followed Him to the hour of His death on Calvary (Mark
15:40, 41). Peter and John alone of the men who had fled
at His arrest in the garden had spent the night in the city
and the women may not even have known of His trial and condemnation until the last fateful morning.[1] But they followed
Him out to the hill of the cross and stood their ground to the
end while the men were in hiding. Peter would be in the depth
of despair, and John would be preoccupied with the care of
His heartbroken mother.

Thus it remained for Mary Magdalene and that "other Mary"
to keep the last vigil near the tomb where He lay until failing
light warned them to withdraw (Matthew 27:61). She was
now the foremost in that band of women on whom the full
impact of the crisis would fall. The long cheerless Sabbath was
spent in the darkest sorrow that could oppress the heart, but
she had to plan the kind of action which the situation seemed
to require. Therefore "when the Sabbath was past" Mary and
two others went out at once to buy spice and balm (Mark 16:1).
Then in the last hour of darkness before the dawn of a new
day they set out once more to visit the tomb.

"The first day of the week cometh Mary Magdalene early,
when it was yet dark, unto the sepulchre, and seeth the stone
taken away from the sepulchre." It is clear that Mary was not
alone, for the first three gospels furnish the names of three
other women who went with her. All three refer to "the other
Mary," mother of James and of Joses, who had shared the vigil
at the tomb when He was buried (Matthew 28:1; Mark 16:1;

---

[1]Frank Morison, *Who Moved the Stone?* (1st ed., 1930), pp. 93, 94.

Luke 24:10). Mark adds the name of Salome (Mark 16:1; see John 19:25), and Luke supplies the name of Joanna (Luke 24:10; see 8:3). Thus there were four at least in that group of women, and that explains why a plural pronoun was thrust into Mary's breathless message: "They have taken away the Lord and *we* know not where they have laid Him" (John 20:2).

There are minor variations in the statements as to when the women set out, but all insist that it was at the first available moment. The first gospel says that it was "as it began to dawn" (Matthew 28:1), and Luke speaks of "early dawn" (Luke 24:1, R.V.). John says that it was "early, when it was yet dark" (John 20:1). Mark says that it was "very early in the morning . . . at the rising of the sun" (Mark 16:2). Perhaps they set out while it was yet dark, but the sun might break the skyline before they reached the tomb. They would choose that early hour to avoid publicity, for they had come to anoint or embalm the Dead.[2]

The women knew that His body had been wrapped in fine white linen, and that myrrh and aloes had been sprinkled freely between its folds; they knew too that there had not been time to treat the body with the liquid ointments which were customary among the Jews.[3] They thought to add this last act of loving kindness to His reverent burial; they did not know that they had been forestalled by the act of another disciple. The Lord Jesus Himself had made it clear that the cruse of ointment which was broken over His head in the house of Simon was in tender forethought for the day of His burial (John 12:7); there would be no repetition of that rite when His body was laid in the tomb.

We all know the kind of shock which a man sustains when he suddenly encounters something of which he has had no idea, something like the footprint on the sand in Crusoe's story which sets the mind racing in search of an explanation.[4] That was now the experience of this band of women who were startled to find that the stone had been rolled away from the mouth of the tomb. This was the first mention of that stone in John's gospel, but the definite article implies that he spoke of it as well known. The first gospel notes that it was "a great stone" (Mat-

---

[2]Frank Morison, *Who Moved the Stone?* (1st ed., 1930), p. 116.
[3]C. J. Ellicott, *Historical Lectures* (1876), p. 378, footnote 1.
[4]Frank Morison, *Who Moved the Stone?* (1st ed., 1930), p. 227.

thew 27:60); Mark says that it was "exceeding great" (Mark 16:4, R.V.). It had been rolled against the door of the tomb by Joseph before sunset on the Friday (Mark 15:46), and had been sealed by the Jewish rulers before nightfall on the Sabbath (Matthew 27:66). But the Resurrection had occurred in silence within the tomb, and the mighty Captive had now left His prison "leaving behind the gate, the bar, the chain."[5]

The first gospel tells us of the descent of an angel whose task was to roll back the stone; this was followed by an earthquake and the flight of the guard, leaving the tomb open and the garden empty (Matthew 28:2). But it is clear that the women had no idea of this chain of events or they would not have dared to draw near to the tomb at all. They had seen the stone rolled into its place by Joseph and Nicodemus, but they did not know that a guard had been mounted at dusk on the Sabbath. There had only been one problem which had vexed them as they hurried through the darkness: "Who shall roll us away the stone from the door of the sepulchre?" (Mark 16:3). This caused them real anxiety: had they the strength to roll it back? But when they reached the tomb they saw at once that it had been displaced. The first three gospels speak of it as having been rolled away (Matthew 28:2; Mark 16:4; Luke 24:2); but John's word implies that it had been lifted out of its groove before the tomb (John 20:1). The women who had been so preoccupied with the problem of that great stone received a shock for which they were totally unprepared.[6] The door had been unsealed and the vault was open; the one problem which had caused them concern had thus been solved. But there was such mystery in that solution that it would set greater problems at once in train.

The next point of interest lies in Mary's errand to the disciples: "Then she runneth, and cometh to Simon Peter, and to the other disciple, whom Jesus loved." This is the point from which the first three gospels relate the story of the other women with no further reference to Mary Magdalene, while John's narrative pursues the story of Mary Magdalene with no further reference to the other women. There are elements in the nar-

---

[5]Horatius Bonar, *Hymns of Faith and Hope.*
[6]Frank Morison, *Who Moved the Stone?* (1st ed., 1930), p. 117.

rative which we cannot explain because the details are missing, but the women saw at once that something must have occured which would upset all their plans and preparation. Mary's insight would be quickened by the instinct of love, and she came to a clear and rapid decision. How could she know that the body had gone if she did not wait to enter the tomb? How could she fail to see the shroud or the angel if she did not wait to look within? We do not know; but it would seem that she must have entered the tomb with the other women and must have shared the shock which they sustained: "They entered in, and found not the body of the Lord Jesus" (Luke 24:3).

Luke makes it clear that they stood nonplussed and lost in thought for some moments, and it seems that Mary was the first to make up her mind. But she was wrong in the explanation which she conceived, for she thought that hostile hands must have rolled back the stone in order to steal the Lord's body. There may have been a brief consultation with the other women, for she was not likely to act except in the closest concert with them. But the conclusion was so definite that she turned and hurried away at once to find Peter and John. Thus she did not wait for her friends, or she would soon have seen and heard enough to set her mind at rest: "It came to pass, as they were much perplexed thereabout, behold, two men stood by them in shining garments" (Luke 24:4; Matthew 28:5; Mark 16:5). These two angel watchers asked them why they sought the Living among the dead, for the Lord had risen even as He had said. The real explanation of the empty tomb was nothing less than resurrection, and they went on their way with awe and great gladness.

"Then she runneth, and cometh to Simon Peter, and to the other disciple, whom Jesus loved, and saith unto them, They have taken away the Lord out of the sepulchre, and we know not where they have laid him." There must have been a few hurried moments between her first startled recognition of the state of the tomb and her abrupt resolution to go in search of help. Then she turned and ran with her news to His two most intimate disciples while the other women were left to make their great discoveries in her absence. It was a true instinct which made her run to them for help, for they were men; and they were the only men who belonged to His party who were still in Jerusalem. It is in the psychology of this situation that we can see why she did not remain with the other women, for as women there was nothing that they could do to help; John and Peter were men who ought to be informed, and who as men could take the right course of action.[7]

Mary's haste was the first display of the hurried activity which governed the movements of those who came and went on that early morning: they ran, with the anxious haste of great grief or else with the eager speed of great hope. It was all in contrast with the silent calm near the tomb, and their bustling spirit had to be stilled before they were able to grasp the truth. Thus it was that Mary ran in search of Simon Peter and that "other disciple, whom Jesus loved." There can be no doubt that John describes himself with a beautiful naïveté in that brief phrase, but there are two interesting points of contrast in the wording of its self-reference here and elsewhere. The verb employed in this passage differs from the corresponding verb in other contexts, and the reference to "the *other* disciple" is an enlargement of the normal reference to *the disciple* (see John 21:7). The verb conveys the thought of warm personal affection, and the whole phrase suggests that both Simon Peter and that "other disciple" were the objects of such a love.[8] One more interesting detail lies in the fact that the preposition which governs the reference to Simon Peter is repeated for the reference to "the other disciple," and this may be a hint that they were lodged in two distinct places of dwelling.[9] And yet the most natural assumption is that Mary found them beneath the same roof and that she broke her news to them together.

Mary's language shows that she was deeply moved by what she had seen, but that she had not the faintest idea that it spoke of resurrection. She had gone to the tomb to anoint the body, and hers was not the mood to look for mystery or miracle when she found that it had vanished. Her whole outlook is summed up in the vague pronouns which mark the simple, matter-of-fact way in which she spoke, the *they* and the *we* of her news. She could not think who would wish to disturb the tomb, and she used an indefinite phrase which simply indicated

---

[7]C. J. Ellicott, *Historical Lectures* (1876), p. 381, footnote 2.
[8]B. F. Westcott, *The Gospel According to St. John* (1908), p. 289.
[9]*Ibid.*

that someone had interfered: "*They* have taken away the Lord out of the sepulchre."

It is valuable to note that in her eyes the dead body was still "the Lord"; she had not had time to adjust her thoughts to the fact of the cross. Nor could she think where that body might now be found, and she fell back on the plural pronoun in order to express the fact: "And *we* know not where they have laid him." This is the one distinct detail in John's narrative which hints at the presence of the other women. We may compare it with the way in which she phrased the same thought to strangers when she knew that she was alone: "They have taken away *my* Lord, and I know not where they have laid him" (John 20:13). But now she spoke for the others as well as for herself, and her words show how low their hope had sunk. They could only surmise that His body had been transferred to some new site, and they knew not whether it were meant in honor or in disgrace. There was infinite tenderness in the love and sorrow which lie behind those words; there was curious irony in the utter lack of apprehension which they reveal.

The lapse of those three days was part of God's design and was rich in mercy; but it also revealed the full extent of the reaction of the disciples to the fact of the cross. No one represented their distress and surprise, their mistakes and despair, with more vivid realism than did Mary Magdalene; and no fiction could have been so lifelike as the unbridged gulf between her failure in faith and her triumph in love. Jesus, contrary to her dearest longing, had bowed His head and died: how could her faith survive? And yet this same Jesus, whatever else had happened, had set her free from a fate that was worse than death: how could her love perish?

The love which had drawn her to the tomb was the kind of love which emanated from the devoted affection of a warm heart rather than from the more authentic character of grace. Now even His body had gone, and the only resource which still remained was to run in search of comfort to men who were as much in the dark as she was herself. But at least her love was active even when her faith had collapsed, while theirs had been inert from the hour of His death. Perhaps it would be more correct to say that faith was in partial suspense rather than in total ruin, and to conclude that it was the undying energy of love which kept her soul alive. That love survived the dark night of despair and was at length transformed in the power of resurrection reality. But the healing mercies which had so won her heart have now set us free from more than seventy times seven sins: what then ought our love to be in comparison with hers in that hour of grief and despair?

Chapter 29

THE EMPTY SHROUD

Peter therefore went forth, and that other disciple, and came to the sepulchre. So they ran both together: and the other disciple did outrun Peter, and came first to the sepulchre. And he stooping down, and looking in, saw the linen clothes lying; yet went he not in. Then cometh Simon Peter following him, and went into the sepulchre, and seeth the linen clothes lie, and the napkin, that was about his head, not lying with the linen clothes, but wrapped together in a place by itself. Then went in also that other disciple, which came first to the sepulchre, and he saw, and believed. For as yet they knew not the scripture, that he must rise again from the dead. — JOHN 20:3-9.

THERE is a fine touch of artless reality in this passage which could only have been derived from direct and vivid observation. John took up the thread of the story at the point where it crossed his own experience, and the whole tone of his record bears the accent of personal discovery and personal testimony. The full movement is allowed to unfold before our eyes, and we watch each step as though it were near and real.[1]

The two men were filled with concern when they were told that the tomb was empty, and their concern was for the now missing body. But they knew that they ought to see with their own eyes before they tried to think or plan what they should do. "Peter therefore went forth, and that other disciple, and came to the sepulchre. So they ran both together: and the other disciple did outrun Peter, and came first to the sepulchre." Peter at once took the lead and "went forth"; John attached himself to his decided companion, and then both men "went on their way" toward the tomb.[2] They would thread their way through

---

[1]H. C. G. Moule, *Jesus and the Resurrection* (1905), p. 29.

[2]B. F. Westcott, *The Gospel According to St. John* (1908), p. 289.

the streets of the city and leave by the northern gate to run the hundred yards or so down the road. At first they ran at full speed side by side; but as they drew near to the goal, John pressed on ahead. Peter may have begun to flag because he was older and less able to run at such a pace; but a troubled conscience would make it hard for him to keep the pace up as they approached the place where his Master's body had lain.

And so John outran Peter as Ahimaaz had outrun Cushi and came first to the scene where hope was to be born anew. The door of the tomb had been thrown open and the stone rolled back in its groove. Perhaps the sun had now begun to flash its first bright rays into the vault. The three other women had gone away and the watching angels were out of view. Ineffable calm would surround the tomb, and John would lose all sense of haste in that quiet unhurried atmosphere. He would arrive with a mind that was keyed to an understanding of that eloquent mystery.

The first clue to the secret of the empty tomb was the discovery of the graveclothes: "And he stooping down, and looking in, saw the linen clothes lying; yet went he not in.[3] Each word must be examined for its element of truth, for the very details which may seem least important to us are those on which the main emphasis falls in the text. Thus a single word in Greek sums up John's first action, though five words are required to furnish an English equivalent: "Stooping down, and looking in" (see John 20:11; Luke 24:12). He was bending beside the door, looking into the vault where the body had lain; he was looking with frank concern and fixed intent at that which was partly concealed.[4]

John's next impulse would have been to go in, but he hesitated. He was checked by surprise at the very threshold, startled into thought by a sense of the mysterious. He had caught sight of the graveclothes which had been wrapped like a long shroud round the body. The word used makes it clear that this was ordinary seeing; he had seen the clothes at a glance without the least effort on his part to find them. It was not as though

---

[3]For an excellent discussion of this subject, see Henry Latham, *The Risen Master*, on which this chapter is largely based.
[4]B. F. Westcott, *The Gospel According to St. John* (1908), p. 289.

he had come to look for them; it had never occurred to him that he would find them there at all. It was not a surprise to find that the body had gone, but it had not even entered his mind that the graveclothes might still be there. Why should the shroud be left behind when the body had been removed? It would be as hard to explain what was there as it would be to account for what had gone. The body had vanished, but the graveclothes were still in place. This strange discovery filled him with a sense of growing wonder: what could be the explanation?

"And he . . . saw the linen clothes lying; yet went he not in." John had seen enough to fill him with sober surprise, and his mind was in a whirl of awe and wonder. He stood just where he was at the door of the tomb, preoccupied, lost in thought and meditation. He must have thought it strange to find that the graveclothes had been left in the tomb at all, but it seems that he saw something stranger still in the way in which they lay. He took such care to point out not merely that they were there but that they were *lying* (John 20:5, 6, 7). This word commands the most emphatic position in the structure of the sentence. Why should he take such strong notice of the fact that they were "lying"? Why should he pause to mark the fact that they were "lying" at all?

It would have been enough merely to have said that he had seen them unless there was something exceptional, something totally different from what one might have been led to expect. But the author concentrates attention on the graveclothes; their position and arrangement only seemed to add more to their significance. He was fascinated by the fact that they were "lying" in the deserted tomb. The whole context seems to imply that the long loose folds of fine white linen were still "lying" at full length on the ledge where the body had been stretched out. They had not been neatly folded up or piled in a heap; that was what he might have supposed if he had had any idea that he would find them there at all. He was perplexed because they were "lying" in their original manner; yet the body had gone.

There was one more aspect of the situation which may not have impressed itself on his mind in that first startling moment; but it was of the first significance and would compel further thought in due course. A large amount of dry powdered myrrh and aloes, as much as a hundred pounds in weight, had been placed in the folds of the shroud when it was wound round the sacred body. This large weight of spices would have dropped out of the linen wrappings and spilled on the rugged flooring in a conspicuous fashion if there had been the least attempt to disrobe the body or disturb the graveclothes. John could not have failed to observe and record the fact if there had been anything like this in the tomb. But his complete silence with regard to the spices stands out in marked contrast with his detailed comment with regard to the graveclothes. We are forced to conclude that they were still concealed in the folds of the shroud where they had been sprinkled by the hand of Nicodemus.

This fact fills out our sense of the tremendous mystery which held John spellbound at the door of the tomb. The weight of the myrrh and aloes would depress the graveclothes so that they lay flat on the ledge where the body had been, but they were in no disorder. They lay there just as when they had been wrapped round the body, except that they were now somewhat compressed. They were simply lying on the stone slab, with fold on fold in perfect order, but weighed down by the spices. No human hand nor angel touch had been at work; but the body had gone.

The next clue to the secret of the empty tomb was the discovery of the napkin: "Then cometh Simon Peter following him, and went into the sepulchre, and seeth the linen clothes lie, and the napkin, that was about his head, not lying with the linen clothes, but wrapped together in a place by itself." Peter must have been close behind his friend, and so would reach the tomb within a few moments. But while John was still absorbed in a mood of thoughtful wonder at the entrance, Peter went in "without a look or pause."[5] This was just like the man who at other times was in so much haste to reach the Lord on sea or shore (Matthew 14:28; John 21:7); he could not stand and muse when there was a call for action.

This trait appears again in the word which refers to his survey of the graveclothes inside the tomb: he fixed his gaze on them as one who would make out the true meaning of what

---

[5] B. F. Westcott, *The Gospel According to St. John* (1908), p. 290.

he saw. John only saw what he could not help seeing from the door of the tomb; Peter looked with deliberate intent, like a man whose eye was passing from point to point, taking in "the scene and something of its significance."[6] His main object was to find out how the body had been removed, and he fastened his eyes at once on the graveclothes. He was faced with something more than the fact that the shroud was empty: for, like John, he was perplexed by the way in which its folds were lying. There would have been no need to speak again of the appearance or the arrangement of the graveclothes unless there was something special that caught and held the eye. There was indeed something strange and mysterious; and yet it was only half the problem that would confront his gaze.

"Then . . . Simon Peter . . . seeth the linen clothes lie, and the napkin, that was about his head, not lying with the linen clothes, but wrapped together in a place by itself." John at the entrance of the tomb had only caught sight of the graveclothes, whereas Peter, who was inside, saw as well the napkin which had been round His head (cf. John 11:44). John was so absorbed in the recollection when he came to pen this account that no name was mentioned; it was enough for him to write "his head" and to let the pronoun speak for itself. But the napkin was a further sign of something totally different from all that they had feared. It was the more interesting in that it was separated from the graveclothes "in a place by itself."

Luke describes the scene as a whole in words which provide a faint clue as to the situation: "Then arose Peter, and ran unto the sepulchre; and stooping down, he beheld the linen clothes laid by themselves" (Luke 24:12). Luke does not refer to the napkin at all, but he observes with care that the graveclothes had been "laid by themselves." We would wonder why those words were employed and what they meant if John had not told of the presence of the napkin.[7] But his remark that the napkin was "not *lying* with the linen clothes" tells us more still. This is the third statement which avows or implies that the linen clothes were *lying*, and once again it would have been pointless unless it was meant to mark some special feature. It proves

---

[6]H. C. G. Moule, *Jesus and the Resurrection* (1905), p. 29.

[7]Henry Latham, *The Risen Master* (1910), p. 49.

that they were not scattered about the tomb as if they had been thrown aside in haste, for the context makes it clear that they were all in one place.

There would have been no point in the remark that the napkin was not with the graveclothes unless the place where the clothes lay served to define a fixed locality. This may help us to see what the position of the napkin was in relation to that of the graveclothes. The shroud for the body was stretched along the ledge of rock where the Lord had been laid, while the napkin which had been round His head remained apart on a slightly raised shelf which served as a pillow. But the strangest feature of all has yet to be observed.

A rare word was chosen to set before us a picture of the headcloth as it was when Peter saw it, and the choice of a term so out of the common may hint at the abnormal character of the thing which was thus described. The same word had been used in the active voice to describe the way in which the Lord's body had been wrapped up in the graveclothes, and it refers to the thing that was wrapped rather than to the shroud in which it had been wrapped (Matthew 27:59; Luke 23:53). This leads us to infer that the napkin must have been rolled round His head in the same way that the shroud was wound round His body.

However, much more than this is implied by the choice of this word to point out the different appearance of the empty napkin from that of the empty graveclothes. John had to describe what the tomb would look like when the body had gone; he had to bring out the meaning of the empty graveclothes and the folded napkin. Thus he made use of the same term in the passive voice and applied it to the napkin, for the body had now vanished and there would be nothing for it to enfold. The graveclothes were *lying* "by themselves" on the lower level (Luke 24:12), while the napkin was *rolled up* "by itself" on the higher level (John 20:7). It is sometimes thought that this means that it was rolled in the way in which we would roll up a table napkin to fit it for a ring. But the grammar is not conclusive, and the context seems to argue otherwise.[8]

There would be no weight of powdered spices to flatten or depress the folds of the napkin as was the case with the grave-

---

[8]Henry Latham, *The Risen Master* (1910), pp. 89, 90.

clothes. The word employed seems to stress the fact that the folds had not caved in so as to look like the folds of the shroud which had fallen inward. It still bore the shape which it had taken when it was first wrapped round His head; it still retained enough of the circular arrangement of its folds to look like "the roll of a loosened turban."[9] This was not an easy thing to describe, and an author might feel nonplussed; but John found a word for the purpose, and it allows us to see the napkin just as he meant us to see it. There it lay on the rock just as when it had been wrapped round His head, still rolled and round in shape and form. No human hand nor angel touch had been at work; but the head was not there.

John was not slow to follow Peter into the tomb and he at once saw with his own eyes the unique features of the napkin as well as the graveclothes. "Then went in also that other disciple, which came first to the sepulchre, and he saw, and believed. For as yet they knew not the scripture, that he must rise again from the dead." There lay the graveclothes, a little depressed, but still in folds, and not one grain of spice displaced. There lay the napkin, a little apart, but still in rings, and not one roll of cloth disturbed. The air of calm that filled the tomb would make him pause, and then he saw the truth. Once more he chose a fresh word to describe the way in which he saw, for he wanted to convey the idea of intelligence and understanding as well as of visual discernment. He saw the facts, and perceived their meaning; that cleared his mind, and he believed that the Lord had risen.

John's faith as yet was based on what he saw, for he had not grasped the Scriptures which had pointed to His Resurrection. It was that scene before his eyes which made the truth clear and overwhelming. Perhaps, "a sudden throng of memories,"[10] half-subdued, would surge into his mind; perhaps the mighty voice of prophecies, half absorbed, would crowd into his thoughts. He not only saw the empty shroud and napkin, but he suddenly understood their real significance; and he believed with the strength of absolute certainty that they were the tokens of life and not of death.

---

[9]*Ibid.*, p. 36.
[10]H. C. G. Moule, *Jesus and the Resurrection* (1905), p. 33.

There was infinitely more than empty graveclothes and a vanished body; there was Resurrection. There had been no lifeless body for friend or foe to bear away; Jesus Himself had left the tomb in His risen glory. He had emerged from the graveclothes, yet He had not disturbed their folds. He had passed through shroud and napkin with the same ease and power with which He could enter a room while the doors were still shut. This was the solution of the whole mystery: the clothes and the napkin were a silent witness to the mighty fact of Resurrection.

Chapter 30

THE SOBER TRUTH

Then the disciples went away again unto their own home.
— JOHN 20:10

Then . . . Peter . . . departed, wondering in himself at that which was come to pass. — LUKE 24:12.

ONE remarkable but unobtrusive feature in the account of the Resurrection is the reserve which the gospels employ. The Resurrection is always assumed; the process is never described. Human eyes were allowed to watch when the ruler's daughter and the widow's son were restored to life (Mark 5:40, 41; Luke 7:14, 15), but no eye saw inside the tomb of Lazarus at Bethany or of Jesus in the garden when they awoke and rose. However, John saw that the Resurrection had a far more searching significance than mere restoration to life; he saw at once that the Lord had not left the tomb in a revived but still mortal body. His first thought in that case would have been to hurry away in search of Him, and it would have meant that the Lord was still subject to the experience of death. But it was not as though He were bound hand and foot with the graveclothes when He rose from the dead, nor yet as though there were need for angel hands to loose Him and let Him go (John 11:44).

Jesus had passed through the gate of death once and for all, and would never cross its threshold again. His old body had been transformed and was endowed with powers unknown before. He was able to come or go at will, to appear without human means, to vanish beyond human sight. So it was that He had withdrawn from the graveclothes and had left them to bear witness to His Resurrection.

John was to remember afterward how a nascent faith had sprung up in his heart as he stood at the door of the tomb, for he saw and believed. There may have been a pause for some moments inside the tomb while the two men surveyed the scene and took in its meaning. There was nothing that they could do except return in the hope that the Lord would soon declare Himself. Therefore they turned away in quiet faith and wonder, assured that the empty tomb proclaimed His Resurrection.

The first line of meditation is to trace the significance of the empty tomb for John: "Then the disciples went away again unto their own home." John's disarming narrative frankly admits that he had not as yet understood the great words of prophecy in the Scriptures: he had failed to grasp the truth that Jesus had to die in order to break the power of death by His rising again. The simplicity and humility of a transparent character shine through his words. He could rejoice in his recollection of the contrast between the strange blindness which had been his and the understanding which he had since received.

John had been the favorite disciple and had known a special nearness to the Saviour. He had entered into the most intimate fellowship with Him, and had developed powers of insight which made for an awareness of truth not found in ordinary men. He had dwelt so close to the Son of Man that a hint was enough for him to see truth that was still concealed from other minds. He knew with the unargued certainty of a direct insight that it was the Lord who stood on the shore while the other six saw Him in the gray light of early morning only as a stranger (John 21:7). Thus he saw the empty graveclothes and in childlike faith grasped the fact of the Resurrection. He had come in troubled suspense to examine the tomb; he would go with settled resolve to glorify the Lord.

"Then the disciples went away again unto their own home." These words prove that a great change had now come over the friends as a result of what they had seen at the tomb. They had gone out prepared to find the tomb empty, and they had been disposed to think that the body had been removed by rude and hostile hands. That was Mary Magdalene's impression when she had run to let them know of the missing body (John 20:2). But they could not share that view once they had seen the tomb for themselves (John 20:8). They had gone to find out how the body had been removed, and they had been ready to spend the day in search of it. Their first action might have been to report the loss to the owner of the garden so that he could lodge a protest if there had been any interference with his new tomb. They had not been in the mood to sit still until every possible avenue had been explored.

But there was no other course of action that Peter and John could take once they had seen the tomb. The sight of the shroud and napkin had been unexpected and had argued at once against the thought of rough hands and rude theft. They saw that no hostile hand had unwound the long white shroud, laden with its freight of costly spices: they saw, in fact, that it had not been touched at all, but that its folds still lay as they had done when the body was there. New light flashed through their minds as they stood in silence, to wonder and ponder in full view of that scene.

There is one more aspect of the great change which had been wrought in the two men as a result of what they had found out. They might have been tempted to think that the body had been disrobed by friends and then removed by them to a place of greater safety. That was Mary's later and more hopeful idea when she met Him whom she supposed to have been the keeper of the garden (John 20:15). But they could not share that view once they had seen the tomb for themselves (John 20:8). They saw how the linen shroud lay stretched out along the ledge of rock where His body must have reposed; they saw how the napkin lay by itself on the slightly raised shelf which had formed a pillow for His head and shoulders. Neither shroud nor napkin were in the least disturbed, and the napkin was not even depressed. It told them at once that something more than ordered neatness was now before their eyes. They saw that no human friend had arranged the long white folds, lying in the very shape of His limbs.

There was not a single mark that could point to the presence of enemy or disciple in that deserted sepulcher. There was nothing that could suggest how the folds could have been unwrapped at all. Peter and John were convinced that no human means could account either for the vanished body or the empty graveclothes; and thus in turn they were convinced that His body had passed beyond the powers of search. John saw the truth and believed with all his heart in one vivid flash of insight. His first thought was then to return home that he might comfort the mother of Jesus with news of this discovery.

The next line of meditation is to trace the significance of the empty tomb for Peter: "Then . . . Peter . . . departed, wondering in himself at that which was come to pass." The close bond of friendship between Peter and John is never perhaps better displayed than in the storm which had burst with the trial and death of Christ. The bond had been forged on land and water in their early home in Galilee, but it had been braced and strengthened by the common discipleship which had compelled them to follow the Son of Man. The first clear trace of it was when they were sent to prepare a room for the Passover (Luke 22:8). This is confirmed in the understanding which had grown up between them and which was revealed at the time when He spoke of the betrayal (John 13:24). We see them both standing in the palace of the high priest (John 18:16), and then running to the garden where the tomb lay (John 20:3).

Their friendship had survived the dark hour when John thrice heard Peter deny the Lord with oath and curse. Perhaps it was because John was as ready to take Peter for his brother as he had been to take Mary for his mother that Peter did not succumb to the despair which spelled ruin for Judas. We cannot doubt that when the two were side by side within the tomb, gazing in awed surprise at the graveclothes, John would open his heart to Peter in that very moment when he saw and believed. We know that John's brief hint was enough to tell Peter the truth when they saw the Lord by the sea of Galilee (John 21:7); and we might think that such a hint would be enough with the shroud and napkin before their eyes. Peter would leave the tomb and set out for home to muse and marvel on all that he had seen.

"Then . . . Peter . . . departed, wondering in himself at that which was come to pass." Peter would not solve the riddle of the graveclothes or grasp their proof of the Resurrection with the same strong certainty of faith and insight that John had displayed. His mind was not trained for meditation on mystery or miracle and he was a stranger to the subtle gifts of intuition. He saw that the graveclothes in the empty tomb were meant to yield the secret of a glorious mystery, but he might not perceive what it was all at once. He was on the verge of magnificent discovery, but he had not as yet absorbed the full lesson of the vanished body.

Peter was perplexed by the presence of the shroud and napkin, and the significance of their undistrubed appearance seemed to lie just beyond his grasp. He had caught sight of a rift in the clouds which had banked up over the grave, but the full stream of light had yet to pour into his soul. He saw that there was no need to pursue their search for the vanished body, but the secret which alone would explain just why it was missing still escaped him. He was content to leave the tomb, but it was in wonderment of mind rather than in assurance of faith. He had yet to follow John out of the twilight of a partial understanding into the sunshine of a perfect apprehension.

Peter, like Mary and Thomas, stood in special need of a strong personal assurance of the Resurrection. No word had passed between Peter and the Man of Sorrows since he had voiced those words of oath and curse. The last time he had seen His face had been when His eyes turned on him in that look of ineffable love and sorrow. The Lord had been nailed to the cross and had poured out His soul in death; and the course of events had left neither time nor place for Peter to lament the denial or entreat His forgiveness.

His heart must have been wrung with a dreadul remorse when the stone was rolled to the tomb, for Peter did not know that the Lord would rise again on the third day. He had run to the tomb with a trembling desire to make up for the past by his care for the Dead, and it had been in the goodness of God that he should have found the empty shroud and napkin inside the vault. His first humble wonder would be vastly increased with the message which the women received from the angels: "Tell his disciples *and Peter* that he goeth before you into Galilee" (Mark 16:7).

There was exceeding tenderness in that message sent to Simon Peter by name, and it was the prelude to a personal interview with the Risen Master. All the detail of that solemn meeting has been veiled in silence. It is enough that we should know of it, though it only be an elusive reference in the course of another narrative: "The Lord is risen indeed, and hath appeared to Simon" (Luke 24:34). But the first step toward recovery of lost favor had been taken when he turned back from the open tomb and empty graveclothes, musing in his heart if it could really be true that He had left the tomb alive.

The Lord did not reveal Himself to the Jewish rulers of the

common people after He had risen again; that would have been at variance with all His ways. The last sight which the world had of Him was when He hung in shame and weakness on the gallows. It was to disciples alone that He appeared in power and glory after the Resurrection. But the empty graveclothes were a sign which should have convinced all who were aware of the facts.

The whole country was stirred by the drama of the rugged cross (Luke 24:18); so now the whole city was stirred by the report of the empty tomb (Matthew 28:11). The priests were forced to bribe the guards to say that the body had been stolen while they were fast asleep, and that was the rumor by means of which they tried to scotch the sign value of the graveclothes. But the sign had been seen and understood by friends before it could be foiled or undermined by foes. It would matter little if the shroud and napkin were removed and destroyed once their witness had been received and endorsed.

This makes it important for us to remember that while Peter and John were the first to grasp the truth, they were not the first to enter the tomb. They were forestalled by the women who had been so amazed at the sight of the two angels, and the object of their vigil may have been to guard the graveclothes until they had served their purpose (Luke 24:4; Mark 16:5). This would help to explain their words to the women: "He is not here: for he is risen, as he said. Come, see the place where the Lord lay" (Matthew 28:6). There is little change in the form of this message as it appears in Mark: "He is risen; he is not here: behold the place where they laid him" (Mark 16:6). These words are so plain and realistic that there must have been some special feature in view. This strong inherent emphasis would be quite in keeping if they referred less to the ledge of rock where the body had reposed then to the shroud and the napkin which still lay in perfect order though the body had vanished. But the women were so conscious of the presence of the angels that they could pay no heed to the witness of the graveclothes, and they fled with mingled feelings of awe and joy (Matthew 28:8; Mark 16:8). Thus it remained for John and Peter, who saw not the angels, to see and grasp the true meaning of that empty shroud and napkin, and it was in faith and wonder that they returned to their place of lodging until He should appear.

Chapter 31

THE SEEMING STRANGER

> But Mary stood without at the sepulchre weeping: and as she wept, she stooped down, and looked into the sepulchre, and seeth two angels in white sitting, the one at the head, and the other at the feet, where the body of Jesus had lain. And they say unto her, Woman, why weepest thou? She saith unto them, Because they have taken away my Lord, and I know not where they have laid him. And when she had thus said, she turned herself back, and saw Jesus standing, and knew not that it was Jesus. Jesus saith unto her, Woman, why weepest thou? whom seekest thou? She, supposing him to be the gardener, saith unto him, Sir, if thou have borne him hence, tell me where thou hast laid him, and I will take him away. — JOHN 20:11-15.

ENGLISH literature does not often excel the charm of this narrative as it describes the first encounter with the Lord Christ on the Resurrection morning. The whole scene is colored by the fact that Mary had once been the hapless victim of the darkest kind of demon control. There is no worse case on record except that of the man who called himself Legion (Mark 5:9), and we can think out her state of distress in view of his experience.

We are not told just how she was released from that plight of multiple possession; we know only that she owed her rescue to the redeeming ministry of Christ Himself. But no details have been preserved of that momentous occasion, and even this meager information is gleaned only from a casual reference. Luke speaks of certain women who were healed of evil spirits, and in particular he names "Mary called Magdalene out of whom went seven devils" (Luke 8:2). No leper or cripple was ever more grateful for His healing mercy than Mary and Legion; no one ever tried to repay their debt with a love so true and spontaneous as theirs. Legion longed to follow Jesus, but went home at His word to tell his friends all that the Lord had done for him (Mark

5:19). Mary was allowed to follow Him and counted it her joy that she could use her means to provide for His comfort (Luke 8:3). Her gratitude and devotion survived the cross and brought her back to the tomb where at length she made her great discovery.

There is a brief fragment in Mark's account which sums up this experience: "Now when Jesus was risen early the first day of the week, he appeared first to Mary Magdalene, out of whom He had cast seven devils" (Mark 16:9). But John stands alone in his detailed record of that dramatic episode. The style which he adopts is marked by a touch of extreme simplicity; sentence succeeds sentence without one connecting particle before the end of the passage (John 20:18).[1] But few chapters can rival the result which it achieves in chaste beauty of language and feeling.

The first words bring Mary before us in her grief: "But Mary stood without at the sepulchre weeping." She had set out for the tomb while it was yet dark with the other women, fondly hoping to anoint the body with spice and balm. They found that the stone had been rolled away from the mouth of the tomb, and the fear that gripped their hearts was that the body itself had been taken away. Mary left the other women at the entrance to the tomb and ran back to tell Peter and John what had happened. Her friends remained for a while near the tomb where they saw the angels; then they left the garden and made their way to the other disciples who were probably some distance from Jerusalem (Matthew 28:8). This would explain how it was that Peter and John did not meet them as they hurried from the city toward the tomb, though they must have arrived within a few moments of the time when they left.

Peter and John did not remain long at the tomb; what they saw caused them to return with great awe in their hearts. But Mary had followed them back to the garden, and she stayed on alone when they had gone. She had been healed from so dark a complaint that she had clung to the Lord with desperate earnestness. Perhaps the blight which those evil spirits had left on her gentle nature had not even yet been wholly effaced. The shock of His death had plunged her into profound dismay and she may have been in danger of some form of relapse. That would partly explain why she continued to mourn near

---

[1] B. F. Westcott, *The Gospel According to St. John* (1908), p. 291.

the tomb when the others had been content to go their way. The past would crowd her thoughts and make her long once more to hear the sound of the voice that was still.

Thus the unsealed tomb left Mary Magdalene in a mood of blank despair. The one fact which should have made her heart dance for joy found her still numb with grief. She stood without and wept; her tears were the only outlet that still remained for the love which was locked up in her heart.

"And as she wept, she stooped down, and looked into the sepulchre, and seeth two angels in white sitting, the one at the head, and the other at the feet, where the body of Jesus had lain." Deep and sore had been her sorrow, and we can still picture the scene. There was the tomb, freshly hewn from the rock. Inside was the linen shroud which lay just as when it had been wrapped round His body. Nearby was the napkin which was folded just as when it had been wound round His thorn-scarred brow. Just outside the door of the tomb stood Mary, whose eyes were dim with tears. She would make no attempt to go inside as the others had done; she was content to keep her post at the entrance.

At length, just as John had done shortly before, she stooped down and looked in as one who fain would see the place where He had lain. She would peer with the moist vision of tear-dimmed eyes into the tomb, and for the first time she was made aware that she was not alone. Strange and unexpected sight that would meet her gaze! She saw not the empty shroud and headcloth which still lay on that cold stone slab; she saw rather the two angels clothed in white and seated in quiet vigil, one at the head and one at the foot of the ledge where the body had not long since reposed. These would be the angel heralds who had hailed the other women with news of the Resurrection after Mary had run on her errand to the two disciples (Luke 24:4, 5).

Neither Peter nor John saw the angels while they were at the tomb, and this is the only place where they are mentioned in this gospel. Mary saw them with a look of silent contemplation as they sat at the head and foot of that ledge like the two cherubim on the mercy seat between whose wings the Lord of Hosts was wont to dwell (Exodus 25:22; Psalm 80:1).[2]

---

[2] B. F. Westcott, *The Gospel According to St. John* (1908), p. 291.

"And they say unto her, Woman, why weepest thou? She saith unto them, Because they have taken away my Lord, and I know not where they have laid him." There was a pause while she beheld but did not speak; at length it was they who broke the silence. They did not tell her what they had told the other women; they did not speak of the Resurrection nor point to the deserted tomb. But they spoke to her with exceeding gentleness, and tried to stir her faith with a kindly question: "Woman, why weepest thou?"

Surely the sight of those angels would be enough to prove that the tomb had not been despoiled by wicked hands! Surely it would help to call to mind the promise that He would rise again! But no; Mary, true child of a sinful humanity, "all weakness, all mistake,"[3] could not see the truth through that mist of tears. She was still so absorbed in her own grief that she felt no special wonder even at the sight of angel faces or the sound of angel voices. But their gentle query touched her deepest longings, and she replied: "Because they have taken away my Lord, and I know not where they have laid him."

This was almost identical with the news which she had blurted out to Peter and John, but the variations are not without significance. She now spoke of "my Lord" rather than of "the Lord," and she used the pronoun "I" rather than "we" (see John 20:2). A more personal relation had now replaced the first general reference, the sense of loss was hers, and was acute.[4] But the repetition of that former statement shows how her mind was now obsessed by the one fixed idea; those words had gone round and round in her mind until they were the true totality of all her thoughts (see John 11:21, 32). Not the faintest gleam of the truth had yet dawned on her soul. She was only troubled because she knew not where she might find His body. Mary needed far more than the witness of the graveclothes or the presence of the angels. Such things may have convinced Peter and John or the other women, but she was still blind with sorrow.

The next words bring Mary before us in her search: "And when she had thus said, she turned herself back, and saw Jesus standing, and knew not that it was Jesus." Her brief exchange

---

[3] H. C. G. Moule, *Jesus and the Resurrection* (1905), p. 51.
[4] B. F. Westcott, *The Gospel According to St. John* (1908), p. 291.

with the angels came to an end as a conversation which had
nothing to yield. Thus she straightened herself up and turned
back to the garden. It is perhaps beyond us to tell what it was
that made her turn at that moment, but the Greek text is de-
scriptive and emphatic. We might suppose that it was an aimless
movement which told of her disappointment, for she was not
impressed by the angels nor did she care for their understanding
of her sorrow. But we would much rather think that she had
heard the soft sound of a muffled footfall behind her back or that
she had seen the dark lines of a human shadow before her eyes.

Chrysostom imagined that some change of gesture on the part
of the two angels as they saw the Saviour appear would cause
Mary to look round in order to see who was behind. No touch
could have been more real or lifelike, but we cannot be sure of
it. We know only that she turned round to come face to face
with Him whom she so ardently longed to see. Her eyes would
meet His eyes, and she saw Him in His resurrection glory. She
looked with the steady deliberate gaze of distinct purpose, but
she knew not that it was Jesus.

Mary had been in search of the Dead, and she had no power
to discern the truth. There may have been some change in His
aspect; there may have been some veil on her vision. One who
had looked on the angels without alarm might look at a seeming
stranger without concern. These were things which would help
to make her see as though she saw not, and so would deny all
her powers of recognition. Her eyes were still holden and she
knew not that she now stood in the presence of her divine Master.

"Jesus saith unto her, Woman, why weepest thou? whom
seekest thou?" The first known words to fall from His lips in
human hearing after death and resurrection speak with immortal
interest to the heart of mankind. He did not wait to see whether
she would unfold her grief to Him. He spoke to her as the
angels had done, and spoke with words akin to theirs. Perhaps
there was gentle reproof in His use of the same question: "Woman, why weepest thou?" Perhaps there was latent intent to
stir the mists of grief in the further question: "Whom seekest
thou?"

Jesus was deeply aware of her sorrow and the sense of loss
which made her pursue the search; He well knew why she wept
and whom she sought. He did not ask because He had need of
information; it was for her sake that He asked. And His repeti-

tion of the angels' question could be readily understood, for her tears made her grief self-evident. But His further question was a significant revelation, for how could a stranger have known the real nature of her hidden longing? It was addressed to her in a way that went much beyond an expression of sympathy, and the words would imply that He knew the cause of her grief.

The sole object of His questions was to prepare Mary for the grand discovery which would surpass all her desires, and His words were meant to startle her with a sense of mild surprise. They would help to dispel her grief with a mental awakening to the fact that she was in search of the Living among the dead. But this purpose was concealed from Mary, and her response to the questions was a totally different affair.

"She, supposing him to be the gardener, saith unto him, Sir, if thou have borne him hence, tell me where thou hast laid him, and I will take him away." Mary had heard His voice and seen His face, but knew Him not. She offered no answer to His question, for a new thought had flashed into her mind. It was just like a spark, for it kindled a gleam of hope in her darkness. She could only surmise that this Stranger was the keeper of the garden, and this led her to think that the body had perhaps been removed from the family sepulcher. Perhaps it had only been placed there by Joseph for the Sabbath; it might have been transferred elsewhere once the Sabbath was at an end. This thought promptly inspired her next moving appeal: "Sir, if thou have borne him hence, tell me where thou hast laid him, and I will take him away."

Mary addressed herself to the Stranger with this passionate entreaty as one who was at the end of human resource; but love made her blindly declare that if she could find Him she would bear Him away. Her heart was so full that she did not speak of Him by name; she was content to employ a pronoun which would assume that the Stranger knew whom she meant. There is such an artless simplicity in this appeal that it recalls the words of the distracted Shulamite in her appeal to the city watchmen: "Saw ye *him* whom my soul loveth?" (Song of Solomon 3:3). The cry of Job was the tacit cry of her soul: "Oh that I knew where I might find *him!*" (Job 23:3). She knew not that she stood in the presence of the living Saviour while her strength was absorbed in a vain search for His mortal body.

Mary had been strangely misled in that search for the Prince of Life among the dead. But no one who reads this moving story can be impervious to its beauty or its pathos. Hers was a love which could not be destroyed, and its character was shown in her interview with the angels. The sight of an angel had been enough to fill both the guard of soldiers (Matthew 28:4) and the band of women (Mark 16:8) with the utmost alarm. They were startled by the awe of glory which the angel presence would create or impart. But she saw the angels without dismay, without surprise, for fear had been banished from her mind by the power of love.

There had been time for her sorrow to fix itself with absorbing interest and exclusive sympathy on the double fact of an empty tomb and a vanished body, and this unexplained mystery left no room for other thoughts in her mind. Thus she did not even wonder, much less tremble, at the sight and sound of angel beings. They had been messengers of gladness and ministers of comfort to the other women, for they had come "as servants to fellow-servants," bound with them by ties of love and worship to the Lord of Glory.[5] But their sympathy was as little able to bring relief as their appearance had been to cause alarm. Her heart was filled with one consuming interest, and nothing would content her while she knew not where they had laid Him.

The appearance of the angels did not overawe; the interview with the Stranger did not enlighten. Such love was to receive its own reward, not in the discovery of the Dead but in the revelation of the Lord. Mary's experience ought to convince us that human sorrow may be softened with a good hope through grace: for when the Lord Himself stoops to ask us of our sorrows, their comfort has begun.[6]

---

[5]H. C. G. Moule, *Jesus and the Resurrection* (1905), p. 51.
[6]*Ibid.*, p. 56.

Chapter 32

THE RISEN MASTER

Jesus saith unto her, Mary. She turned herself, and said unto him, Rabboni; which is to say, Master — JOHN 20:16.

It was appropriate that the Risen Saviour should show Himself alive for the first time in the early morning on the first day of a new week. Mary had first set out for the tomb while it was still dark, and the sun would not yet be far above the long eastern skyline. But the darkness of the world was a match for her gloom when she came, while the brightness of the day was no match at all for her joy when she left. She thought that the light of the world had gone out in darkness on the day of the cross and it had left her in a state of near despair. The mother of Jesus had felt His death as though it had been a sword thrust through her own soul. The disciples were bewildered and knew not where to turn or what to do.

But Mary was shattered with the knowledge that the Master was dead; she felt as though she were deprived of faith and hope alike by a single crushing stroke of fortune. She was perilously close to despair as she lingered in the garden on that Resurrection morning. Sorrow which paid no heed to the angels held her eyes when she stood in His presence. She saw His face and heard His voice, but knew not that it was Jesus. She could only suppose that He was a servant, only address Him as if He were a stranger. That great sorrow was to observe the truth until it pleased the Lord to make Himself known in living reality. There was but one word from His lips, and that veil of misconception was torn away. "Jesus saith unto her, Mary. She turned herself, and saith unto him, Rabboni; which is to say, Master."

There is exquisite tenderness in that word of revelation and the cry of recognition; her sorrow was transformed with a flash of supreme delight. Details still follow each other with rapid and thrilling simplicity,"[1] and the study of this beautiful narrative still evokes a spirit of wonder and worship.

The first half of this verse records the word of self-revelation: "Jesus saith unto her, Mary." We do not know where the Lord was during the time which had elapsed since His Resurrection, nor can we tell whence He came in order to stand before Mary. We know that He could appear or vanish at will; we know that His movements in His risen body were instantaneous and super-natural. Thus His visible appearance near the mouth of the tomb may have been due to a sudden advent like that in the upper room when evening had come (John 20:19).

Mary did not see Him until she turned away from the angels and would not be aware of the mysterious way in which He had come. He was willing to let her think for the moment that He was the keepr of the garden, for He did not wish to reveal Himself by a dramatic arrival so much as by direct revelation. It gave Him time to mark her tears and read her thoughts, to speak to her and to hear her voice in reply. He meant to make Himself known to her in a few moments, but He could not withhold the truth for one moment longer once He heard her pathetic enquiry. It made Him feel just as Joseph had felt when he could no longer restrain himself in the presence of his brethren. He was moved to the depth of His being, and He could find only one word that would voice His feelings.

He spoke in the familiar dialect of Nazareth and Galilee, and with one word touched the chords of her heart: "Mary." This was just the Aramaic equivalent for a name in common demand. It indicates the medium of His conversation with disciples and companions in the days of freedom when He dwelt in their midst. He had fallen back with perfect insight on the vernacular form of her name so as to stir up her dormant recollection, and that word of personal sympathy would be far more telling than a formal style of address. He knew that this homely appeal would be the most direct way to her heart, and the very accent of His voice would thrill with loving kindness as He called her by name: "Mary."

---

[1]H. C. G. Moule, *Jesus and the Resurrection* (1905), p. 49.

"Jesus saith unto her, Mary." The most tender love was concentrated in that exclamation; it was only one word, but that word was her name. No word could have been more revealing and it broke down all the barriers of reserve or inhibition at once. There was no need for her to ask nor for Him to explain who He was as in the case of Saul of Tarsus; His whole voice would declare what no words could so well express: "I am Jesus" (Acts 9:5).

Mary had heard His voice before, but knew it not. He had addressed her just as the angels had done, but she had remained heedless. He had made use of an ordinary form of salutation and had called her "Woman." There was absolute courtesy in that form of address; it was a word which lacked nothing in grace or in kindness. But it fell on deaf ears, for it was the kind of word that anyone might have used. He had spoken then with the voice of a stranger as He called her "Woman"; He was speaking now with the voice of a shepherd, for He called her "Mary."

Jesus called her by her name in a way that would make the love of His heart and the tone of His voice blend in true appeal. The tender longing and vivid accent in that word would remind her as nothing else could ever do of the Lord who had redeemed her from all her sorrow. It was just one brief word, but that word was enough to tell her all. It would make the truth shine through her darkness, for no other voice that she had ever heard could call her by her name as He did: "Mary."

There was infinite tenderness in that unexpected word of revelation. Perhaps no one had stood in more need of reassurance after the day of the cross than Mary and Peter, and there was a personal appearance to each of them on the very day on which He rose from the dead. In the morning He revealed Himself to Mary before He appeared to her other companions; in the evening He revealed Himself to Peter before He appeared to the other disciples. No one knew the cause and nature of their sorrow better than He, and His whole heart went out to them in their need and trouble.

Thus what pity, what kindness, what ineffable love and longing, express themselves in that one word, "Mary." Not a glimmer of hope, not a thought of resurrection, had shone through the darkness which had possessed her mind. But now the word that told of His conquest of death also told her of His undying interest in her own soul: and this revelation of His loving kindness would surpass even the discovery of His risen glory.

That one word from His lips is all the proof we need that the Shepherd of the sheep whom God brought again from the dead still knows each one who belongs to Him. He that tells the number of the stars and calls them by their names (Psalm 147:4) also knows the members of His flock and calls them by their names (Isaiah 40:26). Every name in the Book of Life is like a seal on the wall of His heart (Song of Solomon 8:6) or like a scar on the palm of His hand (Isaiah 49:16). And on the day of His final revelation to all whom He will raise from the dead He will call them by name just as He called Mary of old: "Jesus saith unto her, Mary."

The next half of this verse records the word of glad recognition: "She turned herself, and saith unto him, Rabboni; which is to say, Master." Nothing in this chapter is more true and lifelike than the unobtrusive details which trace Mary's movements. We learn first how she stood outside the tomb weeping, and then stooped down to look within as though she would see the place where the Lord had lain. There was a brief conversation with the angels, and then "she turned herself back" (John 20:14). This brought her face to face with one whom she knew not; she could only suppose that He was a workman in the garden. A gleam of hope flashed through her mind as she wondered if He could aid her in her search for the missing body, but it seems to have died away almost as soon as it had been kindled. This seems to have caused her to turn away as a woman would turn from a stranger, except for the fact that she turned with an air of listless disappointment.

Then before she could resume her watch near the mouth of the tomb, she heard Him speak again. It was only one brief word that fell from His lips, but that word was her name. The whole tone of His voice would touch the chords of true response; there was music for her in each accent of that familiar utterance. "She turned herself" for the third time (John 20:16), but this time with instant recognition. There stood the Lord, and she knew Him! She was moved to the depth of her being, and she could find only one word that would voice her feelings. She spoke in the familiar dialect of Magdala and Galilee, and His one word she met with her one word: "Rabboni." This was just a local variation for a term of common respect. John affirms that she spoke "in Hebrew" (John 20:16, R.V.) and went on to add in Greek the simple explanation: "which is to say, Master!"

Mary had fallen back with ready instinct on her native patois as if to match the way in which He had spoken her name, and that cry of personal submission would be far more welcome than a formal style of recognition. She knew that this homely address would be the most direct way to His heart, and the very accent of her voice would thrill with loving rapture as she hailed Him by name: "Rabboni."

"She . . . saith unto him, Rabboni." The most ardent love was concentrated in that exclamation; it was only one word, but that word was His name. No word could have been more expressive, and it called forth all the gratitude of worship and adoration at once. Mary had no time to pause and reflect how much might be implied by that cry of recognition, but it was the cry of one whose faith had just been rescued from the verge of despair. She had thought of Jesus as her Master ever since the day when He had released her from demon control. She could trace the only peace which she had ever known from the time when those evil spirits had been expelled. But His death on the cross had made her feel as though her heart had once again been left vacant, and she may have feared lest seven times those seven spirits, worse by far than those which had been expelled, should now seek to reclaim her soul.

Thus when Mary found herself face to face with Jesus, there was unspeakable relief in her cry: "Rabboni." The strict meaning of the dialectal form of that word was "My Master,"[2] and the explanation which John adds in Greek makes it clear that it was the word which a pupil would use of his teacher.[3] Mary poured out her heart in that customary title: it was reverent; it was dignified. But it was the only time that it was ever used of the Lord after that first Resurrection morning because it fell short of the full sense of Lordship. Nevertheless Mary used the word with the most ample meaning it could command and it would call to mind the words of the Saviour Himself: "Ye call me Master and Lord: and ye say well; for so I am" (John 13:13).

---

[2] See Alfred Plummer, St. John, p. 341.
[3] B. F. Westcott, The Gospel According to St. John (1908), p. 292.

It was just one brief word, but that word was enough to tell Him all. It would make the truth shine through her worship, for no other voice that He had ever heard had called Him by that name as she did: "Rabboni."

There was passionate devotion in that spontaneous cry of recognition. We feel at once that it has so much in common with the similar utterance which burst from the lips of Thomas. Mary's failure to recognize the meaning of the empty tomb was akin to his failure to understand the promise of the resurrection, and the discovery of the truth in each case was a thrilling revelation which would surpass the wildest dream. It found Mary in the same mind and mood that were to fire Thomas with that cry of unaffected adoration: "My Lord and my God" (John 20:28). No one knew the depth and fullness of His mercy better than they, and their whole heart went out to Him in His praise and glory.

What wonder, what rapture, what ineffable love and worship express themselves in that one word, "Rabboni"! Mary was attached to Him by ties that would command the love of her heart in more than ordinary measure. She had been a human shipwreck, and it was He who had restored her to normal freedom. He had crowned her with His goodness, and all the love pent up within her heart found voice in that cry of recognition.

That one word from Mary's lips is all the proof we need that the sheep of His pasture may claim Him as their guide on each side of death's dark valley. We were as sheep going astray, but we have now returned to Him as the Shepherd of souls (I Peter 2:25). He is that Good Shepherd whose voice we hear and whom we know (John 10:27), and Him we would follow in all places whither He goes (Revelation 14:4). And on the day of our perfect recognition of Him whom we shall see face to face we shall hail Him by name, just as Mary hailed Him of old: "She . . . saith unto him, Rabboni."

We may well ask whether any but a Jew of the first century, born in Palestine, a disciple of Jesus, a companion of Mary, would have preserved such a detail as the Galilean variation of her word of recognition.[4] But the primary interest in this mov-

---

[4]Alfred Plummer, *St. John* (Cambridge Greek Testament for Schools, 1882), p. 341.

ing story is the way in which that recognition was brought about. The word *woman* as a form of address could not evoke more than the word *Sir* in reply; it was the name *Mary* which at once called forth the cry of *Master!* Mary's cry of recognition has always been welcome to those who would greet Him in the spirit of true discipleship.

Thus George Herbert, the poet and mystic, loved to employ that word. He was appointed to the cure of Bemerton in 1630, and the solemn pledge with which he entered upon his work was thus expressed in one of his letters: "I am so proud of His service that I will always call Him *Jesus, my Master.*" The same thought is found in his quaint little poem called "The Odour":

> How sweetly doth "My Master" sound! "My Master"!
>   As ambergris leaves a rich scent
>   unto the taster,
>   So do these words a sweet content,
> An orientall fragrancie, "My Master"!

And so too John Wesley, the preacher and evangelist, loved to use that word. It was at the Moravian meeting in Aldersgate Street in 1738 that he felt his heart strangely warmed and that he put his trust in Christ and Christ alone for salvation. The change wrought in his soul that night found voice in the words which he wrote in his Journal the next morning: "The moment I awaked, *Jesus, Master,* was in my heart and in my mouth." Blessed shall they be who in the Resurrection on the last day can lift up their eyes and say from their hearts: "Rabboni, my Master!"

Chapter 33

THE ELDER BROTHER

Jesus saith unto her, Touch me not; for I am not yet ascended
to my Father: but go to my brethren, and say unto them, I
ascend unto my Father, and your Father; and to my God, and
your God. Mary Magdalene came and told the disciples that she
had seen the Lord, and that he had spoken these things unto her.

JOHN 20:17, 18.

THE FIRST revelation of the Risen Saviour was in circumstances
which were all in glorious harmony with the very thought of
resurrection. He appeared to Mary in the shelter of a garden,
and it was just after the dawn of a new spring morning. He
called her by her name; she knew Him by His voice. His one
word had been met by her one word, and His tender greeting
had been matched by the joyful welcome of hers. The brief
Aramaic form of address in which He spoke her name had been
answered by the vernacular form of reply in which she voiced
His name.

John does not enlarge on this scene in detail, but it is clear
that the relief and rapture in Mary's heart were forced to seek
an outlet in open and ardent worship. The Face which had been
so furrowed with pain was now alight with the glory of God, and
the Voice which had been muffled in death had come to life with
the cadence of immortality. One brief word of adoring gratitude
was not enough for the pent-up feelings that struggled for release;
her love yearned for tangible expression and sought immediate
demonstration. It would seem that she must have cast herself
down at His feet, ready to clasp them in fervent embrace. She
sought to lay hold of them with the touch that feels, as though
she would assure herself of His reality.

Mary was moved by the same impulse which had prompted

213

the cry of the Shulamite: "I found him whom my soul loveth: I held him, and would not let him go" (Song of Solomon 3:4). It would express the strength and the weakness of her love with a force which He was bound to check. But the words of restraint have always seemed strangely austere, and their meaning has long been in dispute. John's record forgets all about the angels as it moves on to the climax, and they vanish from mind and view to leave Mary alone with the Master in the crisis of her experience.

The first command seems to strike a note of austere restraint: "Jesus saith unto her, Touch me not; for I am not yet ascended to my Father." Mary doubtless heard those words with a sense of sharp surprise, for they surprise us still; and the reference to the Ascension as the reason why that touch was forbidden would only increase the mystery.

It is not as though it were wrong for men to touch the Lord in His Resurrection Body, for we are told in the case of others that they were allowed to touch Him without reserve. Within a few moments of this conversation, when He met the other women by the wayside, He freely permitted them to touch Him: "They came, and held him by the feet, and worshipped him" (Matthew 28:9). The same evening, when He revealed Himself to the astonished disciples in the closed room, He gladly invited them to touch Him: "Handle me, and see; for a spirit hath not flesh and bones as ye see me have" (Luke 24:39). Eight days later, when He appeared to them again, He plainly commanded Thomas to put out his hand and touch Him: "Reach hither thy finger, and behold my hands; and reach hither thy hand, and thrust it into my side" (John 20:27). Such facts rule out any idea that His body could not be touched in its risen glory. Perhaps for that very reason we might have thought that this was a case when we should expect words of invitation rather than of prohibition.

The phrase "Touch me not" is quite inadequate, and it creates a false idea. The whole situation can be made clear by a correct reading of the Greek text: "Do not keep on clinging to me" This verb in the present tense would convey a plain command to stop doing something which in fact she was then doing. It did not mean that she ought not to have touched Him at all, that she was wrong to have held Him in that act of worship. But it would not allow her to prolong the moment of contact; it would prevent her from continued endeavor to feel or hold His limbs.

Mary had fallen down at His feet, but she must now resume her place. She had clasped them with an eager embrace, but she must now withdraw her hand. She who had been so much beyond others in her devotion was not forbidden to do what those others were yet to do, but once she had touched Him and made sure that He was alive indeed, she was gently restrained.

"Jesus saith unto her, Touch me not; for I am not yet ascended to my Father." There was quite a simple reason which might prompt those words of restraint. Mary, a warmhearted and impulsive woman, had passed through a severe emotional crisis and was flushed with glorious excitement in her discovery of the Resurrection. She was prostrate at His feet, clinging to each limb, perhaps clasping and kissing them as though she could not cease. Others might touch Him in order to prove that His presence was a reality; hers was the touch of one who would not let Him go. This display of her feeling was too demonstrative and too preoccupied with the humanity of her risen Master.

John only employs the verb this once, but its regular occurrence in the other gospels shows that it was often used to describe the touch of the lightest finger. Thus the Saviour was asked to touch the eyes of the blind man (Mark 8:22), and the woman was moved to touch the fringe of His garment (Matthew 9:21).[1] This is enough to show how wisely and kindly the Lord Jesus phrased this command. There is not the least sign that He spoke in reproof, as though she had failed in reverence or humility. But she must not go on clinging to Him, must not touch Him at all, lest the wonder of that holy hour should run to waste in misguided emotion.

But His reference to the Ascension affords the main reason why she was to refrain from such contact with His risen body. The words are not without difficulty, and the attempt has been made to explain their real meaning in the following paraphrase: "Do not cling to Me now, for the time has not yet come when I must ascend; there will be time enough to make contact with Me before I go away, but not just now."

But the whole drift of the text is against such a meaning and lies in quite another direction. There is nothing to suggest that

[1]H. C. G. Moule, *Jesus and the Resurrection* (1905), pp. 64, 65.

Mary ever did have such an experience; this was the one momentous interview which she enjoyed, and the words of restraint were meant to make her see that the Resurrection was bound to impose a sense of reserve. This was a new factor which she had not had time to grasp, nor was it an easy lesson for her or for others to learn. They had only known Him as the Son of Man who had dwelt among them in humble manhood, but the hour was coming when they would see His face no more.

After the first tender word of self-disclosure, He went on to reveal the change which was at hand. He would ascend to the Father — that would be the sequel to the Resurrection. Nor was that all: it would condition the new kind of fellowship which would thenceforth exist between the Lord and His people. Therefore He would have her cease to cling to Him with mortal embrace, for He would soon ascend beyond the sight and touch of sense and time. Mary was told that she could no longer live in contact with Him as in His days on earth; she would have to commune with Him in the sphere where spirit meets with spirit. The touch of flesh in the material world of human experience would now yield to the touch of faith in that other world of spirit relationship.

The next command serves to strike the note of tender constraint: "But go to my brethren, and say unto them, I ascend unto my Father, and your Father; and to my God, and your God." These were words of gentle wisdom for Mary and of thoughtful kindness for the disciples. Mary had been highly favored as the first to see the Risen Master and she naturally wished to linger in His presence (cf. Matthew 17:4). It was the kind of hour which could never return, an hour at the gate of heaven itself.

Mary would have been glad to prolong that hour, pouring out her heart in love and worship. But that was not to be; the joy that filled her heart was to find its proper outlet in an act of service. She must rise and run on her way with news for those who were yet in doubt or darkness. She who had borne tidings of the vanished body must now be the herald of His Resurrection. He would not show Himself to those others before nightfall, but their need was never out of His mind. Almost His first thought was for them, and this message was phrased with a peculiar affection.

Jesus spoke of them as He had never done before; He called them His *brethren*. It would have been a word of great kindness in the best of circumstances; it was a word of exceeding grace in view of recent events. Joseph did not disown Jacob's sons as brethren in spite of their hatred and cruelty; nor did Jesus disdain to call these men brethren in spite of their distrust and desertion. It was a new title, and that title, chosen at that time, would tell them as no other message ever could, that His heart was full of love. *Brethren!* He was not ashamed to call them brethren (Hebrews 2:11). He would forgive their sin and would revive their hope, for they were His brethren in spite of all.

"But go to my brethren, and say unto them, I ascend unto my Father, and your Father; and to my God, and your God." It is remarkable that this message refers to His return to the Father rather than His recovery of life. He did not say, "I have risen," but "I ascend." The fact of the Resurrection was not ignored; it was subordinate to a larger idea. The Lord meant to apprise them of the fact that He had not risen again so that He might remain with them on earth. Resurrection was the first step in His exaltation, and He had burst the bands of death so that He might return to the glory which had been His before the worlds were made. But this was a prospect which might perplex His disciples and companions more than ever. Therefore Mary was sent to break the news in these words of cheer and consolation.

The verb changes in tense from the perfect to the present; from "I have not yet ascended" to "I am ascending." It was as though He would anticipate the change that was yet to take place, as though He would regard the change as now, in fact, begun (cf. Luke 24:44). But He was to ascend to their Father as well as His Father, to their God as well as His God; for their union with Him as His brethren gave them a share in the rights of sonship.

However, Jesus maintained His own unique status by means of the pronouns which He employed. It was "*My* Father and *your* Father," not "*Our* Father"; it was "*My* God and *your* God," not "*Our* God." And we ought to mark the order in which the two titles occur as well as the pronouns which go with them. It was in the very spirit of the Messianic saying: "He shall cry unto me, Thou art my father, my God" (Psalm 89:26). The great fundamental relationship in pre-existence and incarnation was that of the Son who communed with God as His Father. The word *Father,* and often *My Father,* as a form of address was in constant use by the Son of Man, but was unknown to prophet or psalmist.

On the other hand, He never employed the phrase *My God* in His normal approach to the Father. It had been wrung from Him in the cry of desolation (Matthew 27:46), and it was to occur in His promise to them that overcome (Revelation 3:12). But this is the only other place where that great title is found on the lips of the Son of Man. The whole phrase, "*My Father . . . and . . . my God,*" is preserved in the compound title of Pauline and Petrine usage: "The God and Father of our Lord Jesus Christ" (II Corinthians 11:31; I Peter 1:3).

Thus we expect to find that the order was My Father and then My God in the case of the Son of Man; but we might think that it would be reversed in the experience of His brethren. The true original relationship of God to man is that of the Maker to the creature rather than that of a father to his children. No one ever spoke to Him as Father, still less as My Father, until the Son of Man taught men when they pray to say "Our Father" (Luke 11:2).

But the Risen Saviour looked on them as brethren and taught them to lift up their eyes as sons rather than as servants. They would have the witness of His Spirit with their spirit, and they would learn to cry as He Himself had done, "*Abba, Father*" (Romans 8:15; Mark 14:36). The whole message would tell them that old things had passed away, and that grace would make all things new. It would tell them what He had told Mary: He had risen again, but earth could not hold Him. He would appear to them, but He would not be with them now as in the days of old. The interval of transition would pass, and then He would ascend beyond their sight.

Such language almost partakes of a covenant character, and is like the divine reverse of Ruth's great vow (Ruth 1:16). He had risen again as the First-born of His brethren, and he would now go to prepare a place for them. All that God the Father had been to Him as the First-born He would also be to them as brethren; for His Father was their Father and His God was their God for time and for eternity.

John rounds off the whole beautiful narrative with an account of her response: "Mary Magdalene came and told the disciples

hat she had seen the Lord, and that he had spoken these things
into her." Mary had done much for the Son of Man in the days
of His flesh, but it was in things which she had shared with
others. She had followed Him from Galilee and had ministered
o Him from her substance; but she was not alone in that devo-
ion or that ministry (Luke 8:3). Other women had stood beside
her at the cross or had gone with her to the tomb: they had
followed Him to the end and they were to find Him almost as
soon as she (Matthew 28:9). But His appearance to her before
His appearance to others was an act of supreme kindness, and
He conferred great joy on her when He chose her as the bearer
of this message.

The Greek text is far more vivid than the English in the way
hat it throws emphasis on her promptitude. John says in effect
that Mary *cometh telling*, and her words in direct speech must
have been "I have seen the Lord" (cf. John 20:25).[2] John does
not refer to its effect on the discouraged disciples, for he was not
among them when she came. But the Markan Fragment is most
lifelike: "And she went and told them that had been with him,
as they mourned and wept. And they, when they had heard
that he was alive, and had been seen of her, believed not" (Mark
16:10, 11). Luke confirms this in words which combine her
news with that of the other women: "And their words seemed
to them as idle tales, and they believed them not" (Luke 24:11).

Mary passes out of historic perception with this message, and
the unbelief of the disciples could not dim the luster of her reward. The Lord Jesus gave the other women also a message for
the disciples: they were to tell them to go into Galilee, for there
they would see Him (Matthew 28:10). But Mary spoke neither
of Galilee nor Judaea, for her message would point their minds
to the right hand of God. It would direct their thoughts away
from the deserted tomb in Joseph's garden to the ascended
throne in highest glory. It would bid them in mind and heart
thither ascend to meet Him in spirit as His brethren in the presence of the Father.

---

[2] B. F. Westcott, *The Gospel According to St. John* (1908), p. 293.

PART FOUR

THEN
CAME
JESUS

Chapter 34

THE THREE TRAVELERS

And, behold, two of them went that same day to a village
called Emmaus, which was from Jerusalem about threescore
furlongs. And they talked together of all these things which had
happened. And it came to pass, that, while they communed together and reasoned, Jesus himself drew near, and went with
them. But their eyes were holden that they should not know
him. And he said unto them, What manner of communications
are these that ye have one to another, as ye walk, and are sad?
And the one of them, whose name was Cleopas, answering said
unto him, Art thou only a stranger in Jerusalem, and hast not
known the things which are come to pass there in these days?
— LUKE 24:13-18

THE fine literary taste of the French critic, Ernest Renan, led
to his claim that the gospel of Luke is the most beautiful narrative which has ever been penned,[1] and there is a special beauty
in this final chapter which makes it one of the finest treasures
which that gospel contains.[2] There is lifelike insight in what
is told just as there is artless reality in the telling. It is full of
movement, and yet without a trace of haste or strain; the facts
speak for themselves in a narrative that is luminous in its simplicity. Mark has the barest outline of this beautiful narrative
(Mark 16:12, 13); it is like his laconic summary of the Temptation episode (Mark 1:12, 13).[3] But Luke wrote with the instinct
of an artist, and his account is one of the gems of literature. We
may still tread that road in the spirit of quiet meditation and
feel the strong pulse of human appeal. We are aware of the
agitation and bewilderment and uncertainty in the minds of the

[1]J. N. Geldenhuys, *Commentary on the Gospel of Luke* (1956), p. 29.
[2]H. C. G. Moule, *Emmaus* (1912), pp. 19, 23.
[3]R. C. Trench, *Studies in the Gospels* (2nd ed., 1867), p. 318.

two disciple travelers; we are no less aware of the intensely personal interest in a genuine personal dilemma on the part of their quite unbidden Companion. His gentleness and courtesy, His insight and concern, His tact and skill are drawn with such strength and restraint as He held them for mile after mile in earnest conversation that our hearts like theirs are strangely warmed with the fire of His resurrection love and glory.[4]

The first object in this narrative is to introduce the travelers on the road to Emmaus: "And, behold, two of them went that same day to a village called Emmaus, which was from Jerusalem about threescore furlongs." Luke begins with a word which often prefaced something new and unexpected (see, e.g., Luke 1:20, 31, 36; 2:25).[5] He would have us behold, observe, take note, of what he was about to write: two men who had been with the disciples were now on their way from Jerusalem to the village of Emmaus. We know very little of these two men, and still less of the reason for their journey. One of the two remains anonymous, but the other is called Cleopas; perhaps he was known to Luke and told him the story. Latham suggests that they belonged to Judaea like Nicodemus and Joseph of Arimathaea. They had the air of men who were going to a fixed home; they could invite a guest to stay the night and the evening meal was ready for them. They did not display the same strong personal affection for Him as the disciples from Galilee; they mourned His loss as a Messianic Leader rather than as their own beloved Master. They did not share that quick insight which love imparts; they knew not that it was Jesus even when their hearts were burning.[6] They had held no prominence in His ministry, but they were in intimate fellowship with the disciples: they were aware of what was in their minds in the morning, and they knew where to look for them in the evening. But they had left Jerusalem some time on "that same day," the day which had dawned with resurrection, and they were on the road to a village which was "about three score furlongs" away, about seven miles in distance. It was not a long walk, and would only require two or three hours to complete at leisure. Evening had not yet come, though the day was far spent when they arrived (Luke 24:29).

---

[4]H. C. G. Moule, *Emmaus* (1912), p. 25.

[5]Alfred Plummer, *St. Luke* (4th ed., 1906), p. 551.

[6]Henry Latham, *The Risen Master* (1907), p. 102.

There was time for a meal, but "the same hour" they rose up to return, and they were in Jerusalem once more in time for the evening appearance. Perhaps it was early in the afternoon when the walk to Emmaus began.

"And they talked together of all these things which had happened." Perhaps they had gone to Jerusalem to share in the Passover and the Feast of Unleavened Bread; they may have known that the Lord was to eat it there with His disciples. But we wonder why they should have left the city at the hour when they did on that "third day" (Luke 24:21). They had no faith in the reality of the Resurrection, and they did not wait for the solution of their problems. Perhaps it was "fear of the Jews" which made them leave (John 20:19); the absence of Thomas may have been for the same reason (John 20:24). The element of disruption was already at work among the disciples; they had begun to disband and would soon be scattered "every man to his own" (John 16:32). These two men were thus "not without grave fault;"[7] they were walking on in darkness when they should have looked for Him Who is the light of the world. It was natural that they should talk together of all that had happened — the death of Him to Whom they looked as the Hope of Israel and the mysterious fact that the tomb in which He had been laid was now empty. They were absorbed in this eager conversation; more than one word implies that they were in earnest debate. They "reasoned" (Luke 24:15) or "questioned" (R.V.) with each other, and their feelings were so deeply engaged that they showed up in "their outward gesture and mien."[8] Their whole attitude in this discussion is a revelation of the secret struggle between hope and fear which went on that day among the now thoroughly bewildered disciples.

"And it came to pass, that, while they communed together and reasoned, Jesus himself drew near and went with them." They were so lost in their conversation about "these things" that they took no notice as a stranger drew near. We can no more say whence He came than we can tell where He went when He left them: but His approach had none of the dramatic qualities of His ultimate withdrawal. He "drew near"; He came from behind: for they assumed that He must have come from Jerusa-

---

[7] R. C. Trench, p. 318.

[8] R. C. Trench, p. 320.

lem as they had done (Luke 24:18). He caught up with them on the road and heard something of their conversation before they were aware of His presence. But His coming was not accidental; He drew near and went with them on purpose. He knew even before He came that they were in the grip of bewilderment, uncertainty and disappointment, and when He joined them He was moved by the look of settled sadness on their faces. Just as He had come to Mary in her tears and sorrow, so He now drew near to these men in their gloom and perplexity. Humble men and obscure enough they may have been, but He was now to give them His time as freely as once He had given it to John and Andrew (John 1:39). Who can tell what power their sadness had in drawing the Man of Sorrows to their side,[9] or what comfort would fill their hearts as He drew near and went with them?

The next object in this narrative is to introduce the dialogue on the road to Emmaus: "But their eyes were holden that they should not know him." The nonrecognition of the Lord on the part of these two men need cause us no surprise; it has indeed all the marks of sober reality. But we ought to observe the way in which the two evangelists account for it. Mark stresses the fact that there was some change in His general appearance: "He appeared *in another form* unto two of them, as they walked, and went into the country" (Mark 16:12). Luke stresses the fact that there was some kind of restraint on their eyes so that they did not know who He was: "Their eyes *were holden* that they should not know Him." It seems right to conclude that both factors were at work in their minds. On the one hand, He may not have been so readily recognized in His resurrection body: there may have been enough change in actual appearance to cause momentary hesitation (cf. Luke 24:37). On the other hand, they may have been so preoccupied with their own thoughts that this would in itself explain their nonrecognition: it would never occur to them that this Stranger was He of Whom they were talking, and they did not even guess from His face or His voice that it was Jesus (cf. John 20:14; 21:4). Mary was so absorbed in her sorrow that she at once formed the impression that He was a gardener, and they were so immersed in their perplexity that they at once reached the conclusion that He was

---

[9]W. Hanna, *Our Lord's Life on Earth* (1882), p. 596.

a traveler. Thus their eyes were "spellbound,"[10] and they did not know Him.

"And he said unto them, what manner of communications are these that ye have one to another as ye walk and are sad?" Perhaps the two men fell silent when they became aware that a stranger had drawn level with them; perhaps they were still so intent on their conversation that they failed to notice Him at their side. Thus it remained for Him to break in on their thoughts with a question which was meant to explore their hearts. It was in this way that He had once asked the Twelve that leading question: "Whom do men say that I the Son of man am?" (Matthew 16:13). And the question which He asked was meant to register sympathy and to elicit confidence: "What communications are these that ye have one with another, as ye walk?" (R.V.). But his words took them by surprise and they at once came to a stop: "And they stood still, looking sad" (R.V.); "They halted, their faces full of gloom" (N.E.B.). The language is picturesque and hard to improve.[11] They had stopped short as if under arrest, and the look on their faces told its story. They were resentful at His intrusion in their affairs and could hardly conceal an element of suspicion at His purpose.[12] At the same time, they wore such a downcast look of gloom and sorrow that a courteous inquiry was the natural consequence. The word rendered in the Revised Version "looking sad" is only found once elsewhere in the New Testament. That was in His remark with regard to fasting: "Be not . . . *of a sad countenance*" (Matthew 6:16). Henry Latham helps to catch the idea with his picture of two Royalists leaving London on foot after the execution of Charles I on January 30th, 1649; they might well be suspicious of a stranger, affected by his question, full of perplexity and sunk in gloom.[13]

"And the one of them, whose name was Cleopas, answering said unto him, Art thou only a stranger in Jerusalem, and hast not known the things which are come to pass there in these days?" Cleopas broke the silence, but his reply shows that he

---

[10]H. B. Swete, *The Appearances of Our Lord After the Passion* (1915), p. 22.

[11]R. C. Trench, p. 320, footnote 2.

[12]H. C. G. Moule, *Emmaus* (1912), p. 40.

[13]Henry Latham, *The Risen Master* (1907), pp. 107, 108.

was by no means pleased. Why should one who was a stranger accost them and meddle in their sorrow?[14] His language in reply was cold, curt and abrupt, and it mainly voiced his surprise that any such question should have been asked at all. This element is underlined in the Revised Version: "Dost thou alone sojourn in Jerusalem and not know the things which are come to pass there in these days?" The pronoun *thou* is emphatic in virtue of its position, but the exact bearing of the word *only* (A.V.) or *alone* (R.V.) is open to some slight doubt.[15] It may imply that He was "the only stranger" in Jerusalem who did not know these things: "Are you *the only person* staying in Jerusalem not to know?" (N.E.B.). Or it may mean that He was "a solitary stranger" who was so withdrawn from things around Him that He did not know what had happened: "Dwellest thou *in solitude* at Jerusalem . . . that thou dost not know?"[16] The point is summed up by Plummer in the alternative readings: "Dost *thou alone dwell* at Jerusalem" or "Dost *thou dwell alone* at Jerusalem?"[17] But each alternative reveals a touch of scorn as well as of surprise for such a question and such a stranger.

Such words on the part of Cleopas show how easily a man who is inclined not to believe will form a wrong mental image even in a situation where he is face to face with truth. He could only think of the Lord Jesus as a stranger, but did this mean that He was a stranger in the city as well? There could only be one topic for their conversation, but did this mean that this Stranger would not know of the things which had happened? Cleopas failed to recognize that a stranger might know these things, yet might not know what they had been talking about. However, his reply was an unselfconscious testimony to two great facts. It proves that the eyes of all who were in Jerusalem were on the Lord Jesus when He died on the cross; this was not something "done in a corner" (Acts 26:26). The facts of His death were known to all who were in Jerusalem; men could never pretend that it did not take place. And it also proves how the things which had happened domin-

---

[14]R. C. Trench, *Studies In The Gospels* (2nd ed., 1867), pp. 320, 321.

[15]Alfred Plummer, *St. Luke* (4th ed., 1906), p. 553.

[16]R. C. Trench, p. 321.

[17]Alfred Plummer, *St. Luke* (4th ed., 1906), p. 553.

ated the minds of the bewildered disciples; it led them to assume that even a stranger would know just what they were thinking. So it was with Mary in the garden; she spoke of "Him" as though even a stranger would forthwith know to whom she referred (John 20:15). There are attractive elements in this single-minded discipleship which we must not ignore. It was to such men that Jesus himself drew near, and in the light of His presence, all their doubt and darkness were soon to be dissolved.

Chapter 35

THE TWO DISCIPLES

And he said unto them, What things? And they said unto him, Concerning Jesus of Nazareth, which was a prophet mighty in deed and word before God and all the people: and how the chief priests and our rulers delivered him to be condemned to death, and have crucified him. But we trusted that it had been he which should have redeemed Israel: and beside all this, to day is the third day since these things were done. Yea, and certain women also of our company made us astonished, which were early at the sepulchre; and when they found not his body, they came, saying, that they had also seen a vision of angels, which said that he was alive. And certain of them which were with us went to the sepulchre, and found it even so as the women had said: but him they saw not. — LUKE 24:19-24.

THE two disciples had been astonished to find themselves accosted by a stranger, and their response to His enquiry had been rather churlish. But He was not disturbed by the rebuff, for He knew what was in their hearts. He was moved by the look of gloom which had settled on their faces and He wanted them to tell Him why they were so stirred and saddened. Thus He ignored all that was curt in the reply to His primary overture and went on to treat it as a natural inquiry. Question had been met by counter question, and that in turn was met by a further question: "And he said unto them, What things?" There is only one word in the Greek text, but the translation may be amplified: What kind of things?[1] This was not to deny knowledge of all that had happened; it was simply designed to draw them out and to make them willing to speak. And this it did; all three resumed their walk and two of them began to speak while He listened. They were scarcely aware of the

---

[1] Alfred Plummer, *St. Luke* (4th ed., 1906), p. 553.

hidden charm and magnetic sympathy of this mysterious Stranger, but their coolness was soon displaced by a warmth and freedom which at first had seemed so improbable. Thus they began in a guarded spirit, but their initial reluctance was soon lost in delightful eagerness to tell every detail. They spoke at length, and what they had to say is a revelation of the confused medley of thoughts passing through the minds of various disciples that day.

Their statement begins with a narrative of recent events: "And they said unto him, Concerning Jesus of Nazareth which was a prophet mighty in deed and word before God and all the people." It was as if they both spoke at once in reply, and their words were full of artless self-disclosure. Their talk when He caught up with them had been concerned with Jesus of Nazareth Whom they described as *a prophet*. This is how He had been acclaimed by the Galilean pilgrims when he rode into the city less than a week before His death: "This is Jesus the prophet of Nazareth of Galilee" (Matthew 21:11). Some looked upon Him as another Elijah and some thought of Him as a second Jeremiah; all were willing to count Him "one of the prophets" (Matthew 16:14). It is strange that no one appears to have seen in Him "that prophet" (John 1:21) whom God had long before promised that He would raise up like unto Moses (Deuteronomy 18:15; Acts 3:22; 7:37): for He was like Moses, "mighty in deed and word before God and all the people." He was indeed "a man approved of God . . . by miracles and wonders and signs, which God did by him" (Acts 2:22), and people had "wondered at the gracious words which proceeded out of his mouth" (Luke 4:22). Nothing that had happened could reduce the impact which those mighty doings and those gracious words had once made. But while they proved that He was "a prophet mighty . . . before God and all the people," they proved no more than this; and in thinking Him to be more, so they implied, they had made a mistake.[2]

"And how the chief priests and our rulers delivered him to be condemned to death, and have crucified him." It was His death on the cross which stood at the heart of their perplexity because it seemed to give the lie to all their trust. It was for

---

[2]Alfred Plummer, *St. Luke* (4th ed., 1906), p. 553.

them as though the Light of the world had gone out and left them in total darkness. What else could they discuss as they left the city where He had been crucified? What else indeed but the fact that He had incurred condemnation at the hands of the chief priests and rulers who were responsible for His execution? Their thoughts were fixed on the action of the Jewish leaders and they did not even allude to the part played by the Roman authorities. Luke had made it clear that the Gentiles had their share in this crime; he alone had mentioned the fact that the Roman soldiers had joined in the jibes while He was on the cross (23:36). But these two men had no comment to make about Gentiles; they had nothing at all to say except about their own rulers. Such silence was significant; they fixed the guilt where it belonged. It was the chief priests and Jewish leaders who had stirred up the people to shout for His death and to call down His blood on them and on their children. And this simple statement by two obscure friends of the Son of Man was to form the pattern for the accusations which were levelled against the Jews by such men as Simon Peter on and after the day of Pentecost: "Him . . . ye have taken, and by wicked hands have crucified and slain" (Acts 2:23; see 3:13; 4:10; 5:30).

"But we trusted that it had been he which should have redeemed Israel: and beside all this, today is the third day since these things were done." These words draw their pathos from the disappointment which they could not conceal. They had been full of hope until His death had put an end to it; all their dreams of national redemption had been buried with Him three days ago. The hope of which they spoke was one which had long been cherished. It had been the inspiration of a godly remnant at the time of His birth. Thus Simeon had been described as one who was "waiting for the consolation of Israel" (Luke 2:25) and Anna had spoken of Him "to all them that looked for redemption in Jerusalem" (Luke 2:38). It was a hope which had increased as His life and ministry unfolded; there were many like Joseph and Nicodemus who believed in secret and who "waited for the kingdom of God" (Luke 23:51). Cleopas and his companion were two of those who had looked to Him to redeem Israel, but His crucifixion seemed to spell the total collapse of all their dreams. The fire of that hope had gone out with His death on the cross, and its ashes were cold

before the dawn of "the third day." There had been a mysterious forecast about "the third day" which neither His enemies
nor disciples had been able to grasp or to dismiss (John 2:19).
His disciples heard Him repeat it more than once (Matthew
16:21; 17:23; 20:19); His enemies could not forget it in spite of
themselves (Matthew 12:40; 26:61; 27:63). Now these two men
referred to "the third day" as if they thought that it might
have brought a crisis; but there was still no change, and hope
had failed.

Their statement proceeds with a reference to current affairs:
"Yea, and certain women also of our company made us astonished, which were early at the sepulchre." This verse marks a
new and distinct train of thought as they turn from His death
on the cross to the events of that morning, and this is more
clearly expressed in the Revised Version: "Moreover certain
women of our company amazed us, having been early at the
tomb." The words *yea, and* (A.V.) fail to point the contrast
which the Greek text requires and which is drawn out by
Plummer in an amplified paraphrase: "*But,* in spite of this disappointment, there is *also* this favourable item."[3] No doubt
the news which the women had brought back from the tomb
was the real cause of the earnest debate between these two
men as they left Jerusalem. They were amazed at what they
had been told by the women who had gone to the tomb at
dawn. And those women were not strangers: they were "of our
company"; they were the least likely of all people to mislead
or deceive their friends by a false and wanton rumor. Luke
describes their visit and records their names with his usual
thoroughness: "It was Mary Magdalene, and Joanna, and Mary
the mother of James, and other women that were with them,
which told these things unto the apostles" (Luke 24:10). Mark
makes it clear that Salome was one of the "other women," and
that their one object was to anoint the Lord's body with "sweet
spices" (Mark 16:1). But while they were *early at the tomb,*
they had not been early enough to find Him there; they found
themselves instead faced with facts so mysterious that men like
the disciples on the road to Emmaus could not credit what
they were told.

---

[3]Alfred Plummer, *St. Luke* (4th ed., 1906), p. 554.

"And when they had found not his body, they came, saying, that they had also seen a vision of angels which said that he was alive." The seal had been broken and the stone rolled away; the body had vanished and the tomb was empty. And yet not quite empty; "two men stood by them in shining garments" (Luke 24:4). These were angels who had sat at the head and the foot of the place where the body had lain (John 20:12). Luke does not describe them as angels, and the disciples on the way to Emmaus could not make up their minds. They did not know whether they should ascribe objective reality to the figures in white array or whether they should dismiss the whole thing as subjective fancy on the part of the women. "A vision of angels": this was indecisive. But the women were quite certain that the angels had told them *that He was alive.* They would never forget how they had bowed their heads in awe and had heard the angels declare: "Why seek ye the living among the dead? He is not here, but is risen: remember how he spake unto you when he was yet in Galilee, saying, The Son of man must be delivered into the hands of sinful men, and be crucified, and *the third day* rise again" (Luke 24:5-7). Luke does not record nor did these two hesitant disciples relate how the Lord had appeared to the women by the way or how the women had held Him by the feet in the deepest worship (Matthew 28:9). But they had run to break the news to those who were in the Apostles' company: "And their words seemed to them as idle tales, and they believed them not" (Luke 24:11). Men who questioned a vision of angels would not listen when they went on to say that they had seen Him too — *alive!*

"And certain of them which were with us went to the sepulchre, and found it even so as the women had said." Luke's account implies that there was some hesitation when the women entered the tomb "and found not the body of the Lord Jesus" (Luke 24:3). Mary Magdalene left them during that short uncertain interval before they had seen the angels, and ran to tell John and Peter that the body had gone (John 20:2). These two men had then run to the tomb to see for themselves, but the other women had left before they could arrive. They saw no sign of the angels, but they saw what others seem to have been too awed to take into proper account: they saw "the linen clothes laid by themselves" (Luke 24:12), "and the napkin, that was about his head . . . wrapped together in a place by itself" (John 20:7). The shroud and the napkin were in "the place where the Lord lay" (Matthew 28:6); all their folds were in place as when they had been wound round His body. Yet His body had gone; He had vanished! This was far more astonishing than the presence of the angels; it was something concrete, plain and material. John grasped the truth: "he saw, and believed" (John 20:8). But Peter was perplexed: "he departed, wondering in himself" (Luke 24:12). The two men turned away and went to "their own home" (John 20:10), the home to which John had taken Mary of Nazareth on the day of the cross (John 19:27). John would not be likely to leave Mary again during that day, whereas Peter was likely to rejoin the company of disciples later in the morning. Thus they would hear Peter's account of the graveclothes, and like him would wonder; they would not hear John tell what he had seen or why he had believed. Each of these facts reflects itself in the conversation of the disciples on the way to Emmaus, and this explains why they confined themselves to the remark that the two who went to the tomb found it all just *as the women had said.*

The two men had spoken at length and their last words unconsciously sum up the whole situation: "But him they saw not." Their gloom on the day of the cross ought to have been replaced by the fullness of joy on that third day: the promise of resurrection, the empty tomb, the presence of angels, and the news that He was alive should have dissolved all their doubts in glorious certainty. They had been so eager in what they told, and yet there was restraint in the telling. They did not tell how the women had seen Him by the way, nor did they tell how the women's report had been treated as an idle rumor. They told as much as they felt that they could, and they held back details which went beyond that point. They had such good strong ground for hope, and they spoke like men who wanted so much to hope; but they ended with a mournful statement, and it sums up their lack of faith and state of mind. "A vision of angels" there may have been, but the one thing certain was that "him they saw not." His body had vanished, and this was the burden of their pathetic retrospect. So it was with Mary as she lingered outside the tomb in the garden: "They have taken away my Lord, and I know not where they have laid him" (John 20:13). But they were perplexed while she was distraught, and they longed to know the answer to their problem. Little did they dream that Him Whom others saw not was now before their eyes; for as yet "their eyes were holden that they should not know him" (Luke 24:16).

Chapter 36

THE GREAT COMPANION

Then he said unto them, O fools, and slow of heart to believe all that the prophets have spoken: Ought not Christ to have suffered these things, and to enter into his glory? And beginning at Moses and all the prophets, he expounded unto them in all the scriptures the things concerning himself. — Luke 24:25-27.

The Lord Jesus had listened in silence as the two men told their story, and He would be deeply aware of each shade of feeling which the telling of that story revealed. They had soon lost their first sense of annoyance at His intrusion and had become strangely at ease in His presence. They found relief from their bewilderment as they shared it with Him, and their manner of speech by the way had all the merit of naïve and spontaneous conversation. It would reveal both their ignorance and their devotion, their lack of faith and the reality of their sorrow. It shows up their perplexity; the news which they had been told was still no more than hearsay for them. Those who told were reliable, but the things which they told seemed so incredible. They were disturbed, perplexed, and at a loss what to believe. They felt much as John the Baptist had felt, and they longed for some word or sign that would solve their problem: was He the Christ, or should they look for another? On the one hand, He had died on the cross; what could they think of that? On the other hand, the tomb was empty; what could that mean? It was for them a most disturbing dilemma; its nature and extent were now fully revealed. And as they fell silent, it was His turn to speak: how would He make the truth known to them? To the woman at the well who wondered about the Christ, He had declared: "I that speak unto thee am he" (John 4:26). To the man who had been born blind and who asked Him about the Son of God, He had replied: "Thou hast both

seen him, and it is he that talketh with thee" (John 9:37).
But His reply on this occasion was as different as the character
of the disciples to whom He spoke.

Luke begins with a brief quotation of the words He uttered:
"Then he said unto them, O fools, and slow of heart to believe
all that the prophets have spoken: Ought not Christ to have
suffered these things, and to enter into his glory?" Luke crowds
his record of this reply into a fourth of the space which he had
allowed for the statement of the two men. Cleopas may have
been his informant, and it is clear that he never forgot the
first words of reproof. No doubt they were spoken with the
accent of kindness, and not in the spirit of censure; if He were
their critic, He was also their friend.[1] No doubt too the word
fools is a harsh and misleading translation; it means foolish,
witless, without sense or understanding. There was pathos in its
use by Paul: "O *foolish* Galatians!" (Galatians 3:1). Almost
the same word had been used by the Lord on another occasion:
"Are ye so *without understanding* also?" (Mark 7:18). They
were dull in mind and slow of heart to believe in spite of all
that the prophets had said. They had heard the Scriptures read
and expounded every Sabbath in the synagogue, and they were
well versed in all the great Old Testament prophecies. This
should have taught them to expect that the Christ would suffer death on the cross and then rise from the dead; but they
had been "without understanding" (Mark 7:18) and had failed
to perceive and grasp the truth. This was at the bottom of their
perplexity; it was something which they shared in common
with all the disciples. "As yet they knew not the scripture, that
he must rise again from the dead" (John 20:9).

"Ought not Christ to have suffered these things, and to enter
into his glory?" The two disciples had been willing to pay
attention to the word of angels, and of women, and of men
like Peter; but they had not paid heed to all that the prophets
had spoken or they would have known that the Christ must
first suffer and then enter into His glory. *These things* refer
to their declaration that He had been condemned and put to
death on the cross by the will of the Jewish rulers; the word
itself stands first in the structure of the sentence in Greek as

---

[1]H. C. G. Moule, *Emmaus* (1912), p. 43.

an indication of its emphatic character.[2] They had assumed that Jesus of Nazareth could not have been the Christ because He had suffered these things; now they were told that He could not have been the Christ unless He had suffered.[3] There was in fact a strong moral necessity why He should first suffer and then enter into glory; He had to pass through the terrors of death before He could triumph in the power of resurrection. He could only redeem Israel if He laid down His life; He could not bring many sons to glory until He had been made perfect through suffering (Hebrews 2:10). The great Messianic Servant Whom God was to extol had first to tread the path of pain as one who was despised and put to grief (Isaiah 52:13-53:12). All this had been made plain by the prophets, but was still an insoluble difficulty in the minds of His most intimate companions. They had been quite incapable of an answer to His question: "How is it written of the Son of man, that he should suffer many things and be set at nought?" (Mark 9:12 R.V.). But what was so dark in their eyes was all clear in the plan of God: He that suffered on the cross was then to enter into glory.

This truth was so fundamental that it formed part of the special teaching of a book like Hebrews: "We see Jesus, who was made a little lower than the angels for the suffering of death, crowned with glory and honour" (Hebrews 2:9). It is a theme which runs through all Christian history, for what was true for the Master is no less true for His servants.[4] Thus Paul and Barnabas encouraged the disciples to continue in the faith with this fact in mind: "We must through much tribulation enter into the kingdom of God" (Acts 14:22). We who are called heirs of God and joint-heirs with Christ must share in the travail of His soul as well as in the glory of His kingdom: "If so be that we suffer with him, that we may be also glorified together" (Romans 8:17). Paul indeed returned to this theme in his last letter in words almost like a credal statement: "It is a faithful saying: For if we be dead with him, we shall also live with him: if we suffer, we shall also reign with him" (II Timothy 2:11, 12). It was the Lord Jesus Who for the joy

---

[2]Alfred Plummer, St. Luke (4th ed., 1906), p. 555.

[3]R. C. Trench, Studies In The Gospels (2nd ed., 1867), p. 327.

[4]Compare the title of William Penn's book, No Cross, No Crown.

that was set before Him endured the cross: He that despised the shame was set down at the right hand of God (Hebrews 12:2). It was in this spirit that Paul could reckon that the sufferings of this present time are not worthy to be compared with the glory which shall be revealed in us (Romans 8:18). Thus a simple statement of fact to two bewildered disciples sums up a law of life with the most far-reaching consequences: "Behoved it not the Christ to suffer these things, and to enter into his glory?" (R.V.).

Luke proceeds with a brief reference to the speech that followed: "And beginning at Moses and all the prophets, he expounded unto them in all the scriptures the things concerning nimselr." Cleopas must have remembered the words in which the Lord began with a clarity which time could not diminish, but he could not quote in detail all that ensued. It is enough to know the drift of that conversation; the journey was sweetened by a fascinating exposition of all that the prophets had spoken. The Son of Man had been saturated with the knowledge and the teaching of the Scriptures; He was at home in its language and its spirit as no other had ever been. He could quote from the law and the prophets with an insight and an application which amazed His hearers, and the last words He had uttered before He bowed His head to die had been words of Scripture. He had felt no hesitation in His reference to the words of prophecy and in His claim that they were now fulfilled before men's eyes (Luke 4:21). But there is no record apart from this momentous occasion of a sustained exposition of all that the Scriptures taught with regard to Him Who was the Christ. It was for the two disciples on the road to Emmaus that He took the key of David and set out to unlock all the Messianic teaching in the Old Testament Revelation. He did for them what He was soon to do for their companions who were still in Jerusalem: "Then opened he their understanding, that they might understand the scriptures, and said unto them, Thus it is written, and thus it behoved Christ to suffer and to rise from the dead the third day" (Luke 24:45, 46).

"He expounded unto them in all the scriptures the things concerning himself." There were many fingers of a prophetic character which all pointed forward to the Christ that should

come.[5] He was the seed destined to crush the head of the
serpent (Genesis 3:15; I John 3:8); He was the lamb God would
provide as substitute and sacrifice (Genesis 22:8; John 1:29).
He was the true Paschal victim whose blood would be shed
for many (Exodus 12:13; Matthew 26:28); He was the great
High Priest who would enter into the holy of holies once and
for all (Leviticus 16:2; Hebrews 9:12). He was like the smitten
rock from which there sprang a stream of living water (Numbers 20:11; John 7:38); He was like the brazen serpent that
was lifted up for life and healing (Numbers 21:9; John 3:14).
He was that star out of Jacob which shone as the herald of a
new day (Numbers 24:17; Revelation 22:16); He was that great
prophet whom God promised to raise up like unto Moses (Deuteronomy 18:15; Acts 3:22). The Psalms had told how He would
come to do the will of God (Psalm 40:7, 8; Hebrews 10:7),
and how the nails would pierce His hands and feet (Psalm
22:16; Matthew 27:35). The Prophecy of Isaiah had made it
clear that He would bear our griefs and carry our sorrows
(Isaiah 53:4; Matthew 8:17), and that He would be led like a
lamb to the place of slaughter (Isaiah 53:7; Acts 8:32). It
was through Him that a fountain would be opened for sin and
uncleanness (Zechariah 13:1; I John 1:7); it was in Him that
the sun of righteousness would arise with healing in His wings
(Malachi 4:2; Luke 1:78). He was prefigured in the symbolic
character of things like the pillar of cloud by day and the
column of fire by night, the blood of sprinkling and smoke of
sacrifice, the seamless veil and mercy seat; He was foreshadowed
in the personal history of men such as Joseph and David, Jonah
and Jeremiah, Daniel and Mordecai. There were indeed count-
less signposts to show that Christ was in all the Scriptures and
that He was no other than Jesus of Nazareth.

This fact was so significant that it formed part of the apostolic
witness from the outset: "Let all the house of Israel know that
God hath made that same Jesus, whom ye have crucified both
Lord and Christ" (Acts 2:36). The Son of Man had been
impregnable in His appeal to the testimony of the Scriptures;
they were the rock on which He had taken His stand against
all the storms of controversy. "Ye search[6] the Scriptures," He
said, "for in them ye think ye have eternal life: and they are

[5]W. Hanna, *Our Lord's Life on Earth* (1882), p. 600.
[6]See the Revised Version.

they which testify of me: And ye will not come to me, that ye might have life" (John 5:39, 40). They sat in Moses' seat, yet they did not believe Him of Whom Moses wrote: "Had ye believed Moses, ye would have believed me," He said; "for he wrote of me" (John 5:46). Men who knew the letter of the Law had no real insight into its truth, and could make no reply to His devastating criticism. Had they never read what Moses wrote? (Mark 12:26). Had they never read what David did? (Mark 2:25). Nothing is so final as the statement which He ascribed in parable to Abraham: "They have Moses and the prophets; let them hear them" (Luke 16:29). But there was a plausible argument which was meant to turn the edge of these words: men would be more likely to repent if one were to visit them from the dead. Then He declared in words of absolute finality: "If they hear not Moses and the prophets, neither will they be persuaded though one rose from the dead" (Luke 16:31). Thus a solemn appeal to the Scriptures bears out the claims of truth with the most far-reaching authority: "To him give all the prophets witness, that through his name whosoever believeth in him shall receive remission of sins" (Acts 10:43).

Thus a seeming stranger to the course of events in those days at Jerusalem passed from Moses to Malachi as He talked with them by the way and "opened . . . their understanding" (Luke 24:45) in the Scriptures. He showed them how the law and the prophets had all foretold that the Christ would suffer before He could conquer; then He showed them how all that they foretold had been fulfilled in Jesus of Nazareth. But though their hearts had burned within as they listened, they knew not that it was Jesus Himself who spoke. If the thought crossed their mind at all, it was only for a moment; they had promptly dismissed such a thing as impossible. Yet this Stranger, mysterious as He had seemed in His apparent ignorance, and vastly more mysterious in His astonishing insight into the law and the prophets: who could He be?

> "They talked of Jesus as they went;
>   And Jesus, all unknown,
> Did at their side Himself present
>   With sweetness all His own."[7]

---

[7]H. C. G. Moule, *Emmaus* (1912), p. 63.

Their eyes were still holden, but they were on the verge of the most momentous discovery. There was nothing about Him in general appearance that would disclose the truth; yet that very morning, He had burst the bands of death in the might of His resurrection power and triumph.

Chapter 37

THE WHOLE COMPANY

> And they drew nigh unto the village, whither they went: and he made as though he would have gone further. But they constrained him, saying, Abide with us: for it is toward evening, and the day is far spent. And he went in to tarry with them. And it came to pass, as he sat at meat with them, he took bread, and blessed it, and brake, and gave to them. And their eyes were opened, and they knew him; and he vanished out of their sight. And they said one to another, Did not our heart burn within us, while he talked with us by the way, and while he opened to us the scriptures? And they rose up the same hour, and returned to Jerusalem, and found the eleven gathered together, and them that were with them, saying, The Lord is risen indeed, and hath appeared to Simon. And they told what things were done in the way, and how he was known of them in breaking of bread. — LUKE 24:28-35.

MANY attempts have been made to identify the village of Emmaus and the problem is still unsolved. The most attractive suggestion dates from the time of the Crusades and points to the village of El Kubeibeh in the beautiful Wady Beit Chanina. This is about seven miles northwest of Jerusalem on the road to Lydda, and fits in with all the details of Luke's record.[1] The two disciples and their Companion would thus cross the line of hills on the northwestern fringe of Jerusalem and approach the village by descent into the Wady. They were deep in conversation and had scarcely noticed that the day had begun to fail; but the sun was low in the west and its last rays already shone on Gibeon, while the moon had begun to rise and shed its light in the valley of Ajalon (Joshua 10:12). "And they drew nigh unto the village, whither they went: and he made as though he would have gone further." Emmaus was the destination which

---

[1]Alfred Plummer, *St. Luke* (4th ed., 1906), pp. 551, 552.

the disciples had meant to reach, but they had heard nothing about the plans of the Stranger Who had traveled with them. It seemed that He must have further to go, perhaps to Lydda or Joppa, for they became aware that He meant to go on alone. It was just as when He had once appeared to the disciples on the Lake of Galilee: "He cometh unto them, walking upon the sea, and would have passed by them" (Mark 6:48). There was nothing unreal in His actions; He would have gone on if they had not asked Him to stay. Their arrival in Emmaus would prove whether His words had taken any mighty hold on them:[2] they would be loath to let Him go if their hearts had really been warmed in such unconscious fellowship with Him that should redeem Israel.

Luke builds up the narrative to its climax in order to describe the moment of discovery. "But they constrained him, saying, Abide with us: for it is toward evening, and the day is far spent. And he went in to tarry with them." Cleopas and his companion had been somewhat gruff and churlish when the Stranger joined them at first, but their hearts had been won by His conversation and they were now eager for His continued company. Thus they pressed Him to stay: "they *constrained* him." Luke employs a word that means to persuade or entreat; it does not mean to coerce or compel.[3] He used the same word in a like context in connection with Lydia. She was baptized; then she besought Paul and Silas to come into her house and to abide with her. And Luke adds: "She *constrained* us" (Acts 16:15). Lydia's argument had been one of moral persuasion: she urged them to become her guests as a sign that they judged her to be an authentic believer. The two disciples used an argument which was one of gentle pressure: they urged the Lord to stay with them on the ground that evening drew on and the day was almost over. Paul and Silas could not resist Lydia's entreaty, nor did the Lord refuse to be persuaded by the disciples: "He went in to tarry with them." Perhaps it was in an inn rather than the home of either of the two men; that would better fit in with His actions as host rather than guest when the table was spread. But though they were eager that He should stay with them, they

---

[2] R. C. Trench, *Studies In The Gospels* (2nd ed., 1867), p. 328.
[3] Alfred Plummer, *St. Luke* (4th ed., 1906), p. 556.

still little knew Whom they were making welcome. "Be not forgetful to entertain strangers: for thereby some have entertained angels unawares" (Hebrews 13:2).

"And it came to pass as he sat at meat with them, he took bread, and blessed it, and brake, and gave to them." A meal was soon prepared, and they would all recline round the table. Luke employs a verb which is peculiar to him in New Testament literature (cf. Luke 7:36; 9:14; 14:8), and the accurate rendering in the Revised Version makes its tense plain: it was "when He *had sat down* with them" that further events took place. He took the loaf and spoke the words of thanks; He broke it in His hands and gave to each his share. Such had ever been His custom, and His actions were all well known to His circle of friends. Thus when He fed the five thousand, "He took . . and blessed, and brake, and gave" (Matthew 14:19; Luke 9:16). It was broken bread with which the multitude was fed; the five loaves were of no avail as long as they were whole. It was as He broke that they were multiplied; they continued to multiply as long as He continued to break. So too, when He supped with the Twelve on the eve of His death, He "took . . . and blessed, and brake, and gave" (Matthew 26:26; Luke 22:19). It was broken bread that He gave to each in turn, and the central feature in what He did was the act of breaking. The bread was a token of His body; it had to be broken just as His body had to be given for the life of the world. And now once more a loaf was placed before Him and before His friends. What did He do? "He took . . . and blessed, and brake, and gave." It was not a miracle, nor a Eucharist; but there were just the same actions, and they are told in the same words.

"And their eyes were opened, and they knew him; and he vanished out of their sight." The disciples of Emmaus may not have seen how the multitude on the hills of Galilee was fed, nor had they been among the Twelve with whom the Last Supper was shared. Yet they may have often sat at table with Him, and who but He would act as this Stranger had done? The way in which He took, and blessed, and broke, and gave, told them the truth, and the eyes that had been holden were now opened that they might see. There was something in His manner just as there was something in His accent which had survived the pains of death, and they knew Him in the breaking of bread just as Mary had known Him when He spoke her name (John 20:16).

They knew at last: it was that same Jesus, mighty in deed and word, Who had been put to death; it was the Christ to Whom the law and the prophets all gave witness. It was a rare moment of high discovery; the last trace of doubt as to His identity had been removed and the truth was revealed. The next moment brought a still more dramatic transition, for He "vanished out of their sight." His place at the table was left empty and He became invisible. Luke employs a word which is found in this verse alone in the New Testament; it was a word with a poetical connotation in the Classics, but it is used here to describe what was sober reality.[4] He had always possessed power to withdraw at will (see Luke 4:30; John 5:13; John 8:59), and this power was clearly heightened in His resurrection body. The word conveys much more than a sudden exit or an unnoticed departure; it was disappearance. He had withdrawn beyond their sight, and they were left at the table alone; "the claims of the invisible world were upon Him, a world into which they could not follow Him as yet."[5]

Luke rounds off the narrative with its sequel in order to relate the return to Jerusalem. "And they said one to another, Did not our heart burn within us, while he talked with us by the way, and while he opened to us the scriptures?" Recognition had been long in coming, and was sudden when it occurred; disappearance had been swift as lightning, and was at once complete. They had no time to kneel down, and no need to hold Him by the feet; He did not wait for their worship, and they well knew that He was real. Their case was quite unlike that of Mary in the garden or the women by the wayside; they had walked with Him for some miles and had engaged in long conversation with Him before the moment of discovery had come, whereas He had revealed Himself to the others with a certain dramatic brevity which called for more tangible assurance (John 20:17; Matthew 28:9). Thus they knew Him; then He was gone. Perhaps there was a pause; they would look at each other in silence and wonder and surprise. Then, as if in concert, each said to the other: "Did not our heart burn within us?" They had felt a strange glow within as He communed with them, opening the

---

[4]Alfred Plummer, *St. Luke* (4th ed., 1906), p. 557.

[5]H. B. Swete, *The Appearances of Our Lord After the Passion* (1915), p. 25.

Scriptures as at last He was to open their eyes. It was like the experience of the prophet Jeremiah: "His word was in mine heart as a burning fire shut up in my bones" (Jeremiah 20:9). We may also compare it with the words of the psalmist: "My heart was hot within me; while I was musing the fire burned" (Psalm 39:3). Recollection of a burning heart was added proof that they had been with Jesus.

"And they rose up the same hour, and returned to Jerusalem, and found the eleven gathered together, and them that were with them." The two men lost no time in idle reverie: "They rose up . . . and returned." They knew now as they had not known before that it was no idle report which the women had brought: the "vision of angels" and their word that "He was alive" were true (Luke 24:23). It was a day of good tidings; they could not hold their peace (II Kings 7:9). They could do no less than rise up and set out for Jerusalem, and the lateness of the hour which they had urged as the reason why He should stay did not now put them off. The last faint light of day may have allowed them to start on their way before evening had come, and the full moon must have shone down before they could reach the city. They would travel with a light step and a glad heart, and would tread out the miles as though they were only half the distance which they had walked but a few hours before. They would indeed walk as fast as they could in the way that people do when they have great and glad news to bear, but the distance could hardly be covered in less than two hours of solid travel. It is clear that they knew where to find the rendezvous of "the eleven," and it is also clear that "the eleven" is an expression which was loosely used to refer to the apostolic band now that it had lost Judas. They found others "that were with them," but Thomas had withdrawn. Perhaps this company had assembled in that same large upper room where He had gone to eat the Passover with the disciples (Luke 22:12), and though He was not there, they had met that evening once more to share a meal (Mark 16:14; cf. Luke 24:41, 42). Little did they know that they were as well to share in news of the greatest moment and joy.

"Saying, The Lord is risen indeed, and hath appeared to Simon." The disciples from Emmaus had hurried to Jerusalem with news which they believed they were the first to bring; but they had been forestalled. Before they could open their mouth to speak, they were welcomed with the greeting that the Lord was indeed alive and had become known to Simon. This fact is not mentioned in the other gospels and no details are furnished here. But if ever a man's faith were likely to fail, that man had been Simon Peter (Luke 22:31, 32). He whose boast had been that he would follow his Master to prison and to death had in fact denied Him thrice with oath and curse. When the cock crew and the Lord turned and looked on him, it broke his heart. He had gone out into the night and wept: but he had no chance to pour out those tears of grief in the presence of that Master. The last words which he had spoken in the hearing of Christ before He bowed His head and died had been words of denial and blasphemy and rejection; there had been no time for the Lord to speak words of gentleness and compassion and forgiveness. He must have been haunted by the bitterness of that memory; his heart would be sore and full of brooding. At dawn on the third day he had run to the tomb with John and had found it empty except for the folded shroud and headcloth. He had returned with a sense of wonder, but his heart was as yet unsatisfied. The day wore on and the strain was almost too great to bear. He left the house again to be alone; it must have been sometime after the two disciples left for Emmaus and before their return. It was then that the Lord appeared to him, and that appearance was in the front rank as evidence of the Resurrection (Galatians 1:18; I Corinthians 15:5). We know nothing as to where it took place or what was said; all we know is the bare fact that He did appear, and we only learn that in an incidental way in this verse. He had at once returned from that momentous interview to let others know that he had now seen the Lord. Him they believed though the women they had failed to believe, and their excited reaction burst out in their first words to the disciples from Emmaus.

The exchange of greetings would die away, but the initial excitement would be increased as the two men told their story: "And they told what things were done in the way, and how he was known of them in breaking of bread." Mark's statement adds a clause which almost seems in conflict with the facts in Luke's record: "And they went and told it unto the residue: neither believed they them" (Mark 16:13). Swete points out that this must either belong to a later account or that it must

refer to some who still held out against the growing evidence of
the Resurrection.[6]   That there were some even in that radiant
company and with yet more compelling evidence who still found
it hard to believe is made clear by Luke himself (Luke 24:41).
But Swete also points out that the joy and wonder of those who
were in the upper room must have grown sensibly as the two
men told their story with the fulness of the oriental love of detail.[7]   They would rehearse what had transpired just as
Cornelius was to rehearse how the angel of God had come to
him (Acts 10:8; see also 15:12, 14; 21:19); and the climax in
their story was the way in which He had made Himself known
to them. The act by which He had been pleased to stir up their
powers of recognition had been in the breaking of bread, and
the repeated emphasis on His manner in the fraction of bread
shows that it held obvious interest for all who had known Him.
We hear nothing more of Cleopas and his companion; their
names disappear from the narrative. But the disciples who had
constrained Him to lodge with them at Emmaus were now with
the company assembled in the upper room where He was soon to
stand in the midst.

---

[6]H. B. Swete, *The Appearance of Our Lord After the Passion* (1915), p. 27
   footnote 3.

[7]*Ibid.*, p. 27.

Chapter 38

THEN CAME JESUS

> Then the same day at evening, being the first day of the week, when the doors were shut where the disciples were assembled for fear of the Jews, came Jesus and stood in the midst, and saith unto them, Peace be unto you." — JOHN 20:19.

LUKE's narrative continues with an account of the Lord's appearance to the ten disciples, and the first words suggest that it must have followed in swift sequence on the arrival of the two from Emmaus: "And as they thus spake, Jesus himself stood in the midst of them, and saith unto them, Peace be unto you" (Luke 24:36). Mark also refers to this occasion in a paragraph which seems meant to cover the whole period from the evening of the Resurrection to the Ascension: "Afterward he appeared unto the eleven as they sat at meat." (Mark 16:14). But it is to John that we owe the primary narrative of the events of that evening, and its atmosphere can be recaptured from his words with a sense of most profound reality. The day had been one of concern and surprise and troubled rumor for the bewildered disciples. Its dawn had been dark and cheerless; they did not know that it was to transform their lives. Their hope had been nailed to the cross with the hands and feet of the Lord Jesus; it lay buried, so they believed, with that sacred body in the tomb of Joseph. But there had been such strange events since dawn that they were in the throes of the deepest perplexity. They knew not what to think, and they hardly knew whom they could believe. The seal on the stone at the grave had been broken, and the guard on duty had fled; the stone itself had been removed, and an angel kept watch by the now open door. The body had vanished, and the tomb was empty: and yet not quite empty, for the graveclothes still lay in their position undisturbed.

251

There were reports that something incredible had happened, tha·
One Who had been dead was now alive; and the evening found
them agitated and alternating between moods of doubt and hope
and fear.

John's first words paint the scene as it was before the Lord
Jesus came, and they start with a note of time: "Then the same
day at evening." Both emphasis and precision make up this
note of time, and a similar expression was used by John on
several occasions (John 1:39; 5:9; 11:49; 18:13). It was the same
memorable day as that which had dawned with the Resurrection,
and the Risen Lord had in fact revealed Himself four times at
least in the course of that day. Early in the morning He had
appeared to Mary in the garden and had charged her with a
message for the disciple company: "Go to My brethren and say
unto them, I ascend unto My Father and your Father, and to
My God and your God" (John 20:17). Then a little later, He
had appeared to the women by the way and had given them a
similar commission: "Go, tell my brethren that they go into
Galilee, and there shall they see me" (Matthew 28:10). Luke
asserts that both Mary and the women did go back and tell the
Eleven: "And their words seemed to them as idle tales, and
they believed them not" (Luke 24:11). Yet they could not shake
their minds free from the reports which they had heard, and the
disciples on the road to Emmaus voiced the general attitude in
their remark: "Certain women also of our company made us
astonished, which . . . came, saying, that they had also seen a
vision of angels, which said that he was alive" (Luke 24:22, 23).
Now the evening of that "same day" had come, and they were
still in a state of suspense. They did not know what to expect
when they all met for the evening meal in that large upper room
in Jerusalem.

"Then the same day at evening, being the first day of the
week." The time can be fixed with reasonable accuracy by a
comparison of the gospels. The word "evening" does not require
us to think in terms of the late evening; elsewhere it is employed
in a context which links it with sunset (Mark 1:32; Matthew
16:2).[1] But it had been "toward evening" and the day was "far
spent" when the travelers came to Emmaus (Luke 24:29). It

---

[1]H. C. G. Moule, *Jesus and The Resurrection* (4th ed., 1905), p. 84.

was while they sat at the table for the evening meal that the Lord had made Himself known to the two in the act of breaking the bread. They had at once set out on the seven miles walk back to Jerusalem, and it must have been some two hours after sunset when they arrived. The Jews always measured a day from sunset to sunset, and this meant that nightfall had brought the start of a new day. But the rule in John's gospel was to make use of the Roman method in the computation of time and to measure a day from midnight to midnight (cf. John 1:39; 4:6; 4:52; 19:14). Thus he speaks of evening as part of "the same day," and it was still "the first day of the week." The short eastern twilight would mean that it was dark except for the clear light of a full moon, and it must have been eight o'clock at least when the two men joined the others in that room in Jerusalem. Only ten of the Twelve were there; Judas was dead, and Thomas was away. There were others also "that were with them" (Luke 24:33), perhaps women as well as men (Acts 1:14). The disciples from Emmaus were not of the Twelve, but they were part of the "company" (Luke 24:22); they were known, and were made welcome.

"Then the same day at evening, being the first day of the week, when the doors were shut where the disciples were assembled for fear of the Jews." Doubtless that company of disciples thought that if it were true that the Lord had risen, He would appear to them even as to others, and the room must have been alive with their eager talk and exclamation. They may not have believed the early report from Mary or the women (Luke 24:11), but could they still remain in doubt when yet other testimonies came in? Peter had just arrived, and had told them that he had seen the Lord (Luke 24:34); the disciples from Emmaus had come a few moments later, and they too had seen Him (Luke 24:35). They must have felt the weight of such cumulative testimony; it could hardly be a mistake on the part of all these men and women. But some were still incredulous in spite of this exciting atmosphere, and they were all nervous as well lest the Temple police should make a swoop and round them up. It was barely three days since they had seized the Lord and then procured His death; and the unhappy disciples who had fled at the time of His arrest must have been plunged into even greater alarm on the day of the cross. Rumors of the Resurrection had now begun to spread, and the attitude of the Jewish leaders was yet uncertain (Matthew 28:11-15). Thus it was not surprising that the disciples were still concerned for their safety: "The doors were shut . . . for fear of the Jews." They were still in the heart of the city where He had been crucified, and they were not to know what new steps His enemies might take. There was fear as well as tension among their ranks, and the doors were shut, barred and bolted, against the Jews.

John's next words paint the scene as it was after the Lord Jesus came, and they start with a fact of space: "Then . . . came Jesus." Conversation was in full tide when a sudden change came and a hush fell upon that room; for lo! Jesus had come! He came, though their faith was dull; He came, though the doors were shut. Suddenly and silently He came, as a spirit might come; there was neither shadow nor footfall to tell of His coming. John does not say how He came, no doubt because he did not know; he is content to state the fact, and that is all. The whole narrative is most impressive in its silence as well as its detail,[2] and there is no attempt to avoid this spirit of deep reserve. It does not say that the doors were opened as when Peter was released from prison (Acts 12:10); it does not even say that He passed through the doors at all. John only states what he knew, and he knew that "Jesus came" when the doors were shut. This was wholly astonishing, full of mystery and of miracle; but it fits in with all else that we know of His movements that day. He had emerged from the graveclothes though no hand had unwound the shroud, and had left the sealed tomb before angels could roll away the stone. He had appeared to Mary in the garden and to the women by the way as though He had come from nowhere, and had vanished as if into nowhere before the eyes of the disciples in the house at Emmaus. The real nature of His resurrection body still lies beyond mortal understanding; but there is no room for doubt that He had now come.

"Then . . . came Jesus, and stood in the midst." The coming of Jesus was no less real and true than its manner had been strange and mysterious. He stepped into the midst, and there He took His stand. There was no place for Him but "in the midst"; He was always at the center in the circle of those with whom He

---

[2]H. C. G. Moule, *Jesus and The Resurrection* (4th ed., 1905), p. 87.

had to do. He had been "in the midst" when His mother found Him as a twelve-year-old child in the Temple (Luke 2:46), and He was "in the midst" between the two malefactors on the right hand and on the left when He hung on the cross (John 19:18). But there was a special sense in which He once promised to be in the midst of His own: "For where two or three are gathered together in my name, there am I *in the midst* of them" (Matthew 18:20). This promise was fulfilled in the Upper Room with singular tenderness; it was as if He would furnish us with a sign of the reality of that promise in all circumstances. He stood in the midst of men whom He called friends and brethren, and He took that place as One Who claimed to be their Lord and Master. They were a band of frail, discouraged disciples, men who had grieved Him much; yet He loved them, and to be in their midst was His great delight. Thus when He came, He did not stand aloof; when they saw Him, it was not on the fringe. They were hardly aware that He had come at all until they saw Him in the midst. It was nothing less than the fact of His presence "in the midst" that was to transform their lives. Incredulity was turned to faith; sorrow was swallowed up in everlasting joy.

"Then . . . came Jesus, and stood in the midst, and saith unto them, Peace be unto you." Each new step in the swift sequence of this wonderful narrative is full of grace. He came, but He did more than come; He stood in the midst. He came and stood in the midst, but He did more than this; He spoke words of peace. They heard the voice they knew so well as He hailed them with the normal salutation with which Jew would greet Jew (cf. Judges 6:23; Luke 10:5). But the very simplicity of this greeting would lend it a special value in the circumstances; it was meant in exceeding gentleness as a proof of His love and care. Among the last words which He had spoken to them in their sorrow on the eve of His death had been words of endless comfort: "Peace I leave with you, my peace I give unto you: not as the world giveth, give I unto you. Let not your heart be troubled, neither let it be afraid" (John 14:27). But they had all failed Him and fled when He was seized and bound, and their hearts must have been sorely burdened on the day of the cross. There was nothing of which they stood so much in need, for what peace could they have when He was dead? The fire and energy of Peter: did that create peace? The love and devotion of Mary: did that afford peace?[3] Now he stood once more in the midst of those who had failed Him, but there was no word of blame nor hint of reproof in spite of their failure. His voice fell once more on their ears, and His first words were words of peace. It was as though He would calm their hearts at once by letting them know all that was in His heart for them.

Thus in the hush of that solemn evening and in the midst of that crowded chamber, there stood the Lord Jesus, that great Shepherd of the sheep brought back from the dead. Wonderful was the way in which He had come, "when the doors were shut"; no less wonderful was the way in which He had spoken, "Peace be unto you." And may we not still share in that scene? May we not yet see Him in the midst? Does not the Lord Jesus still come, perhaps in an hour when we think not? In the dark shadows of grief and loss, in the deep nightfall of guilt and need, will He not stand among us and reveal Himself in His resurrection reality? In spite of the doors which our ignorance would shut or the locks which our prejudice would turn, will He not still appear in our midst if we love Him from our hearts?[4] Our need may be hardly less than that of those first bewildered disciples, but we also may hear Him say: "These things I have spoken unto you, that in me ye might have peace" (John 16:33). Nothing is more wholesome than to have this peace in our hearts, and it is an urgent necessity in a life of honest discipleship. We are meant to let the gospel of peace be the sandal with which our foot is shod (Ephesians 6:15); we are meant to let the secret of peace be the umpire by which our heart is ruled (Colossians 3:15). This is more than poise, or a balanced mind, or a well-adjusted personality, for it consists in a state of heart and speaks of a trust in God. This may transcend our power to explain or describe, yet we may know that it is so. We need, with a need which words can hardly express, to see Jesus in our midst and to hear Him say: "Peace be unto you."

---

[3]H. C. G. Moule, *Jesus and The Resurrection* (4th ed., 1905), p. 95.
[4]H. C. G. Moule, *Jesus and The Resurrection* (4th ed., 1905), p. 83.

Chapter 39

HIS HANDS AND SIDE

And when he so said, he shewed unto them his hands
and his side. Then were the disciples glad, when they saw the
Lord. — JOHN 20:20.

A DEEP hush had fallen on that room in the midst of its excited
atmosphere. No one had heard Him knock; no one had seen
Him come: and yet, Jesus was there; they saw His face, and
heard His voice. But there was no sudden outburst of joy; they
could hardly believe that it was He. Luke explains that their
first sight of Him startled their minds beyond measure: "They
were terrified and affrighted, and supposed that they had seen
a spirit" (Luke 24:37). This was perhaps partly because of their
astonishment that one who had been dead was now alive, partly
because of the sudden mysterious way in which He had come.
They fell into a trance of awe and fear; they could not tell
whether what they now saw were phantom or reality. It was
as when He had come to their aid, walking on the storm-tossed
waters of Galilee: "They were troubled, saying, It is a spirit; and
they cried out for fear" (Matthew 14:26). They were only
assured when they heard Him declare: "It is I; be not afraid"
(Matthew 14:27). The same disciples were now reassured by
still more tangible proofs of reality. They heard Him say: "Why
are ye troubled? and why do thoughts arise in your hearts?
Behold my hands and my feet, that it is I myself" (Luke 24:
38, 39). John does not record these words; he was content to
pass at once from the greeting of peace to the proof of reality:
"And when he had so said, he shewed unto them his hands and
his side. (Luke's account explains why it was "when he had so
said" that He went on to show them His hands and side.) He
stood in their midst, clad in folds of white which would conceal

His limbs from view; and then He drew the robes apart so that they could see His hands and His side. There were the marks of His Passion: deep, hollow, bloodless wounds;[1] no ghostly apparition or disembodied spirit would bear such scars. He that bore the marks of the cross in hands and side was real; it was that same Jesus Who now stood in their midst and met them with the words of peace.

This was meant as a pledge and proof of His sacrificial love on the cross: "He shewed unto them his hands and his side." John speaks of His hands and side, but not His feet; Luke speaks of His hands and feet, but not His side.[2] John alone had seen how His side had been pierced, and he had placed it on record with a note of uncommon emphasis (John 19:34, 35). Thus he would have special reason to take note of that wound, and there is a solemn pathos in his account of the whole scene. The Passion on the cross was over; the darkness in the tomb had ended. The wounds with their pain and fever were healed, and all that was mortal had put on immortality. But the print of the nails was there, and the hole in His side was there. These were the scars of His death on the cross; they were like brands on His body which nothing could efface. And with those hands, once pierced and torn, their sins had been nailed to the cross (Colossians 2: 14); behind that deep cleft from the spear lay the fact that His heart had been riven for them (Psalm 69:20). Those scars in His risen body were in fact signs and seals that He had died to bear our sins (John 1:29; I Peter 2:24). He had been wounded in the house of His friends (Zechariah 13:6), and those wounds were for their transgressions (Isaiah 53:5). The sight of those scars in His hands and side was the final proof of love that has no equal: a love that loved unto death, yea, even "the death of the cross" (Philippians 2:8 — R.V.).

Thus His nail-pierced hands and spear-torn side were proofs of a love which death could not destroy, and would appeal to their hearts with overwhelming effect. All analogies are inadequate, but an illustration may be found in an old law of Moses. When a Hebrew bondman had spent six years in the service of a

---

[1]H. C. G. Moule, *Jesus and The Resurrection* (4th ed., 1905), p. 96.

[2]Luke 24:39. For the omission of Luke 24:40, see the marginal note in the Revised Version, and Plummer, p. 560.

Hebrew master, he could claim his freedom; but if he had married while a bondman, his wife and his children would still belong to his master's household. He might go free, but he would have to go alone. But such a man might love his wife and his children, and he could then refuse to go out free. Then his master would take an awl and bore a hole through the lobe of his ear; and that hole would be the sign that he had become a bondman forever. When his wife and children saw that hole in his ear, they could never doubt how much he loved them (Exodus 21:1-6). So too when Paul wrote to the Galatian Christians, he could remind them how he had been stoned and left for dead outside the city of Lystra: "From henceforth let no man trouble me: for I bear in my body the marks of the Lord Jesus" (Galatians 6:17). And when they thought how his body had been pitted with scars and weals as he labored for them in the Gospel, they could never doubt how much he loved them. Thus when the Lord Jesus stood in the midst and showed them His hands and His side, could they ever doubt the depth and reality of the love that sought to redeem Israel? Perhaps it had once been open to Him as the Servant of God to leave the world and to return at once into the joy of His Father's presence; but He chose to speak of the death that He must die and for that end had set His face toward Jerusalem (Luke 9:51). The scars of the cross in His hands and side would tell them how true it was that having loved His own which were in the world, He had loved them unto the end (John 13:1).

Nothing would so stir the memory of the disciples as those memorials of His Passion: they told of a loving Redeemer and a reconciled Father. They were the ground for His greeting of peace: it was peace won by "the blood of the cross" (Colossians 1:20). But they were faced with what appeared to be impossible, and the glorious paradox was this: those marks of death were now present in One Who was alive; He stood before them as the Lord Who had both died and revived (Romans 14:9). All the visible evidence of sacrifice and atonement was seen in His risen body, and those scars will never vanish from His hands and His side. He now bears them at the right hand of God where He appears in the form of "a lamb as it had been slain" (Revelation 5:6). Thus they are the credentials for our acceptance with God and the authority for His intercession on our behalf (Hebrews 7:25). He has entered within the veil and He appears in the presence of God for us: but He has no need to pray in articulate form as we do, for the wounds in His hands are the sole and sufficient advocates which He employs. The scars of death will never be removed from Him Who is the Lord of Life, and He will come again bearing the marks of His Passion in the glory of His resurrection body. Many in the meanwhile may say, Lo, He is here: lo, He is there: but where are the marks in their hands? "Behold, He cometh with clouds; and every eye shall see Him, and they also which pierced Him" (Revelation 1:7). The print of the nails and the mark of the spear will be the sign that the Christ indeed has come.

This was meant as a pledge and proof of His resurrection life from the dead: "He shewed unto them his hands and his side." John describes His action, but does not relate His words; Luke relates His words, but does not describe His action. They were startled and confused when Jesus came "and stood in the midst" (John 20:19); they knew not what to think: could it be a spirit or a phantom that they saw in the dim lamp light? Their faculty of perception had been clouded with prejudice and unbelief, but He met their doubt and uncertainty with a perfect challenge: "Behold my hands and my feet, that it is I myself: handle me, and see; for a spirit hath not flesh and bones as ye see me have" (Luke 24:39). The scars of the cross would prove to them that they were face to face with One Who was real, and no better means could have been found to convince men who were in the grip of doubt. "And when He had so said, He shewed unto them His hands and His side" (John 20:20; cf. Luke 24:40 R.V.M.). He held out His nail-pierced hands and laid bare His spear-torn side, and those scars would tell them that the Man of the Cross was now the Prince of Life. No phantom or specter would bear the marks of the Passion in hands and side, and those marks were now as real as the wounds themselves had been. They could even handle Him with their hands (cf. I John 1:1), and no one can handle a ghost: a ghost would be no ghost if it were clothed with flesh and bones in the way that He was. The fact of sight would convince them of His identity; the sense of touch would convince them of His reality.[3] Those scars were the infallible proof

---

[3]Alfred Plummer, *St. Luke* (4th ed., 1906), p. 560.

that He was "this same Jesus" (Acts 1:11), and their fears would subside forever.

But their initial reaction was as full of caution as of wonder and Luke tells us how He met their need: "And while they yet believed not for joy, and wondered, he said unto them, "Have ye here any meat?" (Luke 24:41). There is profound insight in this account of their feelings, and Luke stands alone in such notes of psychology. They could hardly believe their eyes, it was too wonderful to be true. Those who at first had been held back through fear were now held back for joy; men who slept for sorrow in the Garden believed not for joy in this large upper chamber (cf. Luke 22:45). But the Lord was aware of this further inhibition of faith and He at once took steps to shake them free from the last hold of doubt. He had once long before taken the daughter of Jairus by hand and had spoken to her as a mother would to a darling child: "Talitha cumi" (Mark 5:41). She heard, and woke up, and arose; and He told her parents to give her food to eat. This would calm their emotional bewilderment and would prove to them the reality of her restoration to life. So now He sought to shake them out of their incredulous surprise and to stir them into healthy action. They could have put forth their hands to touch and feel the scars of the cross, but they may at first have shrunk from contact with One Whom they thought of as a spirit. But He could see that they had shared a meal before He came, and He asked if there were any food still at hand. It would do them good to bestir themselves, and He proposed a proof of His reality which would have been impossible if He were in fact a ghostly apparition.

It must have been a relief for them to have something to do, and they obeyed with alacrity: "And they gave him a piece of a broiled fish, and of an honeycomb. And he took it, and did eat before them" (Luke 24:42, 43). They had often eaten with the Son of Man in by-gone days and they would know His every gesture as He partook of food before their eyes. So it had been with the disciples at Emmaus when He sat down to eat with them: "He was known of them in breaking of bread" (Luke 24:35). So it would be with the disciples at Galilee when He prepared a meal for them on the fire of coals by the sea: "Jesus then cometh, and taketh bread, and giveth them, and fish likewise" (John 21:13). Simon Peter could not help but recall such meals when he looked back over the years: We "did eat and drink with Him after He rose from the dead" (Acts 10:41). So now, He that could be seen and touched could also take food and eat before their eyes: and who ever heard of a ghost or a spirit that could partake of food? He was no longer subject to want or distress; He would never again feel the pangs of hunger: but He retained all the essential properties of His body in a way which no ghost could do. To have seen His spirit would not have been the same as to see Him; it might resemble Him in appearance, but it would not speak of Resurrection. But when they heard His voice and saw those scars, when they found that they could handle Him with their hands and that He could share in a meal before their eyes, their doubts vanished and they were filled with joy.

Mark has a short and surprising reference to this scene in complete contrast with the account in St. Luke or John: "Afterward He appeared unto the eleven as they sat at meat and upbraided them with their unbelief and hardness of heart because they believed not them which had seen Him after He was risen" (Mark 16:14). It may be that this brief fragment with its rougher note of reproach preserves another tradition of the circumstances in which they were troubled and strange thoughts arose in their hearts (Luke 24:38). Perhaps it shows even more clearly the exceeding tenderness that led Him to greet them in peace and to show them His hands and side. This in turn led to a sudden release of joy, and John sums up their feelings in one vivid sentence: "Then were the disciples glad, when they saw the Lord." Moule says that the aorist tense of the verb suggests "an act of joy";[4] and the act of joy was linked with the word of peace. He showed His wounds and spoke of peace; they saw the Lord and knew His joy: the God of hope gave them all joy and peace as they saw and believed (Romans 15:13). The words are as calm and serene as the spirit of the one who wrote them, but his recollection of that scene was still as fresh and fragrant as though it had been yesterday. Their hearts had been made glad in a way that he could never forget, for he could not forget what it had meant to see the Lord. We may wonder if in that hour of joy they

[4] H. C. G. Moule, *Jesus and The Resurrection* (4th ed., 1905), p. 97.

would recall the words which they had heard Him speak in that same room only three nights before: "Ye now have sorrow; but I will see you again: and your heart shall rejoice, and your joy man taketh from you" (John 16:22).

Chapter 40

SO SEND I YOU

Then said Jesus to them again, Peace be unto you: as my Father hath sent me, even so send I you. — JOHN 20:21.

ALL the momentary sense of doubt had vanished from the minds of the disciples when they saw the scars of death in His hands and side. They knew now that it was Jesus, and they were glad; all the pent-up feelings of sorrow and suspense would find release in looks of wonder and words of worship. "Then said Jesus to them again, Peace be unto you." Thus there was a double salutation of peace like the twofold "peace, peace" of which the prophecy of Isaiah had twice spoken (Isaiah 26:3 R.V.M.; 57:19). When He spoke first, they were still awed, and surprised, and afraid; when He spoke now, they had found a new and radiant assurance. Then while the word of peace was still fresh on His lips, He went on to speak yet again: "As my Father hath sent me, even so send I you." All the evangelists have some record of the charge which was laid on them (Matthew 28:19; Mark 16:15; Luke 24:48; Acts 1:8). But John gives it in a form which fits in with his view of Christ as the Sent One:[1] as He had been sent forth from God, so they would now be sent by Him. This is phrased in a style which is common in this gospel (cf. John 10:15; 13:34; 15:9), and it has an immediate antecedent in the words of prayer which He had employed on the eve of His death: "As thou hast sent me into the world, even so have I also sent them into the world" (John 17:18). But while the same word in the same tense was employed in each half of that verse, there are two words in the Greek text for the words HATH SENT and SEND in John 20:21.

---

[1]See John 3:17, 34; 5:36; 6:29, 57; 7:29; 8:42; 10:36; 11:42; 17:3, etc.

The first word is in the perfect tense and conveys the idea of delegated authority; the second word is in the present tense and it implies no more than the immediate relationship between sender and sent. Westcott's study of the two words concludes that in this charge the Lord referred to His earthly mission as the only continuing mission in the Father's purpose: thus He did not give the disciples some new commission; He called them to fulfill the task given to Him by His Father.[2]

"As my father hath sent me, even so send I you." How did the Lord Jesus come when He was sent forth from God? He came in lowliness of mind. It was He Who wove the garland that He was in spirit to wear: "I am meek and lowly in heart" (Matthew 11:29). He was the Equal of God in glory, Fellow of His love, Partner of His throne; but God "spared not" His only Son in order to provide for us men and our salvation (Romans 8:32). God "gave" Him (John 3:16); God "sent" Him (John 3:17). And when He was sent forth by God, He came in lowliness and humility. He came neither in the splendor of an angel, nor yet with the grandeur of a monarch; He was born and cradled in the manger of a country inn at Bethlehem. He Who was rich in all the wealth of heaven chose the lot of the poor and heavy-laden. He trod this earth as a meek and lowly Stranger Who had not where to lay His head. He made Himself of no reputation that He might come in the likeness of men, and He died on the cross in the place of sin and shame where all men deserve to die. It was in the contemplation of such facts as these that Bishop William Walsham How wrote his hymn:

> Who is this, so weak and helpless,
>   Child of lowly Hebrew maid,
> Rudely in a stable sheltered,
>   Coldly in a manger laid?

"As my Father hath sent me." He was sent in the submission of will. He came, not to do His own will, but the will of Him that sent Him (John 6:38). Paul notes with simple wonder that "even Christ pleased not himself" (Romans 15:3). He did always those things that were pleasing to His Father (John 8:29). This was the key to His whole life, and it was well expressed in

---

[2]B. F. Westcott, *The Gospel According to St. John* (18th impr., 1937), p. 298.

His words as a child in the Temple: "Wist ye not that I must be about my Father's business?" (Luke 2:49). His whole heart was absorbed in the need to work the works of Him that sent Him while it was day, for He knew that the night cometh when not even the Son of Man can work (John 9:4). Thus He even forgot the need to eat and drink in His pursuit of this mission. "My meat," He said, "is to do the will of him that sent me, and to finish his work" (John 4:34). This was how He confessed God before men, and so finished the work which His Father gave Him to do (John 17:4); and He died on the cross with the Victor's shout on His lips: "It is finished." (John 19:30). So the stanza of How's great hymn concludes:

> 'Tis the Lord of all creation,
>> Who this wondrous path hath trod;
> He is God from everlasting,
>> And to everlasting God.

"Even so send I you." He sent them out to walk before God in lowliness of mind and in submission of will. Yet it is not always easy to keep these things clearly in sight. We deny the spirit of Him Who was meek and lowly in heart by our spiritual arrogance, for we lift up our heads and think that we are much better than our neighbor. We deny the spirit of Him Who was true and faithful by our spiritual ambition, for we seek our own ends and give little thought to the things that concern others. And the measure in which all this is true is the measure of our failure to walk in the spirit of this command; it means that we misrepresent Him Who was sent from God in the eyes of the world. We ought to be living Epistles, able to be read and known of all men, for there are so many who will judge the Lord from heaven by what they see in us. "Let this mind be in you," Paul plainly exhorts, the mind "which was also in Christ Jesus" (Philippians 2:5). He still seeks to send men out in His Name, to be lowly as He was lowly, selfless as He was selfless.

"As my Father hath sent me, even so send I you." Why did the Lord Jesus come when He was sent forth from God? He came for the salvation of men. He never grew weary in the task of making known the one great reason why He had come: "For God sent not his Son into the world to condemn the world;

but that the world through him might be saved" (John 3:17; cf. 12:47). He came to meet man in the place of need and to lift him to the height of glory: "I am come that they might have life, and that they might have it more abundantly" (John 10:10). He came as the Friend of sinners whom He strove to reclaim and redeem; it was not the righteous, but the sinner, whom He had come to call to repentance (Matthew 9:13). It was indeed all summed up in the words of the prophecy of Isaiah which He had read in the synagogue at Nazareth: "He hath sent me to heal the brokenhearted, to preach deliverance to the captives, and recovering of sight to the blind, to set at liberty them that are bruised, to preach the acceptable year of the Lord" (Luke 4:18, 19). He came as the Shepherd of all who may be lost and the Saviour of all that are out of the way: "For the Son of man is come to seek and to save that which was lost" (Luke 19:10). And this redemptive ministry led at last to the cross on which He died: "To this end was I born, and for this cause came I into the world" (John 18:37). It was in the contemplation of such facts as these that Bishop William Walsham How wrote the lines:

> Who is this that hangeth dying
>   While the rude world scoffs and scorns;
> Numbered with the malefactors,
>   Torn with nails, and crowned with thorns?

"As my father hath sent me." He was sent for the sacrifice of ease. He came as the Man of Sorrows, and was swift to be touched with the feeling of our infirmities. He Who was the Lord of angels wore His life out in the service of men, and the path that He trod was the path of surrender and suffering and sacrifice. He might have passed at once from the Mount of Transfiguration into the joy of His Father's presence; it had been open to Him to return to the glory which had been His before the world was made. But He spoke of the death that He must die in that hour of glory, and He came down from the Mount to His work on the plain of sorrow. Thus the time came when He set His face like a flint to go up to Jerusalem, for He foretold that a prophet could not perish away from that city (Luke 13:33). His death on the cross had been in full view from the hour when He came into the world, and the New Covenant between God and man could only be sealed with the blood that He was to shed. His life on earth is the story of a love that was strong as death: "For . . . the Son of man came, not to be ministered unto, but to minister, and to give his life a ransom for many" (Mark 10:45). So the question in How's lines is answered:

> 'Tis our God, our glorious Saviour,
>   Who above the starry sky
> Now for us a place prepareth
>   Where no tear can dim the eye.

"Even so send I you." He sent them out to live among men with a view to the salvation of souls and the sacrifice of ease. The one supreme purpose for which the Church exists is to bring men to Christ. The Lord Jesus is endowed with all power in heaven and upon earth; it would be as easy for Him to convert a soul as to create a star. But He does not act in arbitrary omnipotence; He has chosen to bind Himself by the limits of what the Church can do. He has no hands or feet as once of old to serve the sons of men, for He is now at God's right hand and we can no longer see His face here on earth. But we are here as His servants, and we are to carry on His mission; and if we fail, souls will perish and His Kingdom will suffer loss. That is why He entreats us by all the mercies of God to give ourselves to Him, even as through the Eternal Spirit He gave Himself to God. He calls for the offering of life and the sacrifice of ease that His Kingdom may come and that His will may be done. He still seeks to send men out in His name, to be loving as He was loving, yielded as He was yielded.

There stood the Lord Jesus in the midst of that band of men. A vast mission was in store for them: just as He had been God's Servant in the days of His flesh, so now they were to be His messengers and ministers to all mankind. They would be faced with a colossal task in the midst of a cold and critical world; they were to preach the Gospel to every nation, and they had to begin in the city where He was crucified. They were a mere handful of men, and they well knew their own weakness; heart and flesh might fail them as they looked out on the future. How then would He tell them? "He showed unto them His hands and His side." They saw the print of the nails in His hands; they saw the mark of the spear in His side. And while their eyes were still fixed on the scars of His death and Passion, they heard Him say: "As my Father hath sent me, even so send I you." It had cost Him the cross; they knew that well. It might cost them the cross; they knew that too. But as they heard His voice while their eyes were on His hands and His side, could they refuse? That voice rings through all the corridors of the centuries which come and go, and it is just as fresh and real today as when Jesus stood in the midst. You are the child of His mortal agony, born of the unknown sorrows of His dying love and Passion. By the wounds and the wrongs which He endured, by the love and the life that He outpoured, He prays you still to hear His voice:

"So send I you!"

Chapter 41

THE HOLY BREATH

And when he had said this, he breathed on them, and saith unto them, Receive ye the Holy Ghost. — JOHN 20:22.

THERE was among the band of men in that room an air of profound quiet and solemn expectation; they knew that it was an hour of unique crisis. Their voice is not once heard in John's narrative; they looked and listened in deep and silent wonder as the Lord stood and spoke to them. John's account began with the foundational statement: "Then . . . came Jesus and stood in the midst" (20:19). Then the record falls into two sections, and each section consists of a symbolical action followed by a fundamental saying. The first action was when He showed them His hands and His side; it was followed by the saying that as His Father had sent Him, so now He would send them. Then there is a second illustration of the same firm direct form of approach: "And when he had said this, he breathed on them, and saith unto them, Receive ye the Holy Ghost." It was well known that the ancient prophets enforced their words by such methods; they had a strong appeal for the Hebrew mind which the Lord did not disdain. This verse in fact describes something which was sacramental in nature and meaning, and there is a beautiful relevance between the outward and visible sign and the inward and spiritual grace.

The first fact to claim our thought in this verse is the symbolical action: "And when he had said this, he breathed on them." What the Lord did was done in a single action; it was meant for the whole group in whose midst He stood. He did not breathe on them one by one; He breathed on the whole body as it were at once. It is wise to bear in mind the fact that there

270

was nothing to limit the significance of this action to the Apostles. Thomas was not present at all, and the others were not alone; Luke plainly refers to "them that were with them" (Luke 24:33). The action itself was unique in the life of the Son of Man, and this is stressed by the word which is used. It stands alone in the gospel memoirs; it was never used on any other occasion in the New Testament. But it is not only that the word is not used elsewhere; there is also the fact that the action itself has no parallel whatever in the gospel records. There were times when He touched the eyes of the blind or the ears of the deaf with moisture from His mouth; but He never breathed on any man in this way apart from this singular occasion. The Apostles in Samaria and Paul in Ephesus were to lay their hands on those who had been baptized and they were to receive the Holy Ghost (Acts 8:17; 19:6); but we never hear of anything similar to this action when He breathed on them and bade them receive the Holy Ghost.

These are facts which make us perceive that this was no ordinary symbol, and there can be little doubt that we must refer to the Old Testament for an explanation. Although the word does not occur anywhere else in the New Testament, it is employed by the Septuagint in the narrative of the creation of man. Thus we are told how God formed man's body from the dust of the new-made earth, and how it lay inert and still, waiting to be quickened by the living Spirit of God. "The Lord God . . . *breathed* into his nostrils the breath of life; and man became a living soul" (Genesis 2:7). The breath of God came upon him and into him; he lived, and rose up in the power of life that came from God Himself. So too Ezekiel describes how he was called upon to stand in that valley of bones, "very many . . . and very dry" (Ezekiel 37:2). Then he saw how bone came to bone; they were covered with flesh and skin; but they still had no life in them. At last he was told to lift up his voice and speak to the wind in the Name of the Lord God: "Come from the four winds, O Breath, and breathe upon these slain, that they may live" (Ezekiel 37:9). That breath came upon them and into them; "they lived, and stood up on their feet, an exceeding great army" (Ezekiel 37:10).

Those two scenes were doubtless in mind when the Lord stood among His friends in that quiet room. Just as the dust in Genesis or the bones in Ezekiel were lifeless without breath, so the disciples were without life or power or vitality until they were filled with the Holy Ghost. And the act of breathing on them was like a sign of new life for those who were dead. It was as though He would impart the breath of life in His own soul to the souls of others. He breathed on them just as God had breathed on the once lifeless clay, or as the winds had breathed on the once lifeless bones. These disciples had grievously failed Him three days before in His hour of trouble; they had all forsaken Him and fled when rude hands placed Him under arrest. And if Peter who had denied Him stood in need of a special restoration, would not all who had failed Him stand in need of a special re-commission? They had forfeited their right to His confidence as the men whom He had chosen to be with Him: but now He breathed on them so that they would vibrate once more with His dynamic energy.

The next fact to claim our thought in this verse is the mysterious saying: He "saith unto them, Receive ye the Holy Ghost." These words explain the real nature of His action in breathing upon them: it was as though He would convey or make over to them the Holy Ghost "as by an act and deed of gift" to instruct and inspire their faith.[1] A breath of wind was a well-known emblem of the Holy Spirit in the Scriptures. The very word means no more than *air in motion,* breath, or wind, or spirit. The Lord Himself used it as an analogy in His conversation with Nicodemus: "The wind bloweth where it listeth," He said; ". . . So is every one that is born of the Spirit" (John 3:8). Luke conveys the same idea in the symbols that marked the Day of Pentecost: "There came a sound from heaven as of a rushing mighty wind . . . and they were all filled with the Holy Ghost" (Acts 2:2, 4). Thus there was a spiritual kinship between the sign He gave and the words that He spoke. This has not been preserved in the English version, but it can be expressed if the verse is read in this way: "He *breathed* on them, and saith unto them, Receive ye *the Holy Breath.*"

Thus the symbol and the saying were cognate in idea, if not in verbal form. The Son of Man was the One in Whom the Spirit of God dwelt in all His fulness, and the descent of the

---

[1] H. C. G. Moule, *Jesus and The Resurrection* (4th ed., 1905), p. 99.

Holy Spirit at the time of His baptism was the outward sign of this fact. God gave not the Spirit by measure to Him (John 3:34); He it was Whom God the Father had sealed (John 6:27). But He had not as yet baptized the Church with the Holy Ghost and with fire (Matthew 3:11), "for the Holy Ghost was not yet given; because that Jesus was not yet glorified" (John 7:39). But the years of humility had come to an end when He hung on the cross and lay in the grave, and the first step in His exaltation to God's right hand was His Resurrection on the third day. The hour had come when the Father had begun and would continue to glorify the Son, and He began at once to speak of the Holy Spirit Whom He was to bestow. But did this scene mean that they were at once endowed with the Holy Spirit? Moule for one felt that he could not say that it was not so; there was surely some infusion or revival of life and power.[2] Thus the choice of the word *receive* supports the view that there was some active response in the way of personal reception. It is the same word as was used in the command: "*Take*, eat: this is my body" (Matthew 26:26; Mark 14:22). This may confirm the view that now, as then, there was an outward sign of an inward grace; it may also imply that the gift was then and there both bestowed and received.[3] It was like an "earnest" of the Spirit,[4] a true foretaste of what was yet to come.

But the absence of the definite article[5] and a wider context favor the view that the primary intention of these words was to foreshadow the gift of Pentecost. "Behold," He declared, "I send the Promise of My Father upon you: but tarry ye in the city of Jerusalem until ye be endued with power from on high" (Luke 24:49). "Ye shall receive power, after that the Holy Ghost is come upon you: and ye shall be witnesses unto me . . . unto the uttermost part of the earth" (Acts 1:8). They were not to embark on their mission at once; they were to wait in the city: and they were to wait so that they might be fully endowed with the Holy Spirit. Thus His words were equivalent in some sense to

---

[2]H. C. G. Moule, *Jesus and The Resurrection* (4th ed., 1905), p. 99.

[3]Alfred Plummer, *St. John* (Cambridge Greek Testament for Schools, 1882), p. 343.

[4]See Ephesians 1:14 where the Spirit Himself is described as an "earnest" of our inheritance.

[5]Compare John 14:26 where both substantive and adjective have the article.

the claim: "I am he that will bestow the Holy Ghost." He had referred to this only three nights before on the eve of His death: "It is expedient for you that I go away: for if I go not away, the Comforter will not come unto you; but if I depart I will send him unto you" (John 16:7; cf. 14:16; 15:26). All these sayings make it clear that the Holy Ghost was His Spirit as well as the Father's Spirit, and they are a strong indirect proof of the Double Procession of the Holy Spirit. We affirm our belief in this doctrine when we recite the Nicene Creed: "I believe in the Holy Ghost . . . Who proceedeth from the Father and the Son." The Greek Church broke away from the Latin Church on the ground that it could not accept this Filioque clause; but the Lord's words as well as His action on the Resurrection evening prove that this clause rests on a strong and sound basis.

"And when he had said this, he breathed on them, and saith unto them, Receive ye the Holy Ghost." No mere mortal man could have spoken those words with authority or could have endowed them with the Holy Spirit. What are we to say then about their use in the Prayer Book Service for Ordination to the Priesthood or Consecration of a Bishop? Hands are laid on the head of the person concerned while the solemn words are spoken: "Receive the Holy Ghost for the office and work of a Priest (or Bishop) in the Church of God now committed unto thee." We are bound to regard those words so spoken as in the nature of prayer, for a Bishop has as little power to confer the Holy Ghost as he has to forgive a man his sins. But their use in this sense reminds us all of the one thing necessary for a true man of God: Bishops may lay their hands on men in the rite of Ordination, but only the Risen Christ can breathe on them and make them servants of the Gospel. This truth is not confined to those who are ordained to the Christian ministry; it holds good for all those who go forth in His Name and at His call. They stand in need of that Holy Breath if ever they are to feel His power. They ought to kneel at His feet in self-conscious poverty until they hear Him say:

"RECEIVE YE THE HOLY GHOST."

Chapter 42

TO REMIT AND RETAIN

Whosesoever sins ye remit, they are remitted unto them; and whosesoever sins ye retain, they are retained. — JOHN 20:23.

THE LORD had breathed on those who were in that room that they might inbreathe the Breath of God. Then He gave them a charge which may reflect His own mighty triumph over the great problem of sin: "Whosesoever sins ye remit, they are remitted unto them: and whosesoever sins ye retain, they are retained." These words to some extent are an echo of the words which He had spoken, first to Simon Peter, and then to all the Twelve: "Whatsoever thou shalt bind on earth shall be bound in heaven: and whatsoever thou shalt loose on earth shall be loosed in heaven" (Matthew 16:19; 18:18). They all knew the kind of authority which the ruler of a synagogue exercised among the Jews; to bind and to loose were Rabbinical terms which dealt with rules and regulations for the conduct of the Jewish community. The same kind of authority would now belong to the leaders of that Church which He was to build (Matthew 16:18); they were empowered to take measures for the conduct of its affairs and the exercise of its discipline. But to remit and retain were terms which went beyond rules and regulations for the proper conduct of Church members; they were concerned with the inner world of conscience and they have a judgment value which was endorsed with a divine sanction. Westcott says that the most probable form of the text points to the use of the perfect tense for both verbs, and that this is meant to convey the idea of "absolute efficacy";[1] there is no interval between the act and

---

[1]B. F. Westcott, *The Gospel According to St. John* (18th impr., 1937), p. 295.

its issue; there is a harmony between the voice on earth and the will in heaven. Thus He bestowed authority for the declaration of the terms of divine absolution or the fact of divine condemnation. Both the extent and the limit of this tremendous commission demand the most careful study.

The first half of this verse refers to forgiveness and absolution: "Whosoever sins ye remit, they are remitted unto them." These words have their counterpart in the earlier saying: "Whatsoever thou shalt loose on earth shall be loosed in heaven." To loose referred to the power to allow or to permit: what was allowed by His servants on earth would be confirmed with His benediction on high. But this power to loose was set out on a very broad plane, and there was no special mention of the problem of sin or the need for absolution. It was not so with this saying on the Resurrection evening: it goes beyond the rules of an external form of fellowship; it deals with the issues of a personal need for forgiveness. The first and chief function of the Church is to deal with the problem of sin: and to remit man's sin is to forgive that man, to set him free from the guilt and curse that sin must entail.

But what is the exact shade of meaning which these words are meant to convey? The Church of Rome holds its doctrine on the Power of the Keys partly on the basis of this saying, and it maintains that to Peter and the Twelve was given the full right of Absolution. But the Scriptures declare that the power to forgive belongs to God alone: "There is forgiveness with thee, that thou mayest be feared" (Psalm 130:4). The scribes were in error when they accused Jesus of a blasphemous utterance when He forgave a man his sins, for they knew Him not as the Son of God. But they stated their case with an orthodox argument: "Who can forgive sins but God only?" (Mark 2:7). The Son of Man indeed had the power on earth to forgive, but He had no power to confer that right upon others. His grand mission in this world was to make a way to save men from their sins, and His Resurrection was the sign and proof that He had achieved this great purpose. Thus one special duty which He enjoined on the Church was to make known the terms of pardon and peace.

The Lord Jesus did not confer upon them the power to forgive any more than the Law conferred upon Aaron as high priest of Israel power to heal the leper. But He did give them the right to declare whose sins God will forgive just as Aaron had the right to pronounce that a leper was cleansed from his disease. Nothing beyond this well-defined right of declaration can be wrung from these words. They will never lend pope or priest authority to say as though it were in his own name: "I absolve thee." There is nothing in the Pastoral Epistles which would suggest that such independent Absolution is part of the Christian ministry. Our task is to declare in the Name of Jesus the terms on which God will forgive, and this was the Apostolic practice. Peter made this proclamation in the house of Cornelius in direct and simple language: "To him give all the prophets witness that . . . whosoever believeth in Him shall receive remission of sins" (Acts 10:43). Paul made it in the synagogue of Antioch in Pisidia with similar directness and simplicity: "'Be it known unto you . . . that through this man is preached unto you the forgiveness of sins" (Acts 13:38). This is the norm; there is no example in the New Testament of what is called Sacramental Absolution. The Lord alone can speak with the authority that commands the blessing: "Son, be of good cheer; thy sins be forgiven thee" (Matthew 9:2).

The next half of this verse refers to discipline and condemnation: "And whosesoever sins ye retain, they are retained." These words have their counterpart in the earlier saying: "Whatsoever thou shalt bind on earth shall be bound in heaven." To bind referred to the power to forbid or to refuse: what was refused by His servants on earth would be confirmed with His authority on high. But this power to bind was set out on a very broad plane, and there was no special mention of the burden of sin or the fact of condemnation. It was not so with this saying on the Resurrection evening: it goes beyond the rules of a temporal form of discipline; it deals with the issues of an eternal destiny. A prime and grave function of the Church is to deal with the burden of sin: and to retain man's sin is to condemn that man, to hold them fast so that they may not pass away.

But what is the exact shade of meaning which these words are meant to convey? The Church of Rome holds its doctrine on the Power of the Keys partly on the basis of this saying, and it maintains that to Peter and the Twelve was given power to shut the gates of heaven. It is argued that a priest has power to retain man's sin so that it will not be removed from him, and the threat which this power implies is at the heart of the wider teaching on penance and purgatory. It is equivalent to the claim that the priest may act as a judge of man's soul; he determines man's destiny both in this world and in the world to come. If a priest has power to retain man's sin, to bind it on his soul so that it may not then be put away, man is in his hands and at his mercy unless he dares to risk his soul and to defy that power. But the priest looks only on the outward facade of a man's life, while God looks on his heart. We judge a man by the fruits which his life brings forth; it is only the Son of God Who can lay an axe to the root of the tree and cut it down. He knows the true nature of sin and sees into man's heart as no earthly priest can ever presume to do; He can judge the soul with unerring certainty, and the keys of hell and of death are at His girdle (Revelation 1:18). When He opens, no man can shut; and when He shuts, none can open (Revelation 3:7). Thus the power to condemn, like the power to forgive, belongs to Him alone; He has never delegated that authority to others. But one special duty which He enjoined on the Church was to make known the facts of judgment and wrath.

The Lord Jesus did not confer upon them the power to consign a man to hell any more than the Law conferred such power on the sons of Aaron. But He did give them the right to declare whose sins God will condemn just as prophets were summoned to declare in what circumstances judgment would come upon Israel. Nothing beyond this well-defined power of declaration can be wrung from these words. They will never give pope or priest authority to say as though it were in his own name: "I condemn thee." There is nothing in the Pastoral Epistles which would suggest that such independent condemnation is part of the Christian ministry. Our task is to declare in the Name of Jesus the terms on which God must condemn, and this was the Apostolic practice. Peter acted in this spirit when he rebuked Simon Magus: "Thy heart is not right in the sight of God. . . . For I perceive that thou art in the gall of bitterness, and in the bond of iniquity" (Acts 8:21, 23). Paul acted likewise when he rebuked Elymas the Sorcerer: "Thou child of the devil, thou enemy of all righteousness, wilt thou not cease to pervert the right ways of the Lord?" (Acts 13:10). This is the rule; there is no example in the New Testament of a judgment pronounced by man as to eternal damnation. Paul wrote twice of those whom he had given up as it were "unto Satan"; but in each case it was "that the spirit may be saved" or "that they may learn not to blaspheme" (I Corinthians 5:5; I Timothy 1:20). The Lord alone can speak with the authority of a verdict that is final: "Depart from me"; "I never knew you" (Matthew 25:41; 7:23).

These words have been enshrined in the Ordinal and have entered deep into the history of the Church of England. It can hardly be too important to understand them aright. The power to bind and loose conferred upon Simon Peter was not confined to him; the same words were addressed to all the Twelve, and one of that band was Judas. Nor could the Twelve claim an exclusive interest in the general privilege of which He spoke, for the circle was much wider when He amplified the first commission in words that dealt with the power to remit or to retain man's sin. Simon Peter would die; the Twelve would pass away; but the Church will endure: these words were not for the Apostolate only, but for the whole living society. Thus they do not confer on the priesthood a power which is denied to the Church as a whole: that lies at the root of sacerdotal teaching about the need for a priestly mediator. No worse or more mischievous doctrine for priest or people can be proposed; nothing has done more to puff up the priest and to pull down the layman. This is why the Absolution in the Service of Morning and Evening Prayer is phrased in the form of a declaration of the terms on which God forgives. It sets out the fact that He "hath given power and commandment to His ministers to declare and pronounce to His people, being penitent, the absolution and remission of their sins." Then at once it goes on to state: "*He*" (not *they*) "pardoneth and absolveth all them that truly repent and unfeignedly believe His holy Gospel." They can pronounce nothing but that those who repent and believe will be absolved; they can threaten nothing but that those who do not repent or believe will be condemned. The great task of the Church in all ages is to bear this witness; there is a sense in which every disciple must act on this Easter command. The sins that we remit, He will remit; the sins that we retain, He will retain: for we are to declare the terms on which God will act in wrath or mercy.

Chapter 43

I WILL NOT BELIEVE

But Thomas, one of the twelve, called Didymus, was not with them when Jesus came. The other disciples therefore said unto him, We have seen the Lord. But he said unto them, Except I shall see in his hands the print of the nails, and put my finger into the print of the nails, and thrust my hand into his side, I will not believe. — JOHN 20:24, 25.

JOHN alone provides this account of Thomas, and the little we know about him is all found in the pages of this gospel. It was Thomas who saw that the death of Lazarus would make Bethany fraught with danger if the Son of Man were to go there in response to the summons from the sisters. Thomas would go with Him, but it would be in a spirit of deep foreboding: "Let us also go," he said to his fellow disciples, "that we may die with him" (John 11:16). It was Thomas who first interrupted the great discourse on the Father's House of many mansions with his own blunt query: "Lord, we know not whither thou goest; and how can we know the way?" (John 14:5). His doubts were a matter of feeling rather than reason; they had sprung from genuine depression rather than from critical unbelief. He was a man who would find it hard to believe even what he would most wish to believe. Henry Latham points out this fact very clearly in his comment that "a person who is exceptionally clear-sighted within a rather narrow range is apt to be more impatient than other people when something is put before him which seems mystical."[1] So it was when Thomas heard of the Resurrection; he thought that it was too good to be true, and his very desire to think it so would not allow him to accept it on hearsay. His was doubt born of a sadness due to his

---

[1] Henry Latham, *The Risen Master* (1907), p. 179.

own intense desire to think that what others had told him was in fact the truth; he longed to know that they had not been self-deceived. Thus he was left to walk in the pensive gloom of moonlight while they were free to bask in the cheerful warmth of sunshine.

We may think first of the reason for his absence on that memorable evening: "But Thomas, one of the twelve, called Didymus, was not with them when Jesus came." John writes with an air of tranquil brevity at the distance of years, and he affords no information at all that would explain his absence; he tells only enough to pave the way for the sequel. Judas Iscariot was not with them either, and that band of twelve was now no longer complete. We know what had become of him; he had gone out with a sense of hopeless remorse and hanged himself. But why Thomas was not there, we know not, nor is there the slightest hint to tell us where he had gone. The disciples from Emmaus had gone away; Simon Peter had been alone: the temptation to separate was a very real one; they would soon have dispersed, "every man to his own" (John 16:32). He had warned them that thus it was written: "I will smite the Shepherd, and the sheep of the flock shall be scattered abroad" (Matthew 26:31). A variety of motives may have prompted Thomas to seek solitude while others sought company; his absence may reflect feelings that were common among them all. It is clear that neither the Lord nor the Ten found fault with Thomas because he was not there. We cannot say whether he was to blame; we are simply left to wonder at his absence. What we do know is that he was kept in suspense for eight slow days while his brethren had the glorious certainty that the Lord had risen indeed.

Thomas must have been much in the mind of his friends after that first evening: "The other disciples therefore said unto him, We have seen the Lord." Would they go in search of him with the news? Did he rejoin them in that room where the Lord had stood in the midst? And was it that very night when he met his friends once more? They were in the first flush of joy, and they hailed him with a simple statement of great gladness. They told him their tidings, lovingly, longingly, as men who had felt the benediction of His presence. They spoke, not once, nor twice, but again and again, as though it could not be too often.

It was continued, repeated testimony; they kept on saying what they knew. Westcott points out that the absence of a pronoun in the Greek text throws the stress on the verb: they could only insist that they had *seen* the Lord.[2] They had seen the scars of the cross — those marks in His hands and His side. They had felt His breath on their face as He bade them receive the Holy Ghost. His face had met their eyes; His voice had met their ears: and all their doubts and fears had been swallowed up in glorious certainty and joy.

Thomas had missed that hour of bliss because he was not there, and we cannot help the feeling that his absence was not wholly accidental; he was away because of some freak or trait of individual temperament. Jesus Himself he loved dearly, however mistaken he may have been as to the fact of His Resurrection. His whole mental outlook affords a true insight into the state of mind which had been shared by all his friends; but in his case this was carried to its logical conclusion. They had all felt the pain of an awful disappointment which lies behind the words of the travelers on the road to Emmaus: "We trusted that it had been he which should have redeemed Israel" (Luke 24:21). But that sense of gloom drove Thomas along the path of a solitary sadness; he tried to cut himself off from others to brood and mourn alone. Perhaps it was a kind of glum independence which passed into stubborn self-will, and it deprived him of the joy of a unique experience.

We may think next of the nature of his feelings on that memorable evening: "But he said unto them, except I shall see in his hands the print of the nails . . . I will not believe." This dogmatic reply does not sound like "an outburst of incredulous surprise";[3] it sounds much more like a deliberate resolve after the whole matter had been discussed at full length in every detail. John only records the end result of much debate, and the very terms in which the verdict was phrased help to fill in the blank.[4] Thomas may have made up his mind slowly enough; then he spoke out brusquely to voice the doubts

---

[2] B. F. Westcott, *The Gospel According to St. John* (18th impr., 1937), p. 296.

[3] Henry Latham, *The Risen Master* (1907), p. 182.

[4] W. Hanna, *Our Lord's Life On Earth* (1882), p. 613.

which he could not allay. He knew that he was now among friends and brethren who could have no earthly reason to pretend or deceive; and yet he met all their statements with a wall of outspoken unbelief. They themselves had been slow to believe the testimony of others, and now they found that he was as stubborn as they had been. They had dismissed the news which the women had brought as though it were an idle tale (Luke 24:11); Mary had come to them as they had mourned and wept, and they believed her not (Mark 16:11). They could not be hard on Thomas when he did not at once believe, and yet he seems to have outstripped them all in his adamant rejection of facts. They had at length believed when they heard how He had appeared to Simon Peter; they believed even before they saw Him with their eyes. And yet Thomas would not believe, though to Peter's testimony there was added that of the disciples from Emmaus, and of those who were his trusted friends and intimate companions.[5] They were the last men in the world who would mock or mislead his faith, and his attitude was wrong, very wrong; but who that knows his own heart will say that it was unnatural?[6]

There was something in him which held him back in spite of his own heart: "'Except I shall . . . put my finger into the print of the nails, and thrust my hand into his side, I will not believe." Unwillingness to let his faith be ruled by theirs would make him prone to doubt whether theirs was in fact soundly derived. He would argue in his own mind that they only believed what they wished to believe, and he would not accept what they told him while their word stood alone. There is no need to think that he accused them of falsehood; that was not his idea: but he could not rid his mind of the fear that they had made some great mistake. Had they seen a phantom? Did they mistake it for reality? He could not rest on what they said that they had seen; he felt that he must have the chance to look and touch as they had done. There may have been mingled feelings of wistful melancholy and stubborn independence in his ultimate attitude, but he was quite convinced that he ought to have the same right to form his own judgment as they had had. The Ten had heard Him say: "Behold my hands and my feet, that it is I myself:

---

[5] *Ibid.*, p. 611.
[6] H. C. G. Moule, *Jesus and The Resurrection* (4th ed., 1905), p. 127.

handle me, and see" (Luke 24:39). Thomas would ask no more and no less for himself — the right to see, and touch, and feel. Westcott points out that he may well have shaped his words about "His hands . . . and . . . his side" in line with what they had told him (cf. John 20:20).[7] And his obstinacy stands out in the repetitions of his demand: "The print of the nails . . . the print of the nails"; "put my finger . . . put my hand" (R.V.).[8]

We need not think that the mind of Thomas was as it were hostile to the miraculous.[9] His was not the Sadducean type of outlook which the Lord had summed up in the saying: "Except ye see signs and wonders, ye will not believe" (John 4:48). But he had misgivings, and he was suspicious lest others should persuade him too lightly. This would drive him back on himself, and would trigger off all kinds of unfortunate repercussions. He was now so anxious to know the truth that he could not reach it at once; his hand trembled so much that he could not grasp it on an impulse. He was prone to doubt simply because he feared, or seemed to fear, lest he should ground his faith on such reasons as were only valid for his brethren. Thus he proposed the most extreme test for himself and said that he would stand by that, just as before he had forecast the most extreme result of a journey to the fringe of Jerusalem and had addressed himself to that (John 11:16). This is as wide apart as the poles from the doubt of the frivolous or the sceptical; it was the doubt of a thoughtful man who liked to feel rock beneath his feet. Doubt may only be a pretext in the case of men who will not face the problem of guilt, but in real doubt there is torment.

Brief as is the record, it is packed with minute traits of definite character, and the result is that Thomas stands out before our eyes as a clear and distinct person. He is no faint shadow of some other member of that band of disciples; we can never confuse him with men like Simon Peter or the sons of Zebedee. His problems and perplexities run through the whole beautiful narrative with a lifelike reality. He was a man whose gloom

[7]B. F. Westcott, *The Gospel According to St. John* (18th impr., 1937), p. 296.

[8]Alfred Plummer, *St. John* (Cambridge Greek Testament for Schools, 1882), p. 345.

[9]H. C. G. Moule, *Jesus and The Resurrection* (4th ed., 1905), p. 113.

doubled when his faith was in halves. He would have proof beyond all doubt, or he would not believe at all. "Except I shall see," he said, "I will not believe." His attitude is underlined with the strongest emphasis by the double negative in the Greek text: "I will *in no wise* believe." Plummer points out that his demand was phrased as though he had no hope. He did not say: "If I see, I will believe"; he said: "Except I see, I will not believe."[10] Thus doubt held his mind in its grip and kept him stretched on the rack of tension; eight days were to pass before that torment was resolved. There are still some who feel tempted to say: "I will not believe." If they have heard of Him by the hearing of the ear and yet have not seen Him with their eyes, there is but one place where their doubt can be resolved and that is at His feet. They need to take their stand with the father who cried out in desperate earnestness and said even with tears: "Lord, I believe; help thou mine unbelief" (Mark 9:24).

---

[10]Alfred Plummer, *St. John* (Cambridge Greek Testament for Schools, 1882), p. 345.

Chapter 44

MY LORD AND MY GOD

And after eight days again his disciples were within, and Thomas with them: then came Jesus, the doors being shut, and stood in the midst, and said, Peace be unto you. Then saith he to Thomas, Reach hither thy finger, and behold my hands; and reach hither thy hand, and thrust it into my side; and be not faithless, but believing. And Thomas answered and said unto him, my Lord and my God. Jesus saith unto him, Thomas because thou hast seen me, thou hast believed: blessed are they that have not seen, and yet have believed. — JOHN 20:26-29.

No ONE could tell when the Lord would stand in their midst again, and how that week was spent or where the Twelve would stay, we do not know. There is very little information as to their way of life during those days apart from the chosen moments when He appeared to them and "shewed himself alive" (Acts 1:3). Thus we see them in the rich light of His presence on the Resurrection evening; then He vanished, and a curtain falls for some days on all of them. They must have been days of wonder and great gladness for all except Thomas: for him, the days would pass one by one while the torture of doubt still racked his mind. But he did not leave his brethren again, for doubt did not destroy the bonds of his devotion to Christ or his communion with them.[1] Perhaps their certainty would tell on him; their happiness would touch his heart: and in this state between doubt and desire, he might be swayed by the course of events.[2] "And after eight days again his disciples were within, and Thomas with them." The "eight days" would include the two extremes, so

---

[1]H. B. Swete, *The Appearances of Our Lord After the Passion* (1915), p. 45.

[2]H. C. G. Moule, *Jesus and The Resurrection* (4th ed., 1905), p. 130.

that this was the next Sunday after Easter. The long Passover Festival must have ended the day before, and it is not clear why they had not set out for Galilee as they had been enjoined (Mark 16:7; Matthew 28:7). They may have been delayed on account of Thomas, and the two words *again . . . within* imply that they had met "in the same place and under the same circumstances as before."[3] They had reassembled in that room where He had appeared to them before: what if nothing were to happen? Would not one man's doubt turn to a distrust still more profound?

The first emphasis in this paragraph is on the presence of Jesus: "Then came Jesus, the doors being shut, and stood in the midst, and said, Peace be unto you." Thomas, like Mary and Peter, stood in need of direct revelation by the Risen Saviour, and that need was to be satisfied. But the Lord did not seek him out while he was still alone as He had done in the case of those others. Thomas had avowed his unbelief in the midst of fellow disciples; it was their testimony which he had refused: therefore he would need to retract his words in their presence and to confess his faith in their hearing. But they were not to know all this when they met once more in that room on the eighth day; they knew only that as Jesus had come before, so He might come again. The doors were shut, but there is no mention that this was "for fear of the Jews" (John 20:19): this had now been dissolved in the knowledge of His Resurrection reality. John's account of what followed was in almost identical language with his account of the earlier appearance, and a literal translation of each verse shows up the minor points of divergence in a way that keeps the narrative alive: "Then *came* Jesus and stood in the midst, and *saith* unto them, Peace be unto you" . . . "Then *cometh* Jesus, and stood in the midst, and *said,* Peace be unto you." The tense of the verbs is reversed, and the second statement in its original form is unencumbered by the preface which had paved the way for the first statement. Thus the words ring out with a marked solemnity: *Jesus cometh.* It was as it had been before: He had come with the same swift and silent advent, without sound of footfall, without noise of movement. He had

[3]B. F. Westcott, *The Gospel According to St. John* (18th impr., 1937), p. 296.

come as if from nowhere, and His sudden entrance to stand in their midst was as though there were no door at all.

His first word was once more that word of Peace, and their hearts must have been full of wonder as He went on: "Then saith he to Thomas, reach hither thy finger and behold my hands; and reach hither thy hand and thrust it into my side; and be not faithless, but believing." There stood Jesus in "the brief and mighty logic" of His risen presence,[4] and Thomas was offered the very proof for which he had asked a week before. The Lord recalled the words which he himself had used, and those very words would prove the identity of Him Who now spoke them.[5] Thomas knew that no one had seen the Lord since he had first uttered those words, and His knowledge of them was in itself overwhelming. He heard that voice which he had known so well; it was identical in accent, articulate in address: and he heard it recite the words of the challenge which he himself had so rashly thrown out. Then he saw Him hold out those hands, once pierced and torn with nails; saw Him lay bare His side, with the deeper wound-print left by the spear. Those were the marks of His identity as the Man of the Cross, the proofs of His reality as the Lord from heaven. And he was to draw near: he was to come, and see, and touch, and feel! He had asked for starkest reality, and now it was offered to him. He was at the border "where faith and unbelief part company,"[6] and in words of mildest reproof, he was told to believe. The Lord knows how long the fortress of the will can hold out when the reason has been convinced, and He added this call to surrender in terms in which exceeding tenderness is mingled with sovereign finality.[7]

This all took place in the lamplight of that room and in the presence of those other disciples: they were silent, looking on with eyes of shining wonder. Would he actually finger those wounds? Would he reverently handle those limbs? We are not told, but there is still room for surmise. That the Lord should

---

[4]H. C. G. Moule, *Jesus and The Resurrection* (4th ed., 1905), p. 132.

[5]H. B. Swete, *The Appearances of Our Lord After the Passion* (1915), p. 46.

[6]Alfred Plummer, *St. John* (Cambridge Greek Testament for Schools, 1882), p. 345.

[7]H. B. Swete, *The Appearances of Our Lord After the Passion* (1915), pp. 46, 47.

have come when the doors were shut was wonderful; perhaps to him it was still more wonderful that He should know what had been in his mind a week before. The Lord had known what was in the mind of Nathanael even though he was still far off under a tree, and it was proof of this knowledge which had convinced Nathanael (John 1:45-51). So He had known what was in the mind of Thomas even though He was no longer visibly manifest when Thomas had spoken, and that would be enough. The Lord Himself was to say that it was because Thomas had seen the scars of His Passion that he believed, but He did not suggest that he had put out his hand to touch them as well. He had stood in their midst eight days before and had shown them His hands and side; we are not told that they availed themselves of the invitation to touch and feel as well. So it was with Thomas; we may safely conclude that the very sight of those scars would be enough. He saw the Lord in His risen reality, with the marks of perfect identity: what need remained for the touch and feel of human contact?

The next emphasis in this paragraph is on the worship of Thomas: "And Thomas answered and said unto him, My Lord and my God." Thomas was a man of strong and passionate loyalty, and was moved to faith or distrust by his feelings rather than his reason. This cry was so swift and spontaneous that it rules out any thought of further delay, and he was as vehement in the utterance of faith now as of doubt before. Doubt had vanished at the very sight of Jesus, like mist at the morning sunrise. His suspense was ended; his reserve was answered; and his inmost being was now released from its stubborn pride and self-isolation. He could have said with Job, and in the same spirit of deep humility: "I have heard of thee by the hearing of the ear: but now mine eye seeth thee" (Job 42:5). He was overwhelmed with repentance and faith; he was overawed with amazement and joy; he was convinced of his wrong and grievous doubt; he was ashamed of his rash and reckless speech. What could he do but fall at the feet of Jesus while the pent-up feelings of his heart found their way to the surface in one glad, brief exclamation of joy?

There is a note of simple grandeur in this confession of faith: "And Thomas answered and said unto him, My Lord and my God." Even before the Lord had bared those wounds or had spoken aloud, Thomas would be aware that his doubts could not stand. But when he heard those words and saw those scars, he could only respond in words of love and of adoration. He had grasped the great facts of His personal relation both to men and to His Father; he had seen that He was both Lord and God. *My Lord!* My beloved Master! He recognized that He Who once was dead is now alive; it was "this same Jesus," once slain, but now risen! *My God!* My almighty Saviour! He recognized that He Who rose again must be divine; He was no less than God Whom death could not enthrall. His words ascend from fact to truth, from Jesus risen to Jesus divine, and he confessed Him in terms of Godhead with an intelligence that was definite, emphatic, and new. Westcott points out that the words are beyond question addressed to Him,[8] and the pronouns invest the words with an impressive character as a personal confession of faith: Thou art *my* Lord: thou art *my* God!

This was the most advanced statement of faith ever made by one of the Twelve; it rose to a height and maturity which far surpassed that of all his brethren in the days of His flesh. Nathanael had once exclaimed: "Rabbi, thou art the Son of God; thou art the King of Israel" (John 1:49). And Peter had declared: "Thou art the Christ, the Son of the living God" (Matthew 16:16). But the words of Thomas outstrip those two famous declarations both in personal quality and in factual perception. No confession of Deity could go beyond his cry, nor can it be explained away. Each word came from his heart, and was equal both in wonder and in worship. Jesus Himself received it as His due; He heard with the tacit recognition that it was both appropriate and true. There was nothing of the caution which Peter felt when Cornelius fell down in an act of worship: "Stand up," he said; "I myself also am a man" (Acts 10:26). There was nothing of the restraint that the angel felt when John fell down in worship: "See thou do it not," he said, "I am thy fellow servant" (Revelation 19:10). Doubt is both cold and cruel, and it often breaks out in some harsh and heartless statement: so it was with Thomas when he had so bluntly declared that he would not believe. But the discovery of truth had warmed his heart with a new and glorious devotion, and he

---

[8]B. F. Westcott, *The Gospel According to St. John* (18th impr., 1937), p. 296.

confessed his faith with an adoring reverence beyond which we can never hope to go.

The Lord did not bestow a benediction on Thomas as on Peter (Matthew 16:17); but He spoke with exceeding gentleness for the sake of future generations: "Jesus saith unto him, Thomas, because thou hast seen me thou hast believed: blessed are they that have not seen, and yet have believed." The first statement is half question and half exclamation:[9] "Because thou hast seen me, hast thou believed?" (R.V.M.; cf. John 1:50; 16: 31). This is not a benediction for the credulous, nor is it the reverse for those who have struggled with doubt; but it has in view those who cannot see as Thomas saw for the cure of genuine misgiving. The truth had seemed like a phantom to him at first because it was seen through a haze of doubt; but he could not reject it when he saw the facts with his own eyes. But a deeper faith is called for today, and a richer blessing now lies in store: for we cannot see as Thomas once saw; we can only believe on the testimony of those who did so see. Thomas saw the wound-prints in hands and side; blessed was he! But we have no cause to envy Thomas, for a richer benediction is ours. Jesus is the One Whom having not seen we love, and in Whom we rejoice with joy unspeakable; for we hear a voice that tells us what we are to do: "He is thy Lord; and worship thou him!" (Psalm 45:11).

[9] Alfred Plummer, *St. John,* p. 346.

Chapter 45

THAT YE MIGHT BELIEVE

> And many other signs truly did Jesus in the presence of his
> disciples, which are not written in this book: but these are writ-
> ten, that ye might believe that Jesus is the Christ, the Son of
> God; and that believing ye might have life through his name.
> — JOHN 20:30, 31.

THESE two verses are in the form of a comment by the Evangelist on the preceding narrative; they are meant to sum up and
round off his account of the Resurrection. Westcott points out
that it is not easy to hit off the precise meaning of the particle
at the beginning of this statement. John looks back over all the
events of which he had written, crowned by the good news of
Resurrection, and goes on to conclude: "So then, as might have
been expected by the reader who has followed the course of my
story, many other signs did Jesus; but of them all, these have
been written that you might believe."[1]   It is clear that John
meant these words to form a dignified conclusion for the entire
gospel. He had written it in order to lead men to believe that
Jesus is the Son of God, and it had reached a true climax in the
words of Thomas: "My Lord and my God" (John 20:28). There
was nothing that he could add to that; what could he say that
would not take something from its graphic effect? He may not
have been a trained or seasoned writer, but his own true instinct
for the effect of the gospel shaped his sense of climax better than
the finest knowledge of the writer's art could have done.[2] But the
primary importance of this statement is the bearing it has on the
real scope of the gospel. It was not his purpose to write a Life
in the formal sense of that word at all; it was simply to make

---

[1]cf. B. F. Westcott, *The Gospel According to St. John* (18th impr., 1937),
p. 297.
[2]Henry Latham, *The Risen Master* (1907), pp. 246-247.

known the good news that His coming spells life for all who will believe.

The first words have to do with the historic character of the *signs* which He wrought: "And many other signs truly did Jesus in the presence of his disciples which are not written in this book." The word sign is the word used by John whenever he spoke of the miracles. In his narrative of the miracles, he was concerned less with their real story appeal than with their sign value, and he always referred to them by the one word which most clearly brings out their true moral purpose. They were signs just because they led men to look below the surface for some deeper revelation of truth; they were like a divine finger-post which pointed to something on beyond. A *sign* was of value not so much for what it might be as for what it might mean; it was meant to give men some fresh insight into the mysteries which underlie the world we see. Thus John chose this word so as to guide our thoughts to the deeper meaning of things, for the value of the signs lay in their power to illuminate the Mind of God. This is clearly implied in the statement in which this word *sign* first appears: "This beginning of miracles (*signs*) did Jesus in Cana of Galilee and manifested forth his glory; and his disciples believed on him" (John 2:11).

John was at pains to lay stress on the authentic character of these signs as fact, not fancy: "And many other signs truly did Jesus in the presence of his disciples." John had just described how the Risen Lord had appeared to the disciples on three distinct occasions; these were "infallible proofs" that He had burst the bands of death and risen again (Acts 1:3). But the Resurrection Appearances are not classed in the same category as signs, and the "infallible proofs" are never called miracles in the ordinary sense of that word. On the other hand, when the Jews first asked Him for a sign, He had pointed them in cryptic language to the Resurrection: "Destroy this temple," He said, "and in three days I will raise it up" (John 2:19). The Jews thought that He spoke of the Temple built by Herod the Great; "But He spake of the temple of his body" (John 2:21). Thus it is clear that the Resurrection itself was the greatest of all the signs, and we should not confuse the sign value of the Resurrection with the Appearances which were the proofs of its reality. But John was also mindful of the many other signs wrought by Him "in the presence of his disciples," and his words glance back in rapid survey of the three years of miracle and ministry.

John readily acknowledged that his account was neither unique nor exhaustive: "And many other signs truly did Jesus . . . which are not written in this book." There was abundant material at his command; there were many signs from which to select: and he frankly says that he had followed the principle of selection. He had chosen seven such signs as he planned this memoir, and each sign was shown to possess its own special significance in the unfolding of His ministry.[3] But he freely admits that there had been many other such signs which he did not include in his gospel, and his words may imply that he was quite aware that there were other books now in circulation. These may have been the three Synoptic narratives; perhaps there were other primitive documents. We may compare the first words in Luke's preface with the last words in this chapter: "Many have taken in hand to set forth in order a declaration of those things which are most surely believed among us" (Luke 1:1). It adds strength to our faith to know that these were but a few of the great signs which might have been chosen, and to know as well that they were all wrought in the presence of men whose testimony is unimpeachable.

The next words have to do with the ultimate intention of the *signs* which He wrought: "But these are written, that ye might believe that Jesus is the Christ, the Son of God; and that believing ye might have life through his name." There were many signs of which there was no record, but these had been chosen for a deliberate purpose. Each had its own significance, and was meant to build up positive conviction of truth. Thus they were meant to form that frame of mind which would first lead to faith and then result in life itself. We may compare John's avowed purpose with that of the Luke's preface: "It seemed good to me also, having had perfect understanding of all things from the very first, to write unto thee in order . . . that thou mightest know the certainty of those things, wherein thou hast been instructed" (Luke 1:3, 4). Luke's purpose was to write an accurate history; John's design was to build up a sound doctrinal conviction. Luke was less concerned with dogma than with fact; John's concern for fact was with a view to dogma. He did not

---

[3]John 2:1-11; 4:46-54; 5:1-9; 6:1-14; 6:15-21; 9:1-7; 11:1-46.

ignore history, for the factual evidence was the basis of his theology; but his gospel, his selection from history, was ruled by the conscious desire to demonstrate his conclusion.

John's first aim was to reach the mind and intellect of his readers: "But these are written, that ye might believe that Jesus is the Christ, the Son of God." He claims that the One Whose Name was Jesus, the Name that spoke of His humanity and His humility, was both *The Christ* Who had fulfilled all the hopes and promises of Israel and *The Son of God* Who had fulfilled all the need and destiny of mankind.[4] These two names or titles represent what were separate issues in the minds of the Jews. They are conjoined on three momentous occasions in His earthly career (Matthew 16:16; John 11:27; Matthew 26:63), and they stand side by side in this culminating statement of the gospel. There were many who looked for a second Moses or a second David, for another Elijah or another Solomon;[5] but they missed the great point to which all the Scriptures are a witness: Jesus Himself is *The Christ*; and He is *The Son of God*. And each facet of this fundamental belief is of equal moment for us. The first chapter of this gospel tells how Andrew found "the Christ" (1:41), and Nathanael "the Son of God" (1:49); but the development of this recognition took place slowly among both friends and foes. There were many who thought that He must be "the . . . Christ" (7:26); there were others who did not think that He met the prophetic requirements (7:31). At last they said bluntly: "How long dost Thou make us to doubt? If thou be *the Christ*, tell us plainly" (10:24). Thus the final question which He had to answer on oath, was put to Him by the High Priest: "I adjure thee by the living God, that thou tell us whether thou be *the Christ, the Son of God*" (Matthew 26:63). And He replied: "Thou hast said; I am" (Matthew 26:64; Mark 14:62). And all the signs, crowned by that of Resurrection, proved that His claims were true.

John's final object was to reach the life and character of his readers: "But these are written . . . that believing ye might have life through his name." The whole gospel proves point by point

---

[4]B. F. Westcott, *The Gospel According to St. John* (18th impr., 1937), p. 297.

[5]Alfred Plummer, *St. John* (Cambridge Greek Testament for Schools, 1882), p. 347.

that the human Jesus was none other than Christ and God, and it must be interpreted by constant reference to this ruling motive. But this is not just an academic matter; it leads on to the most practical consequence: for it is in virtue of this truth that we find life through faith in Him. This shows how the primitive Evangel was in fact the source of highest blessing, and it corresponds with the avowed object of his Epistle: "These things have I written unto you that believe on the name of the Son of God; that ye may know that ye have eternal life" (I John 5:13). Accurate narrative and doctrinal conviction must issue in true moral reality, for He came that we might have *life*, and have it more abundantly (John 10:10).

Does this passage provide a good ending for the apostolic memoir? It does; yet a further chapter was still to be written before it reached its close. We may compare this with Bunyan's comment when the Pilgrims were received into the Celestial City: "I looked in after them, and behold, the City shone like the sun; the streets also were paved with gold, and in them walked many men, with crowns on their heads, palms in their hands, and golden harps to sing praises withal. There were also of them that had wings, and they answered one another without intermission, saying, Holy, holy, holy is the Lord. And after that, they shut up the gates; which when I had seen, I wished myself among them."[6] Was not that a truly artistic conclusion for a great book? The last sentence was a perfect finish. Yet with all his literary taste and spiritual insight, Bunyan did not come to an end just there. He had something more to relate; and there follows the bleak narrative on the fate of Ignorance. This has a literary power of its own, and it concludes the book with a memorable climax: "Then I saw that there was a way to hell, even from the gates of heaven, as well as from the City of Destruction."[7] And so too the final chapter of this gospel has a charm and beauty which we would not willingly surrender.[8] But we are meant to pause with the last words of this chapter while we survey the *sign* of the Resurrection. We see how the Son of Man was "declared to be the Son of God with power" (Romans 1:4): and we believe; we live!

---

[6]John Bunyan's, *Pilgrim's Progress* (Everyman's Edition), p. 193.
[7]Ibid., p. 194.
[8]See A. Yule, *Who Wrote The Fourth Gospel* (1930), pp. 49-50.

BIBLIOGRAPHY

BIBLIOGRAPHY

Crawley-Bovey, A. W. *The Garden Tomb, Golgotha, and the Garden of the Resurrection.* Garden Tomb Maintenance Fund.

Ellicott, C. J. *Historical Lectures on the Life of Our Lord Jesus Christ.* 6th ed., 1876.

Geldenhuys, J. N. *Commentary on Luke.* Grand Rapids, Mich.: Wm. B. Eerdmans Publishing Co., 1951.

Hanna, William. *Our Lord's Life on Earth.* 1882.
Hobart, William K. *Medical Language of Luke.* Grand Rapids, Mich.: Baker Book House, 1954.

Innes, A. Taylor. *The Trial of Jesus Christ: A Legal Monograph.* 1899.

Latham, Henry. *The Risen Master.* 1907.
Loane, Marcus. *It Is the Lord.* London: Marshall, Morgan & Scott, 1965.
_____. *Key Texts in Hebrews.* Fort Washington, Pa.: Christian Literature Crusade, 1961.
_____. *Life of Archbishop Mowll.* London: Hodder & Stoughton, 1960.
_____. *Makers of Religious Freedom in the 17th Century.* Grand Rapids, Mich.: Wm. B. Eerdmans Publishing Co., 1960.
_____. *Mary of Bethany.* Fort Washington, Pa.: Christian Literature Crusade, 1949.
_____. *Masters of the English Reformation.* Church Book Room Press, 1954.
_____. *Pioneers of the Reformation in England.* Church Book Room Press, 1964.

MacLaren, Alexander. *Expositions of Holy Scripture.* 11 vols. Grand Rapids, Mich.: Wm. B. Eerdmans Publishing Co., 1959.
Martin, Hugh. *The Shadow of Calvary.* Swengel, Pa.: Bible Truth Depot, n.d.
Morison, Frank. *Who Moved the Stone?* Grand Rapids, Mich.: Zondervan Publishing House, 1956.

Morison, James. *A Practical Commentary on St. Mark's Gospel.* 1887.

—————. *A Practical Commentary on St. Matthew's Gospel.* 1885.

Moule, Handley C. G. *Emmaus.* 1912.

—————. *Jesus and the Resurrection* (Expository Studies on St. John 20, 21). 4th ed., 1905.

Plummer, Alfred. *Exegetical Commentary on Matthew.* Grand Rapids, Mich.: Wm. B. Eerdmans Publishing Co., 1953.

—————. *The Gospel According to St. John* (Cambridge Greek Testament for Schools). 1882.

—————. *St. Luke.* 5th ed. Naperville, Ill.: Alec R. Allenson, Inc., 1956.

Powell, Frank J. *The Trial of Jesus Christ.* 1949.

Ryle, John Charles. *Ryle's Expository Thoughts on the Gospels.* 4 vols. Grand Rapids, Mich.: Zondervan Publishing House, 1956.

Stalker, James M. *Trial and Death of Jesus Christ.* Grand Rapids, Mich.: Zondervan Publishing House, 1956.

Stroud, William. *A Treatise on the Physical Cause of the Death of Christ.* 1871.

Swete, Henry Barclay. *The Appearances of Our Lord After the Passion.* 1915.

—————. *The Gospel According to St. Mark.* 1913.

Trench, R. C. *Studies in the Gospels.* 2nd ed., 1867.

—————. *Synonyms of the New Testament.* Grand Rapids, Mich.: Wm. B. Eerdmans Publishing Co., 1950.

Westcott, Brooke Foss. *Commentary on Gospel According to St. John.* Grand Rapids, Mich.: Wm. B. Eerdmans Publishing Co., 1950.

Yule, A. *Who Wrote the Fourth Gospel?* 1930.